Transactions and Creations

Transactions and Creations

Property Debates and the
Stimulus of Melanesia

Edited by
Eric Hirsch and Marilyn Strathern

Berghahn Books
NEW YORK · OXFORD

First published in 2004 by

Berghahn Books

www.berghahnbooks.com

©2004 Eric Hirsch and Marilyn Strathern

All rights reserved. Except for the quotation of short passages for the purposes of criticism and review, no part of this book may be reproduced in any form or by any means, electronic or mechanical, including photocopying, recording, or any information storage and retrieval system now known or to be invented, without written permission of the publisher.

Library of Congress Cataloging-in-Publication Data
A catalog record for this book is available from the Library of Congress

British Library Cataloguing in Publication Data
A catalogue record for this book is available from the British Library

Printed in Canada

ISBN 1-57181-615-1 (hardback)

Contents

Preface		vii
Acknowledgements		xiii
List of Abbreviations		xv
Introduction		1
Marilyn Strathern and Eric Hirsch		

Part I: Property

1	Property Limits: Debates on the Body, Nature and Culture *Stuart Kirsch*	21
2	Legal Options for the Regulation of Intellectual and Cultural Property in Papua New Guinea *Lawrence Kalinoe*	40
3	Seeing, Knowing, Owning: Property Claims as Revelatory Acts *Melissa Demian*	60

Part II: Transactions

4	Transactions: an Analytical Foray *Marilyn Strathern*	85
5	Transactions in Perpetual Motion *Tony Crook*	110
6	Negotiating Interests in Culture *Karen Sykes*	132

Part III: Creations

7	Modes of Creativity *James Leach*	151
8	Boundaries of Creation: the Work of Credibility in Science and Ceremony *Eric Hirsch*	176
Notes on Contributors		193
Bibliography		195
Index		217

Preface

Between 1999 and 2002, the authors worked together on a research project that gives its name to the three parts of this book. 'Property, Transactions and Creations' (PTC), came to refer both to the project and to those engaged on it.[1] The book springs from this work, although it is not intended to be a report on it. The same could be said of the way its intellectual impetus comes from Melanesia: the Melanesian experience is stimulus rather than subject matter.[2]

Since the late 1980s/early 1990s, international policy instruments such as the Convention on Biological Diversity (CBD) and TRIPS, an agreement on Trade-Related Aspects of Intellectual Property Rights, have led numerous countries to reevaluate claims to ownership in resources of all kinds.[3] PTC documented some of the strategies through which people deal with the ensuing challenges. It focused on a part of the world – the Pacific and particularly the societies of Papua New Guinea in Melanesia – renowned for the imaginative way in which relations between persons are linked to relations between objects, material and immaterial, and there seemed particular opportunities here for responding to an emergent debate. Among anthropologists this has really only gathered momentum over the last decade, although it touches on long-standing anthropological concerns with resource exploitation and the nature of property relations. New resources and new ways of appropriating them arrived together (as always), in this case under the banner of intellectual property rights (IPR). Papua New Guinea was among many states faced with international pressure to protect outside investment through intellectual property provisions. (In the wake of the World Trade Organization [WTO] agreement on trade-related aspects of intellectual property rights, it honoured its obligation to introduce legislation on copyright and patents in 2000.[4]) But identifying new resources as intellectual property (inventions, trade names, dramatic performances, art) did not stop there. The derivation of patents and copyright from Western law prompted reflection on other resources ripe for recognition. One constellation of these concerns involves what is called 'cultural property'.[5]

These days cultural property has come to refer to knowledge and to a whole range of intangible as well as tangible assets, though it is hardly reducible to the individual act of intellectual creation presupposed by IPR regimes. This was the nub of both local and regional debate. For Papua New Guinean colleagues caught up in deliberations over the new legislation, contributing to the perplexing issue of cultural property was taken to be PTC's prime mission. What had been debatable from the beginning of international interest in the topic was still the central question: whether an IPR model is or is not appropriate for the protection of rights and claims over intangible assets of a particular kind, namely those originating in 'indigenous cultures' or 'traditional knowledge.'[6] The terms are ones with which, like their counterparts from across the world, contemporary activists in Papua New Guinea work.

Coming to grips with the topic meant spreading a broad net. Minimally, claims of ownership over knowledge or similar intangibles are likely to be part of, or modelled on, ownership of other kinds of resources. PTC's research was thus directed towards studying 'new economic relations' at large, with a focus on claims at moments of negotiation and disposal, and hence on transactions in a strong sense of the term. In an arena of attention to cultural matters, with several inflections given to the 'cultural' in cultural property, including questioning what counts as culture, it seemed important to take issues beyond anthropology's own kind of 'cultural analysis'. Culture has in any case become an increasingly awkward analytic.[7] The contributors' concern has been with social relations, with people's dealings with one another, and hence with transactions in a more generalised sense of the term.

Perhaps it was not surprising to find, for example, that rights of disposal are not the same as rights of ownership: when claims are established through reference to social origins, 'non-owners' may have their own distinctive custodial role, and owners may have to consult them before disposing of anything. In Papua New Guinea (PNG), a common image for the different relations here is a distinction between ties traced through women and ties traced through men (as in kin relations, between maternal and paternal or between consanguineal and affinal kin).[8] What was interesting was how often this, and other suppositions about how claims are formulated, turned out to be true of modes of making relationships across otherwise diverse situations and societies. Conversely there was general agreement, within PTC, about which widely used concepts from the outside were particularly problematic. (Derived principally from Euro-American or Western ways of thinking, these are categories found in international discourse as well as in certain kinds of anthropology.) Many of the dichotomies presumed germane to interpretations of 'cultural property' did not hold up: conservation/innovation; borrowing from others/keeping things from others; modernity/tradition. On this last point, there is considerable evidence that what is true of Euro-American modernity is also true of Melanesian modernity: in the context of people's relations with powers they see as lying behind themselves, 'tradition' is a thoroughly contemporary construct. We come back to this in the Introduction. In the meanwhile, the Euro-American presumption that the problem of tradition is the problem of how to transmit culture[9] only partly touches on widespread Melanesian concerns with social reproduction.

PTC's conclusions at once rehearsed and diverged from positions articulated in other studies and in innumerable international documents concerned with 'indigenous cultures' and 'traditional knowledge'.[10] This is hardly surprising, given the manner in which Papua New Guineans initiate, limit and rationalise claims on one another through modes that at once endorse and challenge many of the assumptions behind these two particular categories and their permutations. Needless to say, the categories will continue to circulate in international politics, and often usefully so,[11] and there would be little point in trying to jettison them from there. But processes in the wake of – or in anticipation of – regulatory policies, including the global adoption of IPR protocols, also need to be understood and managed *analytically*. This is because of the way the aims of such policies have been absorbed into local efforts to find (legal, administrative) mechanisms to safeguard 'culture', 'indigeneity' and the rest.

The Introduction takes its cue from these interests and engages with the concept of 'cultural property' as it is understood in the internationalist arena in order to open up some of the debates it contains within. From the outset PTC found itself involved in discussions of general theoretical import, which joined both old and new debates in anthropology – and debates from elsewhere. This is the aspect of PTC's work which is taken up here. As the book proceeds, the topic of cultural property is transposed into seemingly foreign contexts and juxtaposed with interpretations of other practices of possessive ownership, knowledge creation, intellectual transmission, claim-making. The potential field is huge. So a question lies behind this collection: if one is joining debate, what debates might it be interesting to join? The following chapters offer some suggestions. Each contributor pursues his or her Melanesian-derived interests along theoretical trajectories that the Melanesian material has made interesting.[12]

Two local observations remain. First, the volume was being put together when UNESCO announced preparations for a new standard-setting instrument in the area of 'intangible cultural heritage'[13] That was hardly on the horizon when the PTC project was planned in 1997/8.[14] Over three years of the research, Pacific states began to consider region-wide regulation to protect 'traditional knowledge' and 'expressions of culture',[15] significantly altering PTC's horizons. At the same time, one of the largest mining operations in the area underwent a radical reversal of policy at its Ok Tedi site, and in a sense altered PTC's social terrain. All along, fast-changing events have been a challenge to this investigation, a sense of speed equally apparent to Papua New Guineans. Now a sense of speed is experienced as much by village residents as by town ones, although the emphasis which national as well as international rhetoric places on the 'beliefs' of 'local people' often depicts 'village life' as though it were static.[16] This could not be further from the truth. What does endure is people's sense of themselves, and of what gives them life. It is important here to appreciate a characteristic which the country shares with others in the

Pacific: PNG is not a minority (fourth world) nation within a larger state, but an autonomous nation-state itself embracing the distinct identities of myriad local communities.[17] In this context, 'ethnic groups' or 'small ethnic societies', as they are perceived,[18] act as crucial reference points in national discourse on 'tradition'. What emerged for PTC was not the differences between such local communities but the broad similarities in people's social dealings with one another.

Second, in other contexts and from other points of view one would wish to emphasise internal heterogeneity. We should not discount the divergent interests of older and younger generations, of those who aspire to energise the new with the old and those who seek to keep the old apart, nor indeed interests inflected by gender.[19] The very project of 'cultural property' may turn out to have been the prerogative of a few.[20] This in itself is reason enough for departing from the internationalist agenda. It remains to be seen whether shifting some of the frames of analysis will or will not be helpful in the elucidation of power relations.[21]

Where research is designed to illuminate current debate, one problematic may be how to make evident what is already known. The original PTC proposal identified several issues that simply fail to go away. Prime here is the elevation of 'collective' or 'communal' rights as canonical alternatives to 'individual' or 'private' rights. However, while it may not take much to arrive at the issues, documenting their social existence is another matter. In turn, the concepts with which PTC has worked are hardly original to anthropology let alone PTC. But one does not have to be the originator, inventor or author of ideas to give them value: the question is how best they can be deployed.

Eric Hirsch and Marilyn Strathern
Brunel and Cambridge, December 2002

Notes

1. 'Property, Transactions and Creations: New Economic Relations in the Pacific' (UK Economic and Social Research Council research award no. R000237838).
2. PTC Publications directly on Melanesia include Kalinoe and Leach (2001, re-issued 2004); Sykes, Simet and Kamene 2001; Proceedings of the Motupore conference on 'Transaction and Transmission of Indigenous Knowledge and Expressions of Culture', *Melanesian Law Journal*, vol.27, 2000.
3. CBD 1992; for an early anthropological comment on TRIPS (Trade-Related Aspects of Intellectual Property Rights) 1994, see Coombe (1996: 245); on the background to TRIPS, see e.g. Simpson (1997: ch. 6).
4. Patents and Industrial Designs Act 2000; Copyright and Neighbouring Rights Act 2000. Papua New Guinea joined WIPO (World Intellectual Property Organisation) in 1997.
5. With the connotations of 'cultural protection' (see Introduction). International interest in cultural protection acquired a new focus when UNESCO and WIPO

(World Intellectual Property Organisation) joined forces in 1978/9 to agree an approach on the international protection of 'folklore' (Blake 2001). Whereas UNESCO was to concentrate on the protection of cultural heritage, WIPO was to consider the application of IPR to what is now called 'traditional knowledge'. This resulted in a set of *Model Provisions for National Laws on the Protection of Expressions of Folklore against Illicit Exploitation and other Prejudicial Actions* 1982; it has rarely been implemented and nowhere adopted in full (Blake 2001: 28). It was followed in 1989 by UNESCO's *Recommendation on the Safeguarding of Traditional Culture and Folklore*, which also found it hard to gain momentum (Simon n.d., and see Chapter 2, this volume). For the UN Sub-Committee on the Prevention of Discrimination and Protection of Minorities and its Working Group on Indigenous Populations, in 1993 Erica-Irene Daes produced *The Study on the Protection of the Cultural and Intellectual Property of Indigenous Peoples*, which was something of a turning point. Indigenous People's declarations included the 1993 Mataatua *Declaration on the Cultural and Intellectual Property Rights of Indigenous Peoples*. (Texts can be found in Posey 1996; Simpson 1997.) Eriksen (2001) offers a sympathetic critique of UNESCO's efforts, and particularly of the publication, *Our Creative Diversity* (WCCD 1995; also see the volume edited by Arizpe 1996). Questions of cultural appropriation had long been tackled from another direction, namely the politics of identity (for recent discussion: see Merry 2001; Eriksen 2001), and in other quarters, drawing on long standing concerns for instance in the politics of nationhood (e.g. Rowlands 1998; the cases in Cowan et al. 2001: chs 7–10).
6. See, for example, Taylor (2000). For anthropologists, ethnobotany and biological resources were a significant prompt (e.g. Brush 1993, 1994; Posey 1996; Ellen and Harris 1997). The questions at this point were whether IPR could indeed provide remedies for the recognition of indigenous knowledge, values and ways of life that other legal instruments could not (Greaves 1994; Patel 1996). It was not lost on the anthropological community that property claimed in the name of IPR had the potential to impinge on the activities of many ethnographers working in non-Western contexts who make 'culture' their subject matter (Greaves 1995).
7. If indeed it was ever convincingly so (Kuper 1999). The notion of cultures in the plural was anathema to many mid-century British social anthropologists – logically, you could only pluralise social units.
8. Familiar to anthropology in the study of lineal kinship systems, where the claims of non-lineal kin (those outside a person's lineage or clan group) may be accorded special weight as an external 'cause' of the person's life. Compare the argument in the philosophy of intellectual property that the intangible cannot be property in the way chattels or land are yet a person can nonetheless own the proprietary right to the commercial exploitation of an intangible – such as information – as the 'cause' of bringing that (intangible) entity into being (Libling 1978: 104).
9. It is now a well-cited position in the cultural property literature that 'tradition' refers less to the products of cultural life than to modes of transmission. '[T]he social process of learning and sharing knowledge unique to every culture is at the heart of its "traditionality"'; this derives from a submission to the 1992 Convention on Biological Diversity by the Four Directions Council, an organisation of Canadian indigenous peoples, who prefaced it with the remark that 'what is "traditional" about traditional knowledge is not its antiquity but the way it is acquired and used' (cited by Dutfield 1999a: 105, emphasis omitted).

10. Innumerable not only because of the many forums at which debate has taken place, but because numerous countries across the world have addressed the issue of protection and regulation in this field.
11. For example, Matainaho 2000; Tobin 2000.
12. One stimulus here was the manner in which we became aware of the kinds of combinations (of concepts, of tangible and intangible elements) through which Papua New Guineans often provoke further thought or create new entities. What arose from one or two individual reflections came to pervade much of PTC's informal discussions.
13. UNESCO 2001: First Preliminary Draft of an International Convention for the Safeguarding of Intangible Cultural Heritage.
14. A joint conference held by UNESCO and the Smithsonian Institution in late 1999 reassessed earlier (1989) recommendations on the safeguarding of traditional culture and folklore and spurred on the present round of activity, including regional and subregional consultations by UNESCO and WIPO in which Drs Jacob Simet (anthropologist) and Lawrence Kalinoe (lawyer) from PNG were involved.
15. The 'Model Law': see Introduction.
16. Only from certain perspectives are village people in Papua New Guinea – three-quarters of the population – usefully described as 'rural' (as many villagers have lived in towns as urban residents claim village roots).
17. Contra the working definition of 'indigenous' used by UN Agencies, which refers to non-dominant sectors of society (cited by Blake 2001: 60; some of the internal debate as to the meaning of 'indigenous' can be found in Simpson 1997: 22–23). Papua New Guinea has a unique resource in the flexibility of its existing provisions for recognising 'customary law'; uncodified, ubiquitously admissible where its relevance is demonstrated, along with English common law it is part of the underlying law of the country. However, see Busse and Whimp (2000: 20–21), quoting Nonggor (1995), for its frequent overshadowing by common law.
18. 'Ethnic groups': used by the former Chief Ombudsman on PNG in 1997 talking about the protection of 'traditional' dance and music by legislation (reported by Kalinoe 2001). 'Small ethnic societies': used by a National Court judge defending the precedence of 'modern national laws' over certain customary practices that had been admitted as evidence in court (PNGLR 1997).
19. These points were forcefully reiterated by colleagues on several occasions, including Lisette Josephides (n.d.), Martha Macintyre (n.d.) and Katherine Verdery (discussant at the 2002 AAA presentations), and see Jolly (2000). The substantial literature on 'women' in relation to Human Rights discourse hardly needs referencing (discussed, for example, from several perspectives in Part I of Cowan et al. 2001). The reciprocal and divergent interests of women students and men experts in New Ireland and New Britain informed the compilation of Sykes et al. 2001.
20. See for example the Pacific-based (Maori) criticism of Smith (1998), with thanks to Claudia Gross.
21. The displacement of a view of 'communal' claims on collective resources by one which acknowledged 'multiple' claims, for instance, would shift the starting point of any critique based on the exclusion of specific categories of persons from being able to make claims in the first place.

Acknowledgements

The research project (PTC) out of which this volume comes was funded by the UK Economic and Social Research Council (award no. R000237838), whose support is gratefully acknowledged. Capitalising on the record of UK research in Melanesia, the principal investigators (Hirsch and Strathern) were joined by five UK-trained or UK-based social anthropologists (Crook, Demian, Holding, Leach, Sykes) with first-hand experience of PNG. They also enlisted a US anthropologist (Kirsch) who had just completed work on Urgent Anthropology at Goldsmiths, London, and from Papua New Guinea a lawyer (Kalinoe) engaged with property issues; the foremost professional anthropologist in PNG (Simet) became an affiliate. While no one was contracted for more than a year or eighteen months, PTC members remained committed through the three years. Andrew Holding has not contributed to the volume, but his input into the project must get very special mention. Both Lissant Bolton and Adam Reed gave friendship and support throughout, as did Debbora Battaglia. The project also drew on expertise willingly offered by many colleagues within and outside anthropology.

Madeline Watt is owed special thanks as the PTC administrator, and very much more. As Head of the Cambridge Social Anthropology Department, Stephen Hugh-Jones was also an ally, while the office under Sally Reynolds smoothed our way on many occasions. Three of us enjoyed Visiting Fellowships at Clare Hall and thank Gillian Beer for her hospitality. We are grateful to Benedicta Rousseau for help in preparing the manuscript, and to Françoise Barbira-Freedman for her sustaining role at the outset. David Zeitlyn guided our record keeping. Finally, Sandra Bamford's critical judgement is enormously appreciated, as are the good offices of Marion Berghahn and Sean Kingston.

If PTC wanted to make previous anthropological work available in ways it had not been, and available to colleagues in Papua New Guinea, the matter was not of course in its hands. Here we record the stimulus of people from PNG who gave it their own distinctive value. Among many others we would include Lois Stanley Baduk, Ilaiah Bigilale, Sinclair Dinnen, Colin Filer, Sebastine Haraha, Sakarepe Kamene, Jessica Kuambu, Bronya Kumalgo, Siriman Kumbukau, Ru Kundil, James Laki, Oayap Maken, Andrew Moutu, Don Niles, Peter (Porer) Nombo, Jacob Simet,

Elizabeth Suelip, Donna Talvat, Libo Tatias, Julie To'Liman Turalir, Tegela Waine, Sanita Waiut, and the very beginning of it all, Mark Busse and Claudia Gross. The School of Law and Business Studies at the University of Papua New Guinea, and its Publications Unit, proved of great practical help. We are grateful for the assistance of the National Research Institute (NRI); the Institute of Papua New Guinea Studies; the PNG National Museum; the PNG National Cultural Commission and, as consultant to WIPO, Pacific region, Kamal Puri.

Those who contributed to three PTC colloquia included people who contributed in numerous other ways as well: Françoise Barbira-Freedman, Tim Bayliss-Smith, Lissant Bolton, Linus digim'Rina, Susan Drucker-Brown, David Ellis, Colin Filer, Simon Harrison, Stephen Hugh-Jones, Caroline Humphrey, Sean Kingston, Heonik Kwon, Craig Lind, Carlos Mondragon, Mark Mosko, Andrew Moutu, Michael O'Hanlon, Bronwyn Parry, Frances Pine, William Rea, Adam Reed, Helena Regius, Michael Rowlands, Gerhard Schneider, David Sneath, Eduardo Viveiros de Castro, James Weiner; we also drew specifically on the expertise of James Carrrier, Lisette Josephides, Annelise Riles and Paul Sillitoe. Katherine Verdery and Eduardo Viveiros de Castro commented on a presentation of several of the chapters, from which we learnt much.

This is also the moment to acknowledge invaluable financial assistance given to various PTC activities: from the Departments of Law, Anthropology and Sociology, and Language and Literature, at the University of Papua New Guinea; in the UK from the British Academy; the Centre for Learning and Teaching in Sociology, Anthropology and Politics (C-SAP); the Centre for Research in the Arts, Social Sciences and Humanities, Cambridge University; Manchester University Staff Development Fund; the Royal Anthropological Institute; the (Cambridge) Smuts Fund; and also at Cambridge, in diverse ways, Corpus Christi, Darwin College and Girton College.

Some of the contributors have added their own acknowledgements. All of us are aware how much the individual chapters owe to conversations, collaborations and conflicts between us.

List of Abbreviations

BHP	Broken Hill Proprietary
CBD	Convention on Biological Diversity (1992)
CMCA	Community Mine Continuation Agreements
IPR	Intellectual Property Rights
HGDP	Human Genome Diversity Project
NIH	National Institutes of Health (US)
NGO	Nongovernmental organisation
PIC	Pacific Island countries
PNG	Papua New Guinea
PTC	Property, Transactions and Creations research project
OTML	Ok Tedi Mining Limited (Papua New Guinea)
RAFI	Rural Advancement Foundation International
TK	Traditional Knowledge
TRIPS	Trade-Related Aspects of Intellectual Property Rights agreement
UNESCO	United Nations Educational, Scientific and Cultural Organisation
WIPO	World Intellectual Property Organisation
WTO	World Trade Organisation

INTRODUCTION

Marilyn Strathern and Eric Hirsch

One might imagine that divisions between cultures were noncompetitive. Or one might imagine the very opposite, that there are countless situations in which a difference of culture is hauled forward to explain conflicting values, misinterpretations, opposition to certain practices, exclusions that offend and inclusions that offend. But what by definition has long been noncompetitive is the idea that the cultures of the world claim distinctiveness through claiming what belongs to them, rather as people point to their ancestors. Who would want someone else's ancestors? There is a surprising indication that, over the last quarter-century or so, a competition of sorts has crept into cultural claims of precisely this kind: it shows itself every time culture is linked to property. For 'cultural property' has acquired a new currency, an expansion of its old high art or museological sense in terms of national monuments and artistic heritage[1] into a rallying call for protection against misuse, exploitation and even theft, and of anything from designs to medical know-how. Its frequent coupling with a category borrowed directly from law, 'intellectual property', shows some of its new kinship. Rather than 'cultural' separating out one kind of property from another, the new connotations refer to making 'property' out of whatever appears to be culturally important. The further implication is that there are interests in 'culture' which need to be promulgated and defended, and by the same token that there may be rival interests requiring negotiation and remedy.

It is not often that people literally claim other people's ancestors. Outside the rather special environment of museums, more often it is the case that they wish to incorporate some design or invention into something ancestral of theirs. This kind of intellectual traffic has always characterised human intercourse. However, it is not the borrowing or copying or incorporation of art or ideas that gives voice to a problem – that voice lies in the protest of those who see by that act something of theirs being taken away, and often something primordial. To take away is not necessarily to deprive people of continuing use or enjoyment, but it deprives them of exclusive identification, or compromises them through disrespect (Puri 1995). Ancestry can thus be 'stolen' to the degree that its defining features are no longer in fact definitive for the descendants. Such views may be part of a postcolonial agenda, as attested by instances from the literature on the repatriation of items deposited in museums.[2]

For old forms of competition, against which copyright and patent were some kind of guard, take on new guises when people also claim that what is being taken away belongs to them as part of themselves. We do not mean part of their body or possessions (though either of these may supply apt imagery) but part of the social milieu in which they live. This is often translated into the now ubiquitous international language of (ancestral) 'tradition'.[3] Whether or not others appropriate that tradition *as* tradition (their own particular tradition, generalised national tradition) will depend on context. The reverse may be taken as even more problematic, that is, when tradition is *erased* in so far as what is taken is being valued for quite different properties from those it originally encapsulated and thus not for connection to (anyone's) ancestral values at all. There are all kinds of intermediate positions, most notably in the tourist industry, which knowingly promulgates other people's 'tradition' not as new traditions for the tourist customer/consumer but as souvenirs of their having been elsewhere. The ability to value what others also hold precious is not in itself to be decried. The disputes are to what use such borrowings are put and in whose name they are owned.

There are two points here, one with which most anthropologists would quarrel, and one with which they would not. The first is the international[4] concept of 'tradition' and the way it feeds into understandings of culture.[5] Most anthropologists would be critical of any easy translation. But second, not unrelated to their own interests in the matter, they would probably listen very carefully when people claim it is their knowledge that is being taken away.[6] Again, the ability to learn from others is not in itself to be decried (Araho 2000). The disputed issue is the rights, including rights to benefits, that ownership might confer.

Global Momentum

'Cultural property' has in effect moved from its location within the world of national monuments and heritage conservation to fuse with notions of 'cultural rights' (Cowan, et al. 2001). While there is 'nothing unusual about communities mobilizing what power they can command to protect a valued resource, [or] maintain a traditional practice ... What does appear to be new is asserting such claims on the basis of culture' (Winthrop 2002a: 116). But then culture has already come to stand for numerous axes of social differentiation, for any set of distinctive practices. No wonder that ownership in the name of culture attracts media attention and is a focus for diverse local and international interests. Without going into great detail about anthropology's initial explorations,[7] it is worth noting that the fusion (of cultural property and cultural rights) simultaneously engaged with the possible application of intellectual property notions to items of cultural worth *and* with many objections to so doing.[8] In turn, the link with intellectual property rights (IPR) released the notion of property (in this context) from its moorings in material objects, and showed that it could embrace design, expressions of lifestyle, information, ideas (e.g. Drahos 2000).

If the concept of culture has burst its banks in several directions – been given new life – so too has the reach of IPR (e.g. Coombe 1994; Brown 1998; McSherry 2001). Over the same period, 'intellectual property' has moved from an exclusive location within legal discourse into much wider public prominence, an item of media attention and a topic for popular and literary analysis, with 'patent' becoming as well known a term as 'copyright'. The domain of patenting has itself been stretched, first by the creation of new objects, electronic or biogenetic, which both do and do not conform to industrial artefacts, and second by new clamours over the kind of rights that patents confer (among recent consultations in the UK, Nuffield Council on Bioethics 2002; CIPR 2002). The same is true of copyright, where technological developments in reproduction, not least in the communications and music industries, have opened up questions about access and control. Many of the questions have become ubiquitous: intellectual property thinking is as global as the problems spread by its special kind of rights discourse.

A regime of intellectual property rights, then, introduces the possibility that resources may be as intangible as ideas and names or could lie in almost any manifestation of distinctiveness.[9] The question that continues to preoccupy many countries outside the industrial West is whether one can in fact apply intellectual property protection to the distinctive artefacts, performances and repositories of wisdom that identify 'a culture'. Culture bearers, it is implied, have an interest in exactly how these at once tangible and intangible aspects of their lives are made available to others. Concerns of this kind could only emerge in a social situation where such aspects already appear appropriatable – where they are not only translated into items to be shared, transacted or otherwise part of the network of communications between people, but where they begin to take on the character of assets to be owned and exploited. In short, ownership claims emerge in a world of owners. The parallel with the exploitation of natural resources has been a key factor here, and Papua New Guinea's experience is no exception.[10]

Safeguarding heritage, protecting culture (more properly, reifications of culture, as in the phrase 'expressions of culture'), giving status to knowledge because it is traditional: such ideas do not circulate in a vacuum. Contemporary notions of ownership in Papua New Guinea are stimulated by ventures such as mining and logging, which bring new perceptions of assets and proprietorship over them, as does tourism, displays of tradition and perceptions of loss, for instance loss of the kinds of know-how displaced by schooling. Local interests in resources of all kinds (where 'resources' already imply claims to exclusiveness) ride alongside both national interest in the protection of biological assets and international talk of indigenous rights. A seminar held in Port Moresby in 1997 on Intellectual, Biological and Cultural Property Rights (Whimp and Busse 2000) gathered exactly these dimensions together.[11] The occasion was more than an academic exercise: the NGOs who mounted the seminar were aware that the government was anticipating legislation, in line with international requirements to widen the arenas in which commercially recognised copyright and patent legislation would apply. At the time of legislation, in 2000, the PNG National Intellectual Property Rights Committee would have argued for more sophisticated mechanisms for the recognition of cultural practices, but this went beyond the terms of reference. In the meanwhile, WIPO/UNESCO have promoted regional plans for a *Model Law for the Protection of Traditional Knowledge and Expressions of Culture in the Pacific Islands*,[12] to which PNG has contributed.[13] While importantly sidestepping IPR regimes as such, early drafts endorsed notions of 'property rights' in 'expressions of culture' and the identification of 'traditional owners'.

The conjunction of culture, property and rights (cultural property, cultural rights, property rights), and the 'indigenous' or 'traditional' character of many societies seeking international protection,[14] has helped create a phenomenon little short of a global civil movement. Papua New Guinea's recent history here can be put within the framework of the larger one of which it is part. That belongs to the history of relations between developed and developing countries, and between minorities and states.

It was as a point of potential negotiation between such polities that an explicit link between culture and tradition came internationally to the fore in the 1990s (notably after Daes 1993; see Preface to present volume n. 5). It circulated as part of the currency by which new nations, so to speak, could deal with the international community. When culture and tradition could be described as encoding knowledge, they accompanied recognition of biological, environmental and other knowledge-sensitive resources. The question of protection (sustainability, ownership), alongside that of appropriate exploitation (with just reward), thus arose from the association of traditional knowledge with protocols about natural resources which had figured in the Convention on Biological Diversity (e.g. Swanson 1995; Brush and Orlove 1996; Blakeney 1999a). Stimulated by the UN Decade of the World's Indigenous Peoples (1995–2004), the ownership and protection of resources became a rallying call not just in defence of national and local interests but for a conscious promotion of the 'indigenous' as the basis for a special class of claims.[15] Indigeneity, originally tied to being of a place, is now used to back up people's claims to being the original owners of resources (Simpson 1997: 48; Muehlebach 2001). If not the creators of it, they may stand as the reproducers of it. It is now widely accepted that TK (traditional knowledge) counts as an indigenous 'resource'.[16]

In any event, resources are not ipso facto property (Gudeman 1996; Posey and Dutfield 1996). Whether a property right was ever an appropriate mode for the negotiation of interests in resources, however defined, was a question anthropologists raised from the outset of their own involvement in these (TK/IPR) debates. What kinds of relations do property rights imply, what kind of economic regime? Social anthropology's genealogy as a discrete discipline puts debate over property relations near its own beginning (one need cite only Maine and Morgan), specifically in relation to the politico-economic conditions that sustain particular forms of ownership and control.[17] And this has remained its most significant input into present discussions over cultural property.[18] Are the kinds of indigenous resources gathered under the rubric of 'cultural property' most usefully described as intellectual (Gudeman 1996)?[19] Is this, analytically speaking, the most valuable way to accord them value? Who gains, who loses?

There is a further issue. As we have already hinted, the very terms in which 'traditional' rights are claimed already belong to the international community, as indigenous conceptualisations of 'law' or 'government' belonged to colonial regimes. And what is true of their English versions also affects their local counterparts. The point is epitomised in the Tok Pisin (neo-Melanesian) concept of *kastom* by which people indicate what makes them distinctive. Whether or not it is appropriately translated as 'tradition' is a moot point. *Kastom* refers to practices flowing across the generations which (like reproductive power) are to be found in habits, conduct and well-being definitive of the present; in Bolton's (2003) words, *kastom* is not conserved but enacted, and may have a transactable or communicational value in relation to outsiders (Harrison 1999; Mosko 2002).[20] Kalinoe (1999: 35) writes of Papua New Guinea custom that it need not have existed from time immemorial, or without interruption, and is 'fluid, flexible and responsive to social change'. Bolton would further argue for Vanuatu[21] that it is 'the product of the *interaction* between expatriate ideas of culture and custom and ni-Vanuatu conceptualizations of their [own] knowledge and practice' (2003: 52 emphasis added). It does not, in this sense, refer to precolonial processes or representations. At the same time, nonetheless, people may serve their *own* interests in using it to evoke an older era by contrast with modern times, and here the divergent perspectives of older and younger generations, or of men and women, may be highly relevant.[22]

The present volume offers a counterweight to some of the rhetoric of cultural property – not in order to pit local realities against global assertions but in order to think about analytical tools. As we have already implied, 'indigeneity', 'heritage', 'traditional knowledge' and such get filtered through the discourse of an international community that must trade in its own conceptual currency (NGO forums, UNESCO, WIPO). But what may be important politically may be less than useful analytically. One double-headed expatriate stereotype would bother anthropologists of the Pacific. On the one hand, here as elsewhere, one hears a variation on the ubiquitous theme that technology races ahead while society lags behind: 'developing' countries are regarded as held back by entrenched traditions and values that must be changed if they are to catch up. On the other hand, such countries are frequently characterised as having communal and collective forms of ownership which do not fit individualised notions of property rights. For Papua New Guinea, such stereotypes perpetuate a stultifying view of 'traditional communities', with little regard to the realities of (economic) life on the ground. The anthropological literature describes a country abounding in evidence of people's openness to novel social forms, inventiveness in negotiation, readiness to borrow practices – from one another and from outside.[23] Transactions occur in numerous modes and all kinds of assets can be the subject of them. Leaving aside the misnomer 'communal',[24] group or collective interests are only part of a wide range of models for people's dealings with one another over the nurture and disposal of resources, and a totally inadequate description of the relationships at stake. It would be surprising if none of this was not sometimes true elsewhere.

The Model Law must trade in concepts recognisable to numerous governments in the Pacific. But there may be local implications.[25] As far as Papua New Guinea practice is concerned, there is often a trade-off between people attributing a hidden (in that sense intangible) power to something and turning it into a concrete (tangible) presence. Indeed, the management of resources, economic and otherwise, could be undermined by outside attempts at codification (Brown 2003; 1998), that is, by classifying types of objects as though value were inscribed in the object rather than in the social context of its management. Consider for instance the management of 'loss'. Loss could mean much or little, but people's experience of loss of knowledge (say) is only partly matched by compensation regimes, and there is concern that formal 'protection' mechanisms could expose more than they conserved. As elsewhere, anxiety over secret or sacred knowledge points to the need for other forms of protection than a law which will make things public (Simet n.d.).[26] You cannot tell from looking at the cultural classification; you need to know the social relationships involved.

By contrast with such 'indigenous' concerns, the intangible in Western-derived law, epitomised as form of expression, invention, knowledge and so forth, gives rise to a special class of assets (hence the 'intellectual' in intellectual property rights). The class is defined by the fact that rights can be laid to the creative processes that brought them into being. This was where the IPR debate left its stamp on the aims of the authors' research project (see Preface). The way in which 'creativity' is recognised, valued and made the subject of property rights in Euro-American (Western) contexts, opened up questions about innovation, authorship and reproduction in Melanesian ethnography, and in relation to phenomena often considered separately – the arts, performance, ancestral knowledge, science, and so forth.[27] At the same time as it became increasingly clear that IPR was not the way forward for the protection of cultural property, as a domain of Euro-American discourse it proved a stimulating prod to the anthropologists' enquiries.

Throughout, the contributors have been faced with situations that have often appeared familiar, so that the issue is less a matter of recognising a social phenomenon as deciding where to situate the analysis. Anthropologists are all too aware of how ideas, interpretations, models and so forth travel across domains. At the same time, that awareness should sharpen what is already a dual concern in the discipline: the persuasiveness of key concepts prevalent in national or international arenas and, in a different dimension altogether, the utility of such concepts for the analysis of current social realities. It is with this in mind that we have organised the book.

The Three Terms

The book summons three constructs: property, transactions and creations. What is the nature of their salience in the arena we have broadly sketched and how might anthropologists these days wish to deploy them to analytical ends? The first is a key term in international parlance; the other two are of different status. There could have been many more terms than three, and each no doubt has alternatives. But a triad is the minimum structure that can recreate for analysis the kind of incommensurabilities that characterise action and debate in this area.[28] Enacting the point, the contributors have brought into focus constructs that are not of the same order at all. They take up the challenge of delineating something of the pasts and futures of these terms or constructs, creating trajectories that could give them continuing analytical purchase.

There seem to be ever new entities subject to claims based on ownership rights, and property is taken to be the obvious form that ownership will take; its exclusionary possibilities engage economic development and political protest alike. For the social scientist, property has become a dangerously interesting term to use. It travels along with NGOs, human rights discourse, multinational companies and the expanding universe of the life sciences to broker all kinds of relationships between people and the products of people's enterprises. It has international currency as a ubiquitous fact of life. But it also has its own life within the politics of the nation-state, the industrial revolution, and the economies of empire, in addition to disciplinary histories within the sciences of human behaviour, including social anthropology.

What makes 'property' dangerously interesting is the long history of objections to it – political and moral. Indeed it has the capacity to rally protest, and in Europe and America 400 years of protest show no signs of abating. But, as we have said, to step outside the discourse of property – as the contributors to this book have done in other contexts – would be to refuse engagement with a powerful international tool. Instead they have here bracketed it with two other concepts. Transactions and creations allow space for fresh critical discourse. This is not least because of their strangeness. There are situations where *not* to borrow and incorporate the works of others may be the greater blindness. 'Transactions' are borrowed from practices often made evident and public in Melanesia, although often 'creations' can only be revealed as such to the observant. In the process Melanesians would likely insist on the differentiating effects of interaction, and relish the way 'otherness' is made to appear. Indeed, thinking about the life of all these concepts particularly through the ideas of people in Papua New Guinea, whether university scholars, village scholars or no scholars at all, is intended to show what can be learnt through intellectual traffic – and what must be learnt (Araho 2000: 187–88).

In brief, *property* points to a species of reification where the values of ownership and possession become identified with the thing owned or possessed (Hann 1998b). Property implies an entity in some substantive, specific form. This means that as an analytical concept it is more appropriate to some economic regimes rather than others. Heavily overdetermined in so many dimensions of Euro-American society, it is a term on which anthropology has few special claims. *Transaction*, by contrast, has a special place in the anthropological tradition that could well be brought into the foreground. Transaction is not tied to content. Rather like 'communication', it refers to a general human facility or inclination, here the ability to compute ratios of values, that is, render something exchangeable by expressing one set of values in terms of another. But that is only half of it. If we talk of transactions we are also talking of specific social interactions, of events at which such conversions have taken place, and thus of a deal or negotiation which has fixed the values on that occasion. In so far as transactions effect or realise (make present or real) the transactability of items, transactions differ from *creations*. This last is something of an innovative area for anthropologists to address.[29] Indeed, interest in IPR has generated a host of new questions about creativity. For 'creativity' acquires the status of a self-evident value in debates such as those which would bring TK into the picture. No surprise perhaps that we witness everywhere new reifications of peoples,[30] new interest groups with apparently primordial boundaries anxious to draw outside attention to claims framed in terms of indigenous creativity. But perhaps creativity is a special preoccupation of energy-consuming capitalism[31] and thus an interested and specific description of the connections between activities and outcomes. How, then, does the anthropologist approach attributions of ingenuity or agency, the sources of energy to which people point, the power of throwing off balance (after Wagner 1975) conventional relations between convention and invention? To imagine creations as the work of people, embodying their know-how in producing novel effects, simultaneously puts value on enactments, including self-consciously customary practices, and on the creative persons who are valued for what they enact. The relationships here open up interesting questions.

Let us return to the point about familiarity. As will become obvious, being of different orders, the three terms do not compete with or exclude one another; they are distributed, albeit with differing weight, across all the chapters. In this the chapters dovetail with one another, just as at certain moments they dovetail ethnographically. The following outline of individual themes makes some of this evident. But as far as issues of analysis are concerned, rather than pointing to a narrative weaving its way through the contributions, as though they could be strung out in linear fashion, we would point instead to the recurrence or replication of commonly stated problems. This is what it means to live in 'a connected-up world' – not that there are links and sequences, to provide routes and maps, but that wherever one is, whatever aspect of the topic one picks up, the landscape is already familiar, one seems to have been there before. Similar themes recur over and again. At the same time each subsists on a slightly different trajectory of thought and practice. Focusing on these three constructs deliberately exaggerates, and thus makes visible, the divergences between trajectories.

Property, Transactions and Creations

Part I: Property

At the outset, the book confronts the reader with new discourses on property regimes. Stuart Kirsch (Chapter 1) explores three areas key to the way in which Euro-Americans generally think about themselves: the human body, nature, and culture. Examples demonstrate how property concerns are shaped by other concerns in each of these areas. While the new discourses arise in the context of spreading ownership and seemingly endless propertisation, they are thus limited by the very thought practices on which these processes depend. Material from Papua New Guinea shows up the limits. It also shows up people's concerns there in three very distinct ways, and thus introduces something of the plurality of present-day Papua New Guinean life.

The first example is drawn from international responses to an attempt to patent a cell line derived from a Hagahai man from central Papua New Guinea, raising for Euro-Americans questions about the commodification of human bodies and body parts. The second addresses environmental issues, in particular the application of 'tragedy of the commons' arguments which promote propertisation as the means to foster sustainable resource use. Specific attention is paid to legal debates concerning the environmental impact of the Ok Tedi copper and gold mine in the west of the country. The final example draws from debates about the applicability of Euro-American property regimes for indigenous assertions of proprietary rights to culture as they concern policy makers. What are the continuities and disjunctions in debates about the potential commodification in relation to the human body, the management of natural resources and the distribution of environmental risks, and the comparability of different regimes for regulating the flow of cultural traffic? Through these comparisons, the first chapter seeks to clarify the basis on which claims are often made – whether property rights seem a route to economic advantage or, conversely, a solution to problems of equity and the distribution of assets.

Chapter 2 moves to a national context for these confrontations. Lawrence Kalinoe writes from the perspective of a professional committed to the law as an instrument for protection as well as for change, and from the perspective of prospects as they might appear to Papua New Guinean policy makers. The chapter introduces policy-setting concerns over the search for legal methods of regulating intellectual and cultural property sensitive to the special features of traditional knowledge. This process could well differ from what has been happening in other national contexts, for example in Australia, in so far as Papua New Guinea formally recognises customary law as part of the underlying law of the country. Significant issues identified by this chapter include multiple and overlapping claims of ownership; the need to protect local systems of privacy and secrecy, and the inappropriateness of applying cultural property rights legislation too broadly. Kalinoe is not here concerned with interrogating either international or local formulations of 'traditional knowledge'; taking these as given, he keep his interrogation for the spectrum of regulatory instruments which the law could offer. In the course of his argument he queries certain legal categories. For instance – and he draws here on country-wide consultations – distinguishing 'intellectual' from other kind of property emerges as quite problematic. This chapter debates the need for *sui generis* solutions to the challenges and opportunities of intellectual and cultural property rights protection in Papua New Guinea.

Yet similar debates, within and outside the national government, had barely got off the ground when global pressure to standardise intellectual property law led to legislation by the PNG parliament, which paid scant regard to the concerns they raised. The Copyright and Patent Acts leave no room for questions about which conceptual framework would provide the best regulatory means to assess apparently contradictory objectives. For the author's scrutiny of the law is in its own terms a cautionary tale about the competing objectives of protection and promulgation (through IPR), associated as they are with the different contexts of privacy, revelation and commercial development. Copyright and the performance and reproduction of songs provide a local case in point.

Prompted by a situation in Papua New Guinea at once specific and ubiquitous, Melissa Demian (Chapter 3) presents an issue in the philosophy of property. The visual as a domain of knowledge is a contentious one for property claims by Euro-Americans, implying an objectification of the thing observed which removes it from the world of relationships upon which such claims are dependent. Some have argued that the realm of the visual is legitimate in discussions of property because it entails the kind of act of imagination which ultimately lies behind any claim to ownership. But the problem crops up anew when one is talking about forms such as intellectual property. Here the imaginative act is what brings the thing-to-be-claimed into being in the first place; can imagination do double duty as the origin for property and the vehicle for claims to ownership? The problem with relying on the imaginative act to legitimate visual knowledge is that it does not necessarily release us from assumptions about the individual nature of creativity inherent in intellectual property regimes. Relationships may be 'added' through contested claims and litigation, but the original act is still not social in that sense, implying as it does a relation not between persons but between persons (the viewer) and things (the viewed object). The beholder is not reliant on anyone else to participate in the act of beholding.

Evidence from Melanesia introduces complications. From much Melanesian ethnography, 'seeing' emerges as an intersubjective rather than objectifying act; that is, the acknowledgement of a visual manifestation includes in its appraisal other social persons. This holds equally for tangible forms of property (artefacts, land) as for intangible ones (songs, rituals); whether or not human beings are regarded as the authors or owners of the property, they are always implicated as moral – or aesthetic or cosmological – contributors to its appearance. Subsequent claims of ownership thus involve assumptions about the social value of things which may in Western conceptions hold only abstract value. Yet such claims may in a sense anticipate certain kinds of value implicit in intellectual property, which in Euro-American legal milieux must be endowed with concrete attributes in order to be claimed as property at all. Where both property regimes appear to converge is in the moment of revelation which enables a claim to be made. In IPR contexts this moment is a legal one; in many Melanesian contexts the revelation may literally amount to ceremonial or ritual display. But, in both, creating a visible index to property is the point at which property described as intellectual reveals itself to be a mediator of relationships. Property, it is argued, is a communications technology.

Part II: Transactions

The concept of 'transactions' had its theoretical moment in social anthropology at a time when gift exchange wedded economic choice theory to universals in communication. In the first of three chapters on transactions, Marilyn Strathern asks what the concept might contribute to debates over intellectual property. The question is particularly germane where discourse bifurcates into issues of ownership on the one hand and of creativity on the other, and where the same path appears to lead in either direction: an obsession with the difference between individual and collective or communal ('social') claims. Arguably, it is this obsession that enables cultural property to be taken as both like and unlike intellectual property.

Yet opening up transactions lands the anthropologist, as usual, in situations not of her own making. Chapter 4 introduces controversy over individual and collective ownership/creativity through arguments, indigenous to Euro-American thinking, which draw on ideas about commodities and gifts. Traffic in scientific exchange is often imagined as a flow of gifts. In this milieu, concerns about rewards falling to individual initiatives when they have been backed with collective resources (often translated as private versus public interests) have a parallel in disputes elsewhere over exclusive and inclusive claims to cultural property. But the kinds of transactions at stake show up the controversy – the respectives virtues of individual and collective rights – as two sides of the same Euro-American coin. From this viewpoint, it is no controversy at all but a predictable alternation between poles. The chapter seeks ethnographic inspiration from different quarters altogether in order to approach the alternative to these alternations offered by some Papua New Guinea material. In doing so, it returns us to the kinds of embodiment sketched in Chapter 3.

Tony Crook observes the individual/collective poles from another perspective. An ambitious totalizing transaction negotiated between 1999 and 2002, the Ok Tedi Mine Continuation Agreement, PNG, sets out an exchange that will endure long into the future. Sustainable development projects are to be funded in return for agreement to allow mining operations to continue to make profit. This innovative social contract seeks a balance between 'social' and 'environmental' concerns, and between these and commercial interests, and seeks to establish a basis for reciprocity that will never need renewal. It is in effect a transaction in perpetual motion, and it prompts anthropological reflection on the way mechanical notions of balance have influenced understandings of social process (what it takes to keep people in a state of perpetual motion) and on perpetual motion at work in social thinking (categories that go on inventing themselves).

Innovations in the history of social contract thinking reveal an abiding concern with, above all, perpetuating a balance between 'individuals' and 'society'. Chapter 5 considers moments at the close of the eighteenth and twentieth centuries when, in contrasting ways, social life appeared as a system to be managed. It proposes that a quest for perpetual motion has operated as an influential imaginary throughout the development of social contract thinking. Thus images of perpetual motion appear both in Bentham's Panopticon (a penal machine by which a central source of vision ensures the greatest observation of the greatest number of individual cells in orbit around it) and in his Utilitarianism (a code by which Society ensures the greatest happiness for the greatest number of individuals). The trick is to engineer a system that can be immune to the quality of human resources operating it, just as the Ok Tedi agreement operates through an administrative structure that aims to make decision-making social actors immune to claims based on particular interests. It thus requires a formal symmetry (compatibility) between the working parts, as in parties to an agreement. Buried (asymmetrically) in the background of the chapter is a foil to these formulations of the social contract, figured out of three episodes drawn from the Ok Tedi area.

Karen Sykes calls the chapter that follows 'Negotiating Interests in Culture' by way of drawing attention to assumptions about interest which long predate anthropological concern with transactions. If 'interest' is taken to be a ubiquitous phenomenon, what seemingly varies may either be its object or else the kind of person that it summons. In the first view, analysis turns to the way in which interests are negotiated, with the result that all exchanges appear to be the same, from Adam Smith's discussions of human nature in market transactions to present-day accounts of privatisation as a global economic practice. These discussions imply that human nature, manifest in individual intentions, must be enchained productively under legal protections if it is to be protected at all. The second view entails recognising that interest has variously been taken as libidinal (Bourdieu), a public expression of personal desires (Hobbes), a legal concern, title right or a pecuniary stake (Locke), or a theory of negotiated meaning in the transformation of values (Sahlins). But perhaps one could re-seat the concept of 'interest' from the individual person to the transaction, and understand transactions as making meaning by differentiating between interests.

The impetus to this reformulation comes from negotiations about cultural property in New Ireland which operate on the axis of generational difference. Certainly these dimensions polarised people from Lelet. Agreeing both on the object of their negotiations (plans for housing 'culture' in a local museum) and on the kind of person it would make (proper 'heirs' to tradition), it was the interests at stake which emerged with radically different implications for people's ways of being. The chapter takes a cue from Wagner, who argues that a theory of meaningful communication must also make sense. Often 'human nature' gains sway over the governance of the meaningful grounds of interaction because most of what happens in communication demands too immediate a response to have any correspondence with descriptions that might be made of its meaning. Analysis of the negotiation of interest needs to expose the processes of naturalisation which create the grounds by which expression indeed comes to make sense. These New Ireland examples of culture under negotiation show interests founded on an explicit and communicable incompatibility, whose exaggeration was part of a wider series of 'transactions' taken for granted as a confrontation between the generations.

Part III: Creations

When creativity is so valorised, as it is in capitalist rhetoric, is so frequently singled out as a capacity that lies as much behind economic innovation as behind personal development, is so promoted and encouraged as a source of advancement and enrichment, what is the anthropologist to do with it? In Chapter 7, James Leach makes out a case for comparative use: 'creativity' is shown to have some purchase as an analytic concept. What is broadcast in media and government discussions (his examples come from the UK) as a value to aspire to – and an attribute to be rewarded – rests on a cluster of specific notions about how persons combine their efforts with a world of goods and materials that lie beyond them. If we take up the question of combination elsewhere, and Leach's elsewhere is Reite in Papua New Guinea's Madang District, we may find other combinations directed to similar-sounding goals (novelty, regeneration of life). Reite residents are concerned with the mixing of people's efforts with one another. Although the chapter draws its material from very different peoples and societies, these are not its units of comparison; rather, its focus is on types of social action, and it develops the idea of 'modes of creativity' to this end.

One outcome of the exercise is new light thrown on Euro-American dualisms, such as subject and object, mental and material, that drive intellectual property debates. Reite residents have been used to slicing their world in interestingly different ways. The fact that they do not make certain distinctions (such as agency as diacritical of the difference between human and non-human) does not mean their interests are 'communal'. On the contrary, Leach shows the obligations and powers that come from minute attention to discrimination between persons and the origins of what they create in social life. This in turn renders interesting the reasons why business can seem to fail, and why for all their concern with novelty and regeneration, and with money and its growth, new forms of economic activity are often short-lived.

In the final chapter, Eric Hirsch brings us back to earlier themes. Chapter 8 takes up a general problem analysed in science studies and a particular one. The general problem is the way people's creations enter science already separate from non-creations of nonscientific value. The particular problem is exemplified by creations identified through legal procedures, such as patents that confer property rights. Both have been analysed as processes of boundary-work. But what occurs in the establishment of boundaries? Among other things, it invariably involves a complex series of negotiations and transactions. However, when the key issue is viewed as the boundary to inventiveness and its claims to credibility, analytical attention is diverted from transactions themselves. Credibility moves centre stage in the extent to which scientific creations presented through patents (say) are increasingly subject to critique. The link between inventiveness and ownership is challenged, or denied, when outcomes are seen as the consequence of acquired conventional knowledge. Based on recent Melanesian ethnography, this chapter offers a fresh perspective on the dilemma of scientific creations. Analogous processes of boundary-work and credibility contests occur around what appear as Melanesian creations, whether novel social or ceremonial forms. Such entities are neither the sole work of invention nor the automatic product of conventional or traditional practices but very clearly the outgrowth of particular transactions between persons. In short, it is the negotiations and transactions, as relations between persons, which establish credibility.

This Melanesian perspective complements those critiques offered by science studies which have highlighted the limits to imagining creations as the outcome of individual effort. Where transactions establish a boundary between what is and is not credible, they are very much a part of what has been created. Here the chapter revisits the Hagahai controversy, and puts it alongside the judgements of Fuyuge people about what of culture is or is not created in (say) disco dances. Cultural creations in this part of the world become speeded up through new forms which, no less than scientific innovations, require promotion, assimilation and debate.

Endnote

We think it has been important to reiterate the way problems and issues flourish in 'a connected-up world'. As was said earlier, being connected up means not that there are clear sequences to provide routes and maps through the complexities, but that wherever one is, whatever the aspect of the topic one picks up, one seems to have been there before, giving the sense that similar themes recur over and again. In the world of policy makers and NGOs, observers and legislators, voters and opinion formers, it is important to recognise the character of arguments in the mouths of others. What are the social trajectories on which they subsist? In a provocative comment on the one world in which we all live, Weiner[32] points to the work of differentiation: in some situations, and he writes specifically of Aboriginal Australia, 'culture' lies precisely in the relationships, procedures and so forth that burgeon between indigenous communities, governments, NGOs and claimant corporations. The various ways in which Melanesians do and do not make themselves part of that world continue to propel the work of anthropology.

Notes

1. The connotations of most preexisting cultural property legislation. At Papua New Guinea's independence in 1975, the National Cultural Property Ordinance (1965) became the National Cultural Property (Preservation) Act (Busse 2000); the National Cultural Commission was a statutory body set up in 1994 to play an active role in the promotion of the 'traditional cultures' of PNG. UNESCO's 1972 Convention concerning the Protection of the World Cultural and Natural Heritage demarcated specific sites of world cultural heritage, in the same way as cultural property laws are concerned with original artefacts or monuments, and thus with conservation and not with practices of reproduction (cf. Coombe 1993: 264).
2. O'Hanlon (2000: 30-31) observes that while the dominant perception of ethnographic collections is that they are sequestered 'cultural property' this is not only very often a 'Westernised' view but a view from now rather than from then (at the time of collecting). This does not of course erase the inequality and ignorance under which the original transactions were made.
3. Numerous concepts refer to the recognition of ownership rights in tradition, heritage, indigenous knowledge, folkore, expressions of culture etc. The Pacific Region Model Law (see p. xx) proposes a part-time Advisory Body, to be called Pacific Traditional Knowledge and Expressions of Culture Board, while the central administrative body is to have the title Pacific Intellectual and Cultural Property Organisation. It is of course a matter of contention to assimilate access to and deployment of 'traditional knowledge' to a property right. The UN Working Group on Indigenous Populations, participants at the World Intellectual Property Organization Roundtables on Intellectual Property and Indigenous Peoples (1998, 1999), called for adequate protection of the 'traditional knowledge' and 'cultural values' of indigenous peoples without presuming that the relationship was one of property ownership.

4. 'International' is used, here and in the phrase 'international community', to refer to what might better be called *internationalist*: the activities of a certain cadre of extranational organisations, notably the UN and its agencies, multinational companies with a governance mission, and NGOs, aimed at a 'global' agenda (Merry's [2001: 35] 'international civil society').
5. In describing a proliferation of new representational styles, Parkin (2001: 142) concludes that 'there is no evidence of a "traditional" Swahili-Islamic culture', but then wonders if the desire to escape one's own culture and borow from others has not always been a characteristic of this particular 'cultural field'.
6. Or what in some contexts is tantamount to that when it is bypassed and ignored (Sillitoe 1998).
7. Into cultural rights and cultural property: for example, Greaves (1994); Brush and Stabinsky (1996); Brown (1998); Coombe (1998). On diverse relationships between cultural rights and human rights, see the overview of works published in the last decade in Winthrop (2002a: 117–19; Cowan et al. 2001.
8. That is, the pursuit of cultural rights may advocate a *non*-property route. It is obvious that anthropologists are participants here (and have been influential in the shape which UNESCO's concerns have taken). They are increasingly caught up in other people's projects, whether as advocates or critics or consultants, and drawn into confrontations whose terms of debate seem already given (Filer n.d; Weiner n.d.).
9. Or 'personality', as evinced commercially, for example in design rights, trademarks etc. (Coombe 1993).
10. Muehlebach (2001: 435) quotes John Kawowo from Papua New Guinea in this vein (he was speaking as a representative of the Indigenous Peoples Network on Development at the WGIP [UN Working Group on Indigenous Populations] 1997). It is worth adding that what would be true of any region of the world is made especially interesting in this case, given the contribution that Papua New Guinean cultural and intellectual life has made to social anthropology's understanding of itself.
11. The 1994 UN Draft Declaration on the Rights of Indigenous Peoples put together 'cultural, intellectual, religious and spiritual property' (in the context of restitution) (see Simpson 1997: 18; Roulet 1999; and references in the Preface to this volume [n. 4]). Blakeney 1999b discusses the Declaration from the point of view of the relevance of cultural traditions to indigenous people's property rights over plant genetic resources.
12. A sui generis proposal, initiated by the South Pacific Community and developed under the aegis of UNESCO andWIPO (original SPC consultants, Kamal Puri and Clark Peteru; WIPO consultant Kamal Puri). Previous attempts at Model Laws are mentioned at S 19, *Draft Model Law for the Pacific (2001)*. As a general framework for legislation, the Model Law was to be available for individual states to adopt as domestic law. Interested states are: Australia, Cook Islands, Micronesia, Fiji, French Polynesia, Hawaii, Marshall Islands, New Caledonia, New Zealand, Niue, Palau, Papua New Guinea, Samoa, Solomon Islands, Tonga, Tuvalu, Vanuatu.
13. For example, at the Workshop for Legal Experts on Protection of Traditional Knowledge and Expressions of Culture, Noumea, New Caledonia, 2001. The institutional context, by one who has been developing WIPO's role in all this, is given by Blakeney (2000).
14. 'The right to own property is recognised in the [UN] Universal Declaration on Human Rights and the International Convention on the Elimination

of All Forms of Racial Discrimination as a fundamental human right that extends to everyone' (Simpson 1997: 35). Adding that such international legal instruments 'do not draw on the principles of indigenous customary law', he notes that they 'assume that the sovereignty of the National State and the concept of exclusive possession lie at the heart of property rights, thereby denying the existence of collective ownership and the non-transferabilty of ownership, which are central to indigenous property systems' [ibid: 35]. (Exclusivity and transferability are taken, for example by Gray 1991, as conditions for propertisation.) Merry (2001: 35) refers to the 'new legal order' of Human Rights.

15. Not as seamlessly as this might suggest. The UN mounted strong criticism that the IPR regime embodied in the TRIPS agreement of 1994 was at odds with international human rights law (paraphrase from the UN Sub-Committee on the Promotion and Protection of Human Rights, 2000). It called for WTO to take into account existing state regulations under 'international human rights law'.

16. A position TK has secured only recently, as noted, for example, at the UK Commission on Intellectual Property Rights conference on 'How intellectual property rights could work better for developing countries and poor people', Royal Society, 2002 (cf. CIPR 2002: 73); and within the international field of indigenous cultural politics, see Muehlebach (2001). Indeed, it is as well to be reminded of the recency of this move: it was only in 1998 that WIPO set up a Global Intellectual Property Issues Division in order to include 'indigenous peoples' within its purview (Roulet 1999: 129), and 'traditional knowledge' (TK) began to take over from earlier understandings of cultural and intellectual property as a matter of folklore and monuments (see n. 3 above). As Blakeney (1999c; 2000) remarks, this significantly changes the discourse. Folklore was typically discussed in terms of copyright – traditional knowledge points towards patent law and biodiversity rights.

17. Much more recently: Hann (1998b); Macfarlane (1998), van Meijl and von Benda-Beckman (1999), as well as Carrier (1995); Filer (1997a); Harrison (2000); Humphrey (2000a, 2000b); Rumsey and Weiner (2001b); Verdery (2003); and outside anthropology, among others, Rose (1994b); Radin (1996).

18. E.g., Greaves et al., early 1990s; Posey, late 1990s. Debate is percolating back into mainstream anthropological discussion (notably Coombe 1996; Harrison 1997; Brown 2003). And beyond that, into other areas. A book on genetic privacy (Laurie 2002: 319–20), weighing up the advantages of property protection in relation to genetic information, evokes the way in which 'indigenous peoples' have sought to protect their interests in their genetic heritage; it cites the 1993 Mataatua Declaration (see Preface n. 5), and the work of Posey and Dutfield.

19. From the start of taking indigenous peoples into account, the international community recognised the problems of IPR. Indeed Daes's 1993 formula. 'intellectual and *cultural* property', was meant precisely to criticise the assumption that IPR alone was a sufficient instrument for protection (cf. Simpson 1997: 54).

20. Mosko (2002) debates later arguments put forward by Harrison (2000) over the processes of objectification involved. Mosko's paper was first given at the 2nd PTC Colloquium, *Inter-gender and Inter-generational Transactions*, Girton College, Cambridge, June 2002.

21. It is important to discount neither local inflexions nor specific micro-histories. In contrast to much more diffuse renderings in Papua New Guinea, Vanuatu

is renowned for the political work and national prominence accorded to *kastom*. As an outcome of 'negotiation', initially on the part of ni-Vanuatu with colonial expectations, it is particularly liable to change, and Bolton (2003) gives a historical analysis of its fluctuating connotations over the last generation. Many presently observed 'traditional' forms are hybrids of this kind, notably according to Küchler (2002), the New Ireland funeral sculptures known as Malanggan (see Chapter 7).

22. Bolton's thesis is that protecting and enacting *kastom* was for a long time the preserve of ni-Vanuatu men, and mobilised the 'public/domestic' dichotomy through which expatriates explained the difference between the lives of 'men' and 'women' to themselves. Among her critiques of this dichotomy is the anthropological observation that men and women never related to one another in a monolithic way (Bolton n.d.).

23. This is also the sense in which people in PNG are re-evaluating some of their own resources (Whimp and Busse 2000; Sykes et al. 2001). Much is already anticipated for the future (e.g. Kambuou 2000; Matainaho 2000), and PNG is not isolated from intellectual property debates going on elsewhere.

24. 'Community' has of course long been a source of Euro-American radicalism, and has been put to critical use against a range of other constructs (individual interests, private property, as well as [Helgason and Pálsson 1996: 454] market-based monetary exchange, commoditisation and economism).

25. The Model Law represents a major advance in recognising non-individual interests. But a document on the whole welcomed by Pacific Islanders has also led to some close questioning.

26. Indeed, the idea of a public domain (as in arguments over IPR putting knowledge into or taking it out of public ownership) once again becomes problematic.

27. For a critical appraisal of 'creativity' outside the context of intellectual property – including the notion that there is more of it around these days – see the essays in Liep (2001).

28. However innocently any two terms start out, they often up as binaries.

29. Until very recently. Creativity itself 'concerns the novel combination of old ideas' (Liep 2001: 7, after Boden and Koestler).

30. E.g., Weiner (1998; n.d.); Ernst (1999); Hirsch (2001); Filer (2003).

31. Brennan (2000), where the contemporary appears not as an old time (re)enacted anew but as a new time not seen before; where creations (the outcome of knowing how to set up the social conditions which will continue to (re)produce afresh [cf. Küchler 2002: 137–38]) turn into the products of creativity (the unique imaginative spark from within).

32. Weiner (n.d). 'Anthropology, the Law and Recognition Space', prepared for session 'Articulating Culture: Understanding Engagements between Indigenous and Non-indigenous Life-worlds', Australian Anthropological Society conference, Canberra, 2002.

Part I

Property

Chapter 1

PROPERTY LIMITS: DEBATES ON THE BODY, NATURE AND CULTURE

Stuart Kirsch

The concept of property is expanding both in scope, through the creation of novel forms of property, including claims to cultural property, and in scale, ranging from the molecular in the patenting of genetic material to the planetary in the establishment of markets for trading carbon and other pollutants. Yet these claims are simultaneously being called into question in debates about the appropriate limits to property regimes.

There are familiar examples of these debates. In *The Mystery of Capital*, the Peruvian economist de Soto (2000) attributes the genius of capitalism to its ability to convert all things into property, and thereby into capital. He endorses private property and the development of the legal instruments that regulate the mortgaging of assets, reconfiguring the world in monetary terms (see Pietz 1999: 62). Yet to mortgage assets is also to risk their alienation, and in the Third World contexts about which de Soto writes, objections to the privatisation of land ownership are based on the recognition that customary forms of land tenure and informal strategies for securing access to land can provide a measure of security to the poor in an otherwise uncertain world. These concerns were highlighted by recent protests in Papua New Guinea against plans to privatise land holdings, the result of World Bank structural adjustment policies, which led to the deaths of several students.[1]

The three debates about property limits that I consider in this chapter address events in Papua New Guinea, where people make claims on one another through transactions carried out in languages and practices that challenge many of the assumptions that underlie Euro-American property regimes. The first case considers the patent awarded for a cell line extracted from a Hagahai man from the Highlands region. The second case examines the relationship between property and pollution downstream from the Ok Tedi copper and gold mine in Western Province. The third case evaluates the response of public intellectuals in Papua New Guinea to international debates on cultural property rights. These examples cover a range of seemingly incommensurate objects, including genetic material, pollution and culture. The associated debates take place in a variety of forums, including international deliberations carried out through the internet, legal claims argued before the Australian courts, and discussions among scholars, politicians and journalists in Papua New Guinea. They incorporate a wide array of voices, including persons who claim indigenous identities, anthropologists, lawyers, corporate executives, and non-governmental organisations (NGOs).[2] My relationship to these cases also varies. While I was not involved in the Hagahai case, I have participated as both an ethnographer and an advocate for the communities affected by the Ok Tedi mine (Kirsch 2002), and have also contributed to scholarly deliberations on cultural property rights (Kirsch 2001a; 2001b).

This chapter considers these debates about property limits in relation to controversial proposals to mobilise copyrights, patents, and other legal instruments on behalf of indigenous communities by multilateral agencies, including UNESCO and the World Intellectual Property Organization (WIPO). As noted in the introduction to this volume, one impetus for these endeavours was the World Trade Organization's imposition of Euro-American patent regimes on its member states through the Trade-Related Intellectual Property Rights (TRIPS) agreement. Some NGOs and communities that identify themselves as indigenous have endorsed these proposals, while others have objected to them on various grounds.

As Euro-American conceptions of property gain currency through globalisation, debates on property limits reveal the presence of other ideas that circulate along with property forms. These debates are commonly carried out in terms of concepts that are central to how Euro-Americans imagine themselves and the world, including particular conceptions of the body, nature and culture. My argument is that these debates about property limits perversely contribute to the establishment of these concepts in the place of local alternatives.

Property and the Indigenous Body

The first debate was concerned with the potential commodification of human bodies and body parts, including genetic material. It addressed a patent granted to scientists affiliated with the US National Institutes of Health (NIH) on 14 March 1996 for a cell line extracted from the blood of a Hagahai man from the Schrader Mountains in Papua New Guinea. It contained a variant of the human T-cell virus HTLV-1, which does not cause leukaemia like other varieties of HTLV-1. The immortalised cell line had potential utility and economic value for the development of diagnostic tests and vaccines (Bhat 1996: 30). While the patent conformed with

NIH policy at the time, it was withdrawn a year later (Bhat 1996: 30; Friedlaender 1996: 22).

The medical anthropologist associated with the patent argued that it protected the economic interests of the Hagahai from whom the cell line was derived.[3] Making these rights explicit was considered essential given the findings in the case of *John Moore v. Regents of the University of California* (1991), in which an individual's claim to a cell line derived from his tissue was rejected by the courts (Rabinow 1996a). Unlike Moore's claim, which was based on his rights as an individual, the Papua New Guinea claim was made on behalf of the Hagahai as a whole.

The patenting of the Hagahai cell line was subsequently criticised by the Canadian NGO, RAFI (Rural Advance Front International).[4] RAFI focuses on the socioeconomic implications of new technologies, especially biotechnology. In particular, it opposes the patenting or licensing of all life-forms.[5] RAFI noted that the Hagahai patent included the individual's entire cell line, including his DNA. Following the logic of the Moore decision, RAFI argued that this genetic material no longer belonged to the man from whom it was extracted, but through the patent granted to NIH had become the property of the United States government. This led to their assertion that the scientists had 'patented a human life', which initiated a global e-storm in which anthropologists, biologists and indigenous rights groups expressed their views on the appropriate limits to property regimes with respect to the human body and genetic material (Riordan 1995; Taubes 1995).[6,7] The scientists associated with the patent disputed RAFI's allegation, explaining that the breadth of the patent was required because HTLV-1 cannot be supported outside of an immortalised cell line.[8]

Debates about the Hagahai patent coincided with RAFI's criticism of the proposed Human Genome Diversity Project (HGDP). This endeavour was designed to supplement the research of the Human Genome Project, which analysed genetic material from a small number of individuals in mapping the human genome.[9] The scientists who organised the HGDP sought genetic information from a broad sample of marginal or minority populations (Weiss 1996; Cunningham 1998). They described their project as 'urgent' because many of their target populations were considered vulnerable or 'endangered' (Lock 1994: 605).[10] While the scientists associated with the HGDP privileged DNA as the tangible form in which biological diversity should be preserved, RAFI and other critics of the project fetishised genetic material as a form of identity, leading them to treat DNA as cultural property.

Rabinow (2002: 140) has observed that multinational corporations and NGOs, despite claiming opposite positions on the political spectrum, reinforce the same 'view of the body, the self, ownership and truth', including the supposition that genomes contain information which can be treated as property. Similarly, Strathern (2001: 152) has noted that the language used in these debates 'tends to universalise certain Euro-American assumptions about property and ownership'. The difference between the Moore and the Hagahai cases is instructive, however: whereas claims about Euro-American bodies are made on the basis of individual rights, the rights of groups or populations are invoked with reference to peoples identified as indigenous. All of the participants in these debates followed the Euro-American assumption that property rights are held by *individuals* in the West, but *collectively* by indigenous peoples.

The claim that the Hagahai represent a distinct biological population has an instructive social history. When several Hagahai men ventured into the Western Highlands town of Mt. Hagen in search of medical assistance in 1983, the PNG media referred to them as members of a 'lost tribe' (Kirsch 1997b).[11] The patent on the Hagahai cell line subsequently naturalised their social status as a distinct population by claiming that they possessed biological characteristics that differentiated them from their neighbours. Their relative isolation consequently became a key construct both *socially* in their identification as a 'lost tribe' and *biologically* as a distinct population (Jenkins 1987). Given the probability that the Hagahai were exposed to the virus by a host from another population, the natural history of the variant of HTLV-1 may actually contradict their social status as a 'lost tribe'.[12] There is no biological evidence to suggest that this T-cell virus is unique to the Hagahai; its distribution may extend to neighbouring populations or other parts of the Highlands and can only be established through additional biological research. Whereas the anthropologist responsible for the patent argued that the Hagahai have property rights to the variant of HTLV-1 by virtue of their *separation* and *difference*, the presence of the virus may actually indicate their *connection* to others.[13,14]

Discussion

Absent from the debates about the patenting of Hagahai DNA is any consideration of differences in how the human body is conceived in Melanesian and Euro-American contexts. Kopytoff (1996: 64–65) has noted that human bodies are treated as potential property in many cultural contexts. Since the abolition of slavery, the American legal system no longer recognises property interests in the body (Greely 1998: 488), demarcating a significant limit to American property regimes.[15] However, American patent law treats human DNA no differently from other complex organic chemicals.[16] Genetic material is relegated to the biological commons and the individual donor is not recognised as having sustained a loss if it is patented or otherwise claimed as property. In contrast, UNESCO maintains that the human genome is part of the shared heritage of humanity and consequently objects to property claims and other efforts to profit from human genetic material (Greely 1998: 489–90).

Euro-American concerns about the appropriateness of treating the body or body parts as property may be contrasted with Melanesian ideas about bodies and transactions. Many societies in Papua New Guinea recognise specific male and female contributions to procreation, commonly identified as bones and blood. These contributions create entitlements that are realised in the form of limited claims on one's offspring and what they produce. People also make claims on the accomplishments of other persons and their offspring by virtue of bridewealth contributions that make reproduction socially possible. The resulting claims to other persons and their productive capacities are largely incompatible with Euro-American assumptions about the 'possessive individual' derived from Lockean conceptions of labour and property (Macpherson 1962). Nor are Melanesian notions of entitlement made on the basis of axiomatic or 'natural' claims to membership within a particular social group. In contrast to Euro-American conceptions of the body, the individual, and society as universal and natural categories, in Melanesia the rights to bodies are socially produced through exchange.[17]

An individual's genetic material is simultaneously a singular configuration *and* the outcome of overlapping genetic histories. Euro-American debates about the ownership of Hagahai DNA were divided in part along these lines. Even where the individual is colloquially conceived as a bounded unit, genetic material might be seen to belong to either a particular person or to the genetic commons. But with respect to communities identified as indigenous, the same material was seen to belong to a particular group or population.

None of these efforts to impose appropriate limits to property regimes accommodates Melanesian treatment of the body in terms of investments from parents, contributions to bridewealth, and other transactions. While the patent of the Hagahai cell line was vigorously opposed by Melanesian public intellectuals (e.g. Liloqula 1996; Sengi 1996), when asked to comment, the Hagahai focused on their relationship to the anthropologist associated with the patent (Ibeji and Gane 1996). They viewed the proposed transactions in terms of the social practices through which persons make claims on one another, organising productivity and the flow of valuables in relation to the circulation of bodily substances.

The debates about the patenting of Hagahai DNA were carried out in terms of rights that were considered 'natural' and a priori by their Euro-American proponents, rather than the kinds of contingent social relations through which comparable claims are negotiated in Melanesia. The decision to withdraw the Hagahai patent by the National Institutes of Health was made with reference to questions about the appropriate limits to Euro-American property regimes rather than Melanesian ideas about how persons make claims on one another. These debates operated in terms of a limited set of understandings about human bodies and body parts, including Euro-American individuals, Melanesian groups or populations, and the concept of the biological commons. The Hagahai controversy was also the first public debate about cultural property rights in Papua New Guinea (Alpers 1996: 32), stimulating the debates that are the subject of the final case discussed in this chapter.

Property and Pollution

The next case considers property claims made in relation to the environment. A familiar example is the concept of natural resources, which is predicated on viewing certain aspects of the environment – e.g., a stand of pine trees, a deposit of coal or a school of fish – as potential property. As the Hagahai case suggests, biotechnology facilitates the conversion of the environment into natural resources at an entirely new scale, at the level of the genome. The following examples have an effect parallel to that of biotechnology, but at the opposite end of the spectrum, enabling property models to operate at a planetary scale. In contrast to property regimes that regulate the distribution of things with positive value or 'goods', this case is about the establishment of value in things that are harmful, what Beck (1992) calls environmental risks or 'bads'. While pollution is commonly conceptualised in terms of damage to property, it is now also seen to mobilise a kind of property right. Examples include emissions trading between power plants in the United States and proposals for an international market in carbon as the means to manage greenhouse gases and their contribution to global warming.

Amendments to the US Clean Air Act in 1990 created a market-based system that was designed to reduce air pollution from power plants more economically than is possible through systematic regulation (Altman 2002: C1). Economists urged the government to target those companies that would have the greatest reduction in the volume of their emissions in relation to their expenditure on pollution controls. A power plant that burns coal with a high sulphur content might more economically reduce the volume of pollutants released into the atmosphere by installing an expensive 'scrubber' than a plant that burns coal with a relatively low sulphur content. Initial estimates of the cost to reduce sulphur dioxide emissions, the cause of acid rain, by ten million tons per year were as much as US$15 billion, but this goal was reached for substantially less. A trading company enables utilities to buy and sell allowances for sulphur dioxide emissions on spot and futures markets, effectively establishing a property right to pollute.

The response to this system has been largely favourable although significant problems remain. Some of the dirtiest plants considered it too expensive to install pollution controls and purchased the rights to continue high emissions of sulphur dioxide. The absence of control over the distribution of these plants created 'hot spots' in regions overexposed to sulphur dioxide. Focusing markets on a single category of pollutants can exacerbate other environmental problems. Efforts to reduce sulphur dioxide emissions can increase reliance on hydroelectric power, which increases the sedimentation of rivers, harming fish populations (Rose 2000). Laws that require the installation of modern pollution controls during equipment upgrades have had the perverse effect of keeping old, inefficient plants in operation, although recent policy changes will permit upgrades without requiring reductions in emissions. Some critics of these regimes argue that affected communities rather than corporations should have the right to distribute permits to pollute, which they could use or sell (Altman 2002: 13).

Comparable arrangements have been proposed for managing carbon dioxide, which is responsible for global warming. Carbon trading is one of the 'Clean Development Mechanisms' proposed in the 1997 Kyoto accord. It is intended to balance carbon capture and emissions by establishing a system of credits and debits. Industrialised countries with high levels of emissions would pay corporations or other countries to set aside 'carbon sinks', usually in forest preserves where carbon can be stored.[18] These initiatives establish the right to pollute as a form of property regulated by market forces. However, debates concerning the impact of the Ok Tedi mine in Papua New Guinea reveal other aspects of the relationship between property and pollution.

Pollution Downstream from the Ok Tedi Mine

The Ok Tedi mine was the subject of contentious litigation regarding its environmental impact from 1994 to 1996. Representing 34,000 plaintiffs from Papua New Guinea, the case was adjudicated in the Victorian Supreme Court in Melbourne, where Broken Hill Proprietary (BHP), the majority shareholder and operating partner of the mine, is incorporated (Banks and Ballard 1997). The legal claims against the mine did not turn on questions of damage to property because the Australian courts were unable to hear claims about land held under customary tenure in Papua New Guinea (Gordon 1997: 153). Alternatively, lawyers for the plaintiffs made the novel argument that people living downstream from the mine had suffered a loss due to the mine's impact on their subsistence economy. Judge Byrne (1995: 15) endorsed their claim, determining that:

> to restrict the duty of care to cases of pure economic loss would be to deny a remedy to those whose life is substantially, if not entirely, outside an economic system which uses money as a medium of exchange. It was put that, in the case of subsistence dwellers, loss of the things necessary for subsistence may be seen as akin to economic loss. If the plaintiffs are unable or less able to have or enjoy those things which are necessary for their subsistence as a result of the defendants' negligent conduct of the mine, they must look elsewhere for them, perhaps to obtain them by purchase or barter or perhaps to obtain some substitute.

The courts recognised in subsistence production a set of rights, relations and values comparable to those which organise the ownership of property in capitalist societies. The ruling established a precedent that recognised subsistence rights.

An out-of-court settlement of the case against the Ok Tedi mine was reached in 1996. However, dissatisfaction with the implementation of the settlement agreement prompted the communities downstream from the mine to return to the courts in Melbourne in 2000. They accused BHP of violating its commitment to halt riverine disposal of tailings and other mine wastes, which have caused extensive environmental damage downstream. While 1,400 km² of rain forest along the Ok Tedi and Fly Rivers is already dead or under severe stress, the damage is expected to spread further downstream, eventually covering 2,040 km² (Higgins 2002), and potentially as much as 3,000 km² (Parametrix, Inc. and URS Greiner Woodward Clyde 1999: 8). Changes to the river system will eventually stabilise, but local species composition is not expected to return to pre-mine conditions, with much of the rain forest along the river becoming savannah grasslands (Chapman et al. 2000: 17).

In a report commissioned by the Prime Minister of Papua New Guinea, the World Bank recommended the early closure of the Ok Tedi mine once programmes to facilitate the social and economic transition to life after the mine are implemented. When BHP (now BHP Billiton) indicated its intention to withdraw from the project, both the government of Papua New Guinea, which relies on the Ok Tedi mine for 18 percent of its foreign exchange earnings, and the communities downstream, which seek additional compensation for damages and opportunities for development, recommended that the mine continue operating until 2010, by which time the ore body will have been exhausted (Higgins 2002). The PNG parliament subsequently passed the Mining (OK Tedi Mine Continuation (Ninth Supplemental Agreement)) Act of 2001, establishing the conditions of BHP Billiton's exit from the mine, which will continue to operate independently. BHP Billiton subsequently transferred its 52 percent share in the mine to the Sustainable Development Program Company that it established in Singapore (see Crook, this volume).[19]

The new trust company has been described as a 'poisoned chalice' (Evans 2002) because it relies on the continued operation of the mine (including the disposal of more than 80,000 tons of mine tailings per day into local rivers) to pay for development programmes. The primary purpose of the trust is to provide BHP Billiton with indemnity from future claims regarding damage to the environment that will result from the continued operation of the mine. The Mining Act limits corporate liability to the value of the trust, even though it is unclear whether the economic returns from BHP Billiton's shares in the mine will be sufficient to offset the damages that will result. A cost–benefit analysis of this relationship was commissioned by the PNG government and completed in 2001, although the results were never made public. The Mining Act also provides the Ok Tedi mine with unprecedented power and authority to establish environmental standards for its operations and procedures for measuring and reporting compliance. Even given the influence of neoliberal economic policies that promote corporate self-regulation, the agreement represents an extraordinary transfer of rights from the state and ordinary citizens to a private company (Divecha 2001). Despite the environmental problems downstream, no changes to the current operating procedures are planned.[20] The Mining Act effectively conveys a right to pollute to the Ok Tedi mine in return for the transfer of BHP Billiton's assets to the trust.

The Mining Act also legalised new arrangements between the mine and the affected communities, known as the Community Mine Continuation Agreements (CMCAs). The CMCAs refer to the rights of two groups of people, identified as the 'land owners' and the 'land users'. These categories are my gloss of the distinction made by the Yonggom people, who live along the Ok Tedi River, between *ambip kin yariman,* persons who own land along the river, and *animan od yi karup*, the people who derive food (*animan*) and money (*od*, also shell valuables) from the same land. Previous negotiations between the mine and these communities reached an impasse during the implementation of the 1996 settlement agreement. The mine was willing to provide compensation for environmental damage only to those persons who owned the land along the river where the damage had occurred. Lawyers for BHP argued that there is no provision in common law for the payment of compensation for damages to persons who are not the rightful property owners. When the lawyers for the local plaintiffs asked me to assist with the implementation of the settlement, I objected to the restriction that BHP had imposed on the payment of compensation, noting that the case had been argued on the basis of subsistence rights rather than damage to property. If only those persons identified as property owners were eligible for compensation, a substantial proportion of the persons who previously made use of the land and resources in question would be excluded. The validity of this argument was eventually acknowledged and the rights of both the 'land owners' and the 'land users' were included in subsequent agreements between the mine and the affected communities. With the passage of the PNG Mining Act of 2001, these categories were given the force of law, providing formal recognition of subsistence rights in Papua New Guinea. This case suggests that damages from pollution are not limited to property claims and that other relations between persons and land should also be considered.

Yonggom relations to land also differ from Euro-American property models in another respect.[21] While the relationship between the *yariman* and his land may be translated as ownership, it has other meanings as well. The central actor in divinations held to seek the cause of a persistent illness, or *anigat*, is the *anigat yariman*. This role is filled by the senior kinsman or guardian responsible for the patient's well-being. Similarly, the sponsor of an *arat* pig feast is known as the *arat yariman*. The *yariman* relationship is based on the responsibilities of kinship, guardianship, and sponsorship. Given that *ambip kin* refers to both a particular bloc of land and the specific lineage or clan which holds the rights to that land, *ambip kin yariman* indicates the person or persons responsible for lineage or clan land. This relationship has figured significantly in recent efforts by lawyers representing the communities located downstream from the mine to challenge the validity of the Community Mine Continuation Agreements.

The CMCAs authorised any 'person representing or purporting to represent a Community or clan' to bind its members to the agreement, 'notwithstanding ... that there is no express authority for that person to sign or execute the Community Mine Continuation Agreement on behalf of the members of the Community or clan concerned'. This would legally commit the members of his or her village to the agreement without necessarily having secured their consent. The members of future generations would also be bound by the agreement. Among the provisions of the CMCAs was the obligation to 'opt out' of continuing legal action against the mine, which seeks to enforce the terms of the 1996 settlement agreement, including the requirement to implement the most practicable form of tailings containment. The lawyers for BHP Billiton included this provision in the CMCAs in order to facilitate the corporate exit from the Ok Tedi project by preventing the people living downstream from participating in the lawsuit.

A hearing was scheduled in Melbourne in February 2002 to evaluate the request for an injunction against the implementation of the CMCAs. In advance of these proceedings, the lawyers representing the communities downstream from the mine asked me to provide expert advice regarding the relationship between the political authority of elected or appointed officials in contemporary villages and the rights to land held under customary land tenure systems recognised by PNG law. Most of the villages downstream from the Ok Tedi mine were established during the colonial era. The authorisation of a village representative to bind the members of that village on matters concerning the disposition of land threatens to bypass the provisions of customary land tenure. It is a requirement of customary law in PNG that decisions concerning land that is held under customary tenure must incorporate the views of all of those persons who have ownership rights to the land in question.

In contrast to land-owners, village representatives acquire their political authority from the government or other electoral processes. They lack authority over the disposition of land, which among the Yonggom is held by individuals in association with particular lineages or clans rather than by the village or community as a whole. Given that the Community Mine Continuation Agreements are fundamentally concerned with damage to local land and rivers, they necessarily invoke customary land rights. In documents prepared for the hearing in February 2002, I argued that village representatives, even if democratically elected, lack the authority to bind other persons to decisions affecting the disposition of their land. Consequently, it was my view that the signatories to the CMCAs did not have the authority to commit the other members of their village or community to the agreement, including the obligation to 'opt out' of the on-going lawsuit.

Immediately prior to the February hearing on the validity of the CMCAs, lawyers for BHP Billiton and the Ok Tedi mine agreed not to enforce the contested provision of the CMCAs that would require the people living downstream from the mine to 'opt out' of the legal action without first providing the lawyers for the plaintiffs with sufficient notice to return the matter to the courts for review. In effect, the lawyers for the Ok Tedi mine and BHP Billiton temporarily conceded to the injunction sought by the lawyers for the plaintiffs. This agreement allows for the continued participation of the people living on the Ok Tedi and Fly Rivers in their legal action against BHP Billiton and the Ok Tedi mine.

Discussion

The examples from the Ok Tedi case suggest that Euro-American property models fail to register the social consequences of pollution, including impacts on subsistence practices. They do not accommodate local constructions of responsibility towards the land and they remain at odds with customary land tenure. Yet by contesting Euro-American assumptions about property in the courts and by seeking compensation from the mine for pollution, the Yonggom and their neighbours accepted a particular view of 'nature' as a legitimate object of human management. Implicit in this perspective is the assumption that development is a fundamental good (see Chapter 5). The result is the transformation of the environment into an object of science, planning, and politics (see Scott 1998).

The debates about the future of the Ok Tedi mine also invoke the 'tragedy of the commons' argument that privatisation promotes sustainable resource use (Hardin 1968). The threat of environmental degradation is used to justify private property, which is naturalised as the most efficient form of stewardship. Yet privatisation can also lead to environmental degradation (Feeny et al. 1990). In the Ok Tedi case, the mine mobilised new property rights to pollute even though it was responsible for the environmental problems downstream. Despite its shortcomings, the 'tragedy of the commons' model remains influential and has even been applied to planetary levels in calls for the management of the 'global commons' as the solution to international environmental problems (Goldman 1998). The resulting vision of the planet as a single ecosystem raises important questions about the recognition of different social interests (Milton 1996).

While the view derived from Locke (1960 [1698]) is that property is created through the addition of labour to nature, these new forms of property mobilise the right to add pollution to the environment. Their emergence substantiates Beck's (1992) claims about the reorganisation of modernity around the management of environmental risks. The Ok Tedi case challenges the 'tragedy of the commons' argument that increased propertisation is the most efficient means of addressing the problems of environmental degradation.[22]

Property in Culture

Proposals for recognising cultural property rights represent a powerful set of conventions. The timing of these initiatives has already been noted. The World Trade Organization has imposed a standardised intellectual property regime (TRIPS) at the international level, which simultaneously protects Disney cartoons, the texts of authors, patents on pharmaceuticals, and innovations in biotechnology. Critics have noted that TRIPS may require developing countries to purchase the modified forms of material that they previously used without restriction. This is the case for certain pharmaceuticals and genetically engineered varieties of seed, for which their contribution to the original form of the commodity is not legally recognised (Shiva and Holla-Bhar 1996).

Proposals to protect cultural property rights are intended in part to correct such imbalances by providing legal protections to communities that are comparable to those available to corporations. Whereas disputes about cultural property rights are increasingly common in North America (Brown 2003) and Australia (see Chapter 2), they remain largely hypothetical in Papua New Guinea. Consequently this section of the paper addresses general debates about cultural property rights rather than a particular case study.

A fundamental weakness of initiatives designed to protect cultural property rights is the tension between their universalist scope and local projects and concerns. The language used by UNESCO, WIPO and other multilateral agencies is framed in oppositional terms, following generalisations about the differences between Euro-Americans and societies identified as indigenous, including private versus collective forms of ownership, interest in commodification versus relations organised through reciprocity, and individual creativity versus inherited traditions. These binary oppositions beg the question of cultural difference among communities identified as indigenous. This particular interpretation of tradition also perpetuates stereotypes about their cultural conservatism, ignoring their capacity for innovation and invention.

Objections to cultural property rights typically operate at the level of the universal as well. One concern is the need to protect the 'cultural commons', the objects and ideas that have already entered the public domain (Brown 1998: 198; see also Brush 1999). Limiting access to cultural property may be incommensurate with liberal political values that emphasise the free exchange of ideas and information, although comparable mechanisms to protect intellectual property are regularly used to defend corporate interests. There are also practical impediments to the assignation of ownership rights when multiple and overlapping claims exist (see note 14). These problems include the definition of membership within particular communities. Brown (1998: 204) urges caution with respect to proposals that would empower the state or multilateral bodies to monitor genre boundaries or police ethnic identity. Regulations or policies designed to benefit particular cultural groups might also be exploited by corporations or other parties to the detriment of the communities whom the policies were originally intended to support (Dominguez 2001: 183). The potential for corporate abuse of cultural property rights schemes has led some NGOs to argue that they should be seen as a plot of the powerful rather than a potential 'weapon of the weak' (Tauli-Corpuz 1999).

The transaction costs associated with formal systems for regulating cultural property rights would also impose significant constraints on the sharing of ideas (Brush 1996: 661–63). An interesting proposal to mitigate this concern involves restricting the scope of cultural property rights to commercial applications (Rosen 1997: 255–59). These smaller domains might be more amenable to tailored solutions (ibid: 256). While this would presumably reduce the general threat to the public domain or 'cultural commons', it would be incommensurate with Melanesian expectations, which include the right to withdraw material from circulation and to limit or restrict access to secret or sacred cultural property (see Chapter 2).

Even if cultural property rights could be successfully mediated by the market, structural limitations might prevent these procedures from benefiting the very communities whose interests they are intended to serve. Dove (1994: 2) relates the Southeast Asian parable of the peasant who finds a diamond but is obligated to sell the gem to his local patron, who pays him but a fraction of the stone's value and profits enormously when the stone is resold.[23] Dove argues that the communities that cultural property rights proposals are designed to protect generally lack the knowledge, political resources and economic networks required to take advantage of the opportunities seemingly afforded to them. Development at the local level is contingent on the reform of the political and economic conditions responsible for inequality. Dove (1996) also suggests that payments for cultural property rights would erode and ultimately destroy the basis on which these communities produce anything of significant value to the rest of the world, their underlying difference.[24] However, this argument is tenable only if local agency is ignored, including widespread Melanesian desires for greater participation in the global economy.

An alternative to the formulation of universal models for cultural property rights is to develop policies or legislation that build on local precedents. Arguments about cultural property rights are usually framed by the problems of Euro-American profiting (or profiteering) from the restricted ownership of knowledge and things in the forms in which they are produced, while denying comparable rights to persons and communities in places such as Papua New Guinea. Yet the motive for establishing cultural property rights is not simply to bring indigenous ownership in line with Euro-American options by providing the same legal rights to Motuans over their tattoos that Disney has over its cartoons, or controls over certain varieties of sago to their cultivators that biotech firms have over the hybrid seeds that they produce. For example, an early proposal by two Papua New Guinean public intellectuals sought to use customary claims of ownership to limit the performance of particular songs and dances to group members, rather than licensing them for use by others (Kalinoe and Simet 1999).

Could Melanesian ways of investing in relationships and recognising multiple ownership serve as the basis for protecting local knowledge and practices? This would require cultural property rights policy or legislation to take the form of Melanesian claims to what they produce, use and transact. This is the premise of *sui generis* systems of cultural property rights, as Kalinoe (Chapter 2) argues. While recognising indigenous mechanisms for protecting cultural property rights might enrich Euro-American legal discourses (Rosen 1997: 258; Barron 1998), in practice 'a *sui generis* system developed in Papua New Guinea would be virtually useless in protecting the exploitation of traditional knowledge elsewhere in the world, unless other countries agree to adopt similar laws' (Busse and Whimp 2000: 24).

Discussion

These debates reify culture in relation to property claims. While Harrison (1992) identified parallels between the Euro-American category of intellectual property and Melanesian traffic in ritual knowledge, he subsequently observed that most cultural property has undergone a transformation from 'goods' into 'legacies', the value of which is largely associated with the past (Harrison 2000). More generally, Dominguez (1992) and Jackson (1995) have described the hegemonic effects of the Euro-American concept of culture, which leads to the reproduction of local beliefs and practices in relation to imported categories. One consequence of this process is that only select aspects of local lives are recognised as 'cultural', while the remainder are ignored. Claims to cultural property are shaped by Euro-American conceptions of culture, including the emphasis on performance.

Local alternatives to the concept of culture include the Tok Pisin term *pasin* or 'fashion', analogous to ethos (Sykes 2001: 3–8). *Kastam* or 'custom' refers to a codified and generally oppositional form of collective self-reference (Keesing 1989). The Motu equivalent is *kara*, or 'way'. These concepts are largely ignored by cultural property rights discourse. To ensure their recognition by universalist proposals to protect cultural and intellectual property rights, Melanesian ideas and practices must be represented in language that is commensurate with Euro-American standards (Busse and Whimp 2000: 24; see Povinelli 2002).

Conclusions

Property claims now extend from the molecular to the planetary. Claims to cultural property are similarly pervasive (see Brown 2003). Paradoxically, the expansion of property claims occurs at a time when challenges to the conventional justifications for property regimes are also on the rise. While patents are seen to provide economic rewards for creativity and capital investment, recent studies have questioned their efficacy in stimulating innovation (Nelson and Mazzoleni 1997).[25] Other research challenges the widespread assumption that the standardisation of property rights by the state facilitates economic development (van Meijl and von Benda-Beckmann 1999). Property regimes may also constrain new economic opportunities by placing 'needless restrictions on securities transfer and capitalist expansion' (Maurer 1999: 365–66).

Despite these negative appraisals of property regimes, new efforts to mobilise the kinds of protections afforded to authors, inventors and corporations to culture have been proposed by multilateral organisations and

NGOs. Critics of these proposals question whether these measures are in the best interests of the communities that they are intended to benefit. Also at issue is whether property can be both the cause and the solution to social and economic problems.

The resulting debates over the appropriate limits to property regimes operate in terms of familiar Euro-American categories, including the body, nature and culture. Whereas Euro-American claims to genetic material are made in terms of individual rights, the ownership of genetic material from communities identified as indigenous is collectively attributed. Alternatively, the human genome may be treated as part of the biological commons. Yet these views exclude Melanesian understandings of the body that emphasise transactions between persons.

With regard to the relationship between property and pollution, arguments derived from the 'tragedy of the commons' model assert that privatisation is the most appropriate response to the challenges of sustainable resource use. The expansion of the commons leads to contradictory applications of the property construct in the creation of positive value in the form of natural resources and negative value through pollution. The use of property rights to manage both production and destruction is challenged by many communities in arguments about the value of place (Escobar 2001), including ideas about kinship and belonging that may invoke the duty of care. However, even these objections may render 'nature' the legitimate object of human management.

Conventions for recognising some forms of cultural property are already in place. The legitimacy of heritage protection, including sacred sites, art and other material manifestations of culture is widely recognised. These practices are institutionalised to the point of nation-making in museums. However, at the margins of this process are intangible forms of heritage, including music, dance, and other performance genres, whose standing as cultural property remains contested (although see UNESCO 2003). Cultural property claims operating at the more abstract level of ideas, designs, and language are increasingly seen to be impracticable and undesirable, if not potentially detrimental (Brown 2003). Yet in Melanesia, these conventions and the debates they engender have the consequence of reifying the Euro-American concept of culture.

In *Property and Persuasion*, Rose (1994a) reminds us that property claims depend on the effective communication of possession. When the objects of property claims 'seem to resist clear demarcation', which is the case for ideas, elaborate systems of registration are required, including patents and copyrights (Rose 1994a: 17). Definitional agreement must precede the recognition of property claims.

These concerns are clearly relevant to the histories of people on the margins of common law, as they were the basis for claims of adverse possession supported by assertions like *terra nullius*, in which indigenous land claims were not deemed to rise to the level of property. In the debates on property limits discussed here, it is notable that while the same communities may now be engaged participants, they still bear the 'burden for social commensuration' (Povinelli 2001: 329–30). To assert or object to particular property claims, they must acknowledge the entities that are invoked.

Examination of these debates in the context of Melanesia, where the language and practices of transactions operate according to assumptions that challenge Euro-American property models, reveals a significant consequence of the globalisation of property forms. While the debates described here represent important political struggles over the appropriate limits to property regimes, they operate in terms of Euro-American categories of the body, nature and culture that travel along with property, and thus potentially limit the very means by which property claims might be made or contested.

Notes

1. Comparable examples from elsewhere in the region abound (e.g., van Meijl and von Benda-Beckmann 1999).
2. It has been argued that the primary beneficiaries from cultural property rights debates have been the scholars and NGOs who have carved out a niche for their work in these arenas. Rabinow (2002: 143; see also 147 fn. 7) has criticised scholars for being unwilling to acknowledge their position in the larger 'market' for ideas.
3. Carol Jenkins was employed by Institution of Medical Research in Goroka. She was well known to the Hagahai through her biomedical research and her help in bringing medical aid to the community since 1983. Hagahai blood samples were sent to Gadjusek, a colleague of Jenkins at NIH who had previously been awarded a Nobel prize for his research on the fatal wasting disease kuru, which affected another Highlands group in Papua New Guinea during the 1950s (Anderson 2000; Hirsch 2002 and this volume). Gadjusek and Jenkins were named on the US version of the patent along with a third colleague.
4. RAFI is now known as the ETC Group (http://www.rafi.org/main.asp).
5. See also RAFI's criticism of Brent Berlin's ethnobotany project among Mayan communities in Mexico (Belejack 2001; Brown 2003).
6. The term 'e-storm' refers to a flurry of electronic mail that moves rapidly through multiple networks of users and user-groups. It has the capacity to spread profligately in a very short period of time.
7. Greely (1998: 490), the Stanford lawyer who chaired the North American ethics subcommittee of the Human Genome Diversity Project (HGDP), has argued that comparisons between the patenting of a gene or a part of the genome and the commodification of humanity muddle the distinction between genes and persons.
8. Immortalisation refers to the process of establishing a line of cells that can reproduce indefinitely outside of the human body under laboratory conditions.
9. The organisers of the HGDP were primarily interested in human evolutionary history, asking, 'who we are as a species and how we came to be' (Cavalli-Sforza in Lock 1994: 603).

10. The risks were said to include physical threats to their survival and assimilation into neighbouring populations, both of which would diminish their value to geneticists (Lock 1994: 605). Hayden (1998) has questioned the political implications of representing organisms by their genes. If biodiversity is perceived solely in terms of DNA, is the threat of extinction of a population or species reduced to a problem of information management? The equation of organisms and their DNA might lead to the preservation of genetic information in lieu of protecting endangered plants or animals, or providing assistance to human populations whose lives might be at risk (Hayden 1998). Santos (2002: 83) has also argued that treating indigenous peoples as sources of information problematically relegates them (and their bodies) to the public domain, 'naturalising' them in the process. However, Weiss (1996: 28) has disputed the claim that the HGDP values DNA at the expense of its carriers: 'We cannot, and do not, think for a moment that the HGDP is a substitute for efforts to protect and enhance human populations everywhere, no matter how small or economically disadvantaged'.
11. A Papua New Guinean anthropologist who visited the Hagahai shortly after their visit to Mt. Hagen concluded that, 'these people were not a "lost tribe," but a group which has kept very much to themselves for reasons other than ignorance of the world around them' (Mangi 1988: 60). An expatriate anthropologist who subsequently carried out research with the Hagahai reached similar conclusions: 'What is apparent is that the Hagahai, protected by physical and social barriers, remained relatively uninfluenced by outside forces until the early 1980s' (Boyd 1996: 106). Yet the isolation of the Hagahai was far from complete. They had regular contact with their closest neighbours, the Pinai (Boyd 1996: 105). Thirty men out of a population of fewer than 300 had intermittently been employed on a nearby cattle station since the 1970s (Boyd 1996: 131). The Hagahai actively contributed to the impression that they were very isolated in order to elicit sympathy and support (Jenkins in Fishlock 1993: 20). Their claims were uncritically accepted by the PNG media, who reported the discovery of a 'lost tribe' (Kirsch 1997: 62–63).
12. An earlier application for a patent on another variant of HTLV-1 from the Solomon Islands was subsequently withdrawn (Bhat 1996: 30).
13. This was also evident in the proposals for the HGDP project: by identifying 'primitive isolates' as their unit of study, the project made a number of questionable assumptions about their genetic homogeneity and their differences from neighbouring communities. Similar concerns have been raised about the DECODE project in Iceland (Pálsson and Harðardóttir 2001).
14. These relationships are indicative of the general problem associated with the assignation of property rights to groups: how to delineate appropriate boundaries. Who owns kava, for example, the root used in Fiji, Vanuatu and other parts of the Pacific to produce an intoxicating beverage that has both ceremonial significance and iconic status for identity? Despite the large number of potential claimants, the circulation of kava beyond this region is often described as an infringement on cultural property rights (Puri 2001). Cultural property rights claims commonly make reference to objects or ideas that historically have a broader distribution. Exclusive claims to cultural property can only be fashioned by arbitrarily privileging the rights of one group while excluding competing claims. This is comparable to what Strathern (1996), in reference to scientific authorship and claims to invention, calls 'cutting the network'.

15. Kimbrell (1996: 135) points out that US restrictions on 'patenting human beings [are] based on the Thirteenth Amendment of the Constitution, the antislavery amendment, which prohibits ownership of a human being'. Similar restrictions apply within British common law. These ideas may be changing. Court cases in the US and the UK on posthumous requests to use the gametes of a deceased relative for procreative processes have raised challenging questions about the right to inherit genetic material as property (Strathern 2000).
16. Exceptions are granted for inventions that are regarded as contravening 'public morality' (Greely 1998: 489).
17. Strathern (2001: 162) describes Melanesian sociality in these terms: 'everyone is enmeshed in a set of relationships predicated on exchanges of wealth between persons in recognition of the bodily energy and activities persons bestow on one another'.
18. Carbon sequestration companies create monetary value for the carbon stored in trees and soil. Subsidies for carbon sequestration act like other subsidies for social or environmental goods, e.g., farming subsidies that support a fallow period for agricultural land. The difference is that they seek to *indirectly* balance undesirable processes across the planet. One recent carbon trade involved the payment of US$25 million to offset carbon dioxide released into the air by Entergy Corporation, a major electricity supplier, to farmers in the Pacific Northwest who agreed to use the 'direct seed' method of planting. They were compensated for offsetting 30,000 tons of carbon dioxide released from Entergy power plants by avoiding ploughing, which releases soil into the atmosphere and increases erosion (Environmental Defense 2002).
19. The outstanding shares in the Ok Tedi mine are held by the PNG government (30 percent, including 12.5 percent on behalf of the province and 2.5 percent on behalf of land-owners from the mine area) and 18 percent by the Canadian mining company Inmet (Ok Tedi Mining 2003).
20. The Ok Tedi mine has operated a dredge in the lower Ok Tedi River since 1998, but dredging only removes approximately one quarter of the material released into the river (Ok Tedi Mining 2003).
21. Filer (1997a: 162–64) has described how ideas about land ownership in Papua New Guinea have changed over time. The Tok Pisin *papa bilong graun* of the colonial era characterised this relationship in the idiom of kinship. This was condensed into the term *papagraun* after independence in 1975, and subsequently anglicised as *landona*. In this form, the idiom of kinship is no longer marked. Land ownership in Papua New Guinea is increasingly associated with populist sentiments (Filer 1997a: 164), including protests against land privatisation schemes in the capital of Port Moresby.
22. The US Environmental Protection Agency has recently proposed a pollution credit trading programme for water, which would provide mining companies with the option of purchasing pollution credits instead of limiting the discharge of tailings and other mine wastes into local waterways (Perks and Wetstone 2003: 15–16).
23. Parables should not be mistaken for history. Consider a contrasting account from Papua New Guinea, describing historical events rather than fiction. During the peak of the Mt. Kare gold rush, during which thousands of Highlanders staked out individual claims and extracted gold worth millions of dollars (Vail 1993), a father-and-son team of entrepreneurs from Australia flew to Mt Hagen, intending to buy gold at low prices from 'natives' who were

ignorant of its true value. Several weeks later, the pair complained bitterly to the media about their experiences, for they had spent their life savings purchasing brass shavings from enterprising Hageners, who misrepresented the metal as gold from Mt Kare. At issue is not whether Papua New Guineans are more resourceful than Indonesian peasants, but whether local options should be constrained on the basis of a parable. Nor is it clear whether the act of finding a stone is an appropriate analogue for the accumulation of indigenous knowledge.

24. Dove (1996) writes about biodiversity; the reference to culture is mine.
25. For example, the economic benefits conferred by patents may discourage innovation in the pharmaceutical industry by providing economic incentives to companies for making small modifications to established drugs when their patents expire, rather than expending resources to develop new medicines.

Chapter 2

LEGAL OPTIONS FOR THE REGULATION OF INTELLECTUAL AND CULTURAL PROPERTY IN PAPUA NEW GUINEA

Lawrence Kalinoe

> We the people of Papua New Guinea, united in one nation, pay homage to the memory of our ancestors, the source of our strength and origin of our combined heritage, acknowledge the worthy customs and traditional wisdom of our people which come down to us from generation to generation, pledge ourselves to guard and pass onto those who come after us, our noble traditions.
>
> Preamble to the Papua New Guinea Constitution

Initial Concerns

The impetus for the intellectual property legislation now in place in Papua New Guinea comes from its international law obligations following accession to the WTO and TRIPS in 1996 and subsequently WIPO in 1997. Earlier, in 1993, Papua New Guinea also ratified the 1992 Convention on Biological Diversity (CBD). Amongst other things it calls for the recognition and preservation of the role of indigenous communities in the creation, maintenance and utilisation of their biodiversity, indigenous knowledge and technologies for their own survival and sustainability, particularly in the face of technological advancement and bioprospecting in plant (and human) genetics. This is now a significant factor, since it introduces indigenous cultural property and traditional knowledge dimensions into any eventual promulgation of comprehensive IPR laws. That eventuality is still in the future.

Within Papua New Guinea, concerns had been raised from around 1996 onwards that certain aspects of local cultures, particularly traditional songs, music and dances, were increasingly used without authorisation and outside traditional contexts – seen by many Papua New Guineans to be unacceptable. A former Chief Ombudsman of Papua New Guinea[1] is reported as saying: 'In many ways, our traditional music and dances are unique. They must be recognised and accepted as such, encouraged and promoted, and above all must be protected.... I must admit that introducing traditional music and dances into modern music using modern instruments can become a mockery.' He called on the government to take immediate steps to protect traditional music and dance by legislating 'to ensure that the traditional music and dances belonging to a certain ethnic group are protected for their [own] purposes'. No doubt, it is public comments like this that have prompted the Papua New Guinea National Cultural Commission (NCC) to develop a national cultural policy to consider regulating the access and use of cultural material, including traditional songs and dances.[2] This was intended to feed into the National IPR Committee (NIPRC) established in preparation of impending legislation.[3]

I suggest that we pause here and first consider what exactly legislation is to legislate over. Speaking from a Papua New Guinean perspective, we must understand the exact nature of the material at issue (is it, in the epistemological sense, cultural property, intellectual property or traditional knowledge, tangible or intangible?) and be clear about the purpose and aim of the legislation. Pertinent questions to ask are: What is our understanding of indigenous cultural and intellectual property? What are the foreseeable consequences of introducing an IPR regime (copyright in particular) for indigenous cultural and intellectual material, which we can call 'property' for the time being? What are the foreseeable consequences and effect on the societies or social grouping which have rights over these materials? Are these possible effects desirable and, if not, what other options are available? Only then can we press ahead with confidence. Secondly, a wider issue lies in what appear to be two different sets of objectives applied to the regulation of indigenous intellectual and cultural property rights, not only in Papua New Guinea but generally in the world. These opposing objectives consist of, on the one hand, protection and preservation of traditional culture, and on the other, creating an opportunity for indigenous people to obtain economic benefits. Can a conventional IPR regime in fact do both? I take these considerations in turn.

The Intergenerational Aspect of Indigenous Cultural and Intellectual Property

To understand the material we are dealing with, let me make the following rather axiomatic but yet essential point. It is this. In most indigenous communities, particularly in Papua New Guinea, the past is always ever present, and by comparison with non-indigenous societies, it is more apparent, visible and real because it is one's link with the past that gives one practically everything that one possesses in the present. Let me illustrate this. As we all know, land (that is, customary land) is the basis of life for the vast majority of people; it is the land that gives them what they have; it feeds and sustains them, physically and spiritually. The 'root title' to this land comes through recognised kin links, followed by various other relationships such as connection to a mythical ancestor that perhaps first walked or worked the land, mountain, valley, forest or canoed down the river. Evidence stretches many generations back, right through to the origin of people in the area concerned, intertwining with mythology and cosmology. Indeed in customary land tenure law involving groups, it is currently the case that a group's ownership of land hinges on its ability to know its social history, and the further that one goes back in the generations, the stronger 'ownership' claims become. In customary land dispute cases, the courts in Papua New Guinea and Australia call this 'traditional evidence' (see Re Fishermen Island Case [1979] PNGLR 202). The group that fails in knowing and reciting its genealogy, for instance, may well lose ownership or land use rights and hence livelihood on that land, mountain, valley or water. That's how real and serious it is. It is the link with the past generation that sustains the present and will continue to sustain and enhance future generations to come. The future generation will be at great risk if it does not know the previous one, and therefore the present generation is duty bound to ensure that the future knows its antecedents and all other related customs and traditions. And this will continue to be so, well into the twenty-first century, unless the current customary land tenure system in Papua New Guinea is changed or superseded by some other system.

Indigenous cultural and intellectual material is like that. This is particularly true of secret/sacred cultural material and knowledge, some of the material over which we are trying to legislate (to offer protection from improper use or to generally regulate access). The general value in these materials (including knowledge) is that they act like a mirror of the past and a guiding light for the present, by which the present life is lived out, and where, amongst other things, it sets out the norms and rules by which people have to live and propagate themselves. Therefore, without these materials (and knowledge), people will be living void and empty lives with a bleak future to face: it 'is a testimony of the past without which the present would have no future' (Puri 1997: 5). Although Puri is particularly speaking with reference to the value of folklore (cultural and intellectual property) amongst the Australian Aborigines, in my view what he says is of equal significance to indigenous communities in Papua New Guinea.[4] This is the reason why, in the preamble, the framers of the Papua New Guinea Constitution intentionally reminded all Papua New Guineans to make it their business to pass worthy customs and traditions 'from generation to generation', and particularly for the present generation to pledge 'to guard and pass onto those who come after us, our noble traditions'.

The formulation and eventual enactment of standard IPR laws for Papua New Guinea is neither difficult nor problematic. What is difficult and problematic is how to accommodate and/or deal with indigenous cultural and intellectual property, commonly known as folklore (or expressions of folklore for indigenous artistic and literary works) previously, and more recently, known as traditional knowledge. Going by the reaction from several provincial seminars held by the NCC throughout Papua New Guinea, the main concern appears to be how best to regulate access to and use of indigenous cultural and intellectual (property) material, rather than, say, copyright in literary or published works such as books and cassettes, or patents and trade marks. Papua New Guineans want to pass laws to first protect the use of their cultural and intellectual (property) material – and if there is to be any economic gain made from the use of this 'material', they want to be adequately compensated too.

Unfortunately, it is not that easy to simply pass laws to grant these indigenous Papua New Guineans their wishes. This is because there are so many other issues, which must be carefully looked at first before the laws are enacted. I have already raised some of these issues in the form of questions. Let me now bring forward, for discussion purposes, one of the main conceptual matters. Although the intangible material in indigenous intellectual and cultural 'property' with which we are concerned appears at first glance to be intellectual property in the conventional sense, when one takes a closer look the 'intellectual' aspect of it diminishes, and instead what shines through is a special kind of 'property': not property in the sense of being 'owned' but as inhering in a social group. The 'property' aspect of this material, by common law standards, is abnormal because most of the items that fall under this category are inalienable. No one person, or generation, has any right by choice, to alienate this variant of 'property'. It survives the group for it is the group's heritage.

If such thinking lies behind calls for cultural preservation, there are grave concerns over an IPR regime's capacity to regulate or deal with misuse or unauthorised use of indigenous cultural property and related traditional knowledge. The essence of IPR is succinctly stated by Torremans and Holyoak (1998: 12) when they say:

> Intellectual property rights are first of all property rights. Secondly, they are property rights in something intangible. And finally, they protect innovations and creations and reward innovative and creative activity.

IPR may present the opportunity for the fair economic exploitation of indigenous intellectual and cultural property and related traditional knowledge, and that option should be made available to those sections or individuals of the indigenous communities who wish to pursue that end. Yet I have reservations over the IPR regime's capacity to regulate or deal with misuse or unauthorised use of indigenous cultural property and related traditional knowledge. A distinction between intangible traditional cultural property (i.e., the secret/sacred heritage material) and practical traditional knowledge should, I suggest, be utilised, and we can perhaps exempt the secret/sacred material from the general IPR regime, leaving that to be addressed by some other legal mechanism. If we do not take that approach, it is highly likely that we may end up facing the problems or difficulties,[5] that various Australian Aboriginal groups have faced. The case of *Yumbulul v. Reserve Bank of Australia* (1991: 2 [Intellectual Property Reports] 481) will demonstrate this.[6] Let us look at the circumstances (rather than the law) of this case and learn some 'object lessons' from it.

A Case from Australia

Terry Yumbulul is an Australian Aboriginal artist and a member of the Galpu clan in the Northern Territory. He had passed through various levels of tribal initiation and revelatory ceremonies conducted by the Galpu clan and, through that process, acquired the clan's various secret/sacred material, including traditional designs and their meanings. Particularly at the last initiation rite that he went through, he was conferred the authority to craft an object called the Morning Star Pole (hereafter referred to as the Pole). The Pole is a sacred Galpu clan object. The right to craft and paint one is jealously guarded, so that it is restricted to those who have properly undergone the various initiation processes and are eventually 'authorised', in the manner in which Yumbulul had done so and had been authorised.

The particular design that Yumbulul crafted and painted depicted a yam leaf symbolising a yam spirit man climbing up the pole, taking with him the spirit of a deceased person to the Morning Star. The Pole was made out of a cotton wood tree, surmounted with a lorikeet crown and cockatoo feathers as symbols of the rays of the Morning Star. Expert evidence received by the court established that Morning Star Poles play a central role in Aboriginal ceremonies such as those for honouring the deaths of tribal elders and generally in harmonising relationships amongst clans.

This Pole that Terry Yumbulul carved and painted was licensed and put on permanent public display in the Australian Museum in Sydney. An agent commissioned by the Reserve Bank of Australia obtained authorisation for purposes of copyright from Terry Yumbulul (not the Galpu Clan!) and the Morning Star Pole was then used by the Bank and was printed on a $10 bank note, commemorating the Australian Bicentenary. Following the release of the commemorative bank note, Mr Yumbulul was strongly criticised by his people (the Galpu), arguing that he, or any authorised Pole maker for that matter, were obligated and duty bound to ensure that the Pole that he carved was not used or reproduced in a manner that would, in their judgement, demean and undermine, and hence bring into disrepute, the significance of the Pole and discredit its integrity. In their view, Yumbulul has failed them in this instance, by allowing it to be reproduced on a bank note. This prompted Yumbulul to go to court, asking the court to invalidate the assignment of the copyright, arguing that when he gave the authorisation via the agent he did not really understand what he was doing and therefore the assignment should now be invalidated on the basis of unconscionability.

The primary issue for the court to determine was whether there has been a valid assignment of copyright. The court found that the Pole was an original artistic work by Terry Yumbulul (as opposed to the Galpu Clan who authorised him to carve and paint it) within the meaning of the Copyright Act and therefore decided that when he gave his authorisation, through the agent, for the Bank to reproduce his artistic work, he had validly assigned copyright. In the related case of the same facts, where Yumbulul sued the agent who had obtained copyright from him on behalf of the Central Bank, *Yumbulul v. Aboriginal Artists Agency* (1991) 21 I.P.R. 481, French J of the Federal Court at Darwin, in dismissing Yumbulul's case, made the following pertinent, observations (at p. 490): 'There was evidence that Mr Yumbulul came under considerable criticism from within the Aboriginal community for permitting the reproduction of the [design].... And it may... be that Australia's copyright laws do not provide adequate recognition of Aboriginal community claims to regulate the reproduction and use of works which are essentially commercial in origin.'

There are significant lessons to learn. First, in my view this case exposes the danger posed by conventional copyright laws for clan-held[7] secret/sacred heritage material, both in its tangible form and in its intangible form (the associated knowledge). When one of its own members, unilaterally decides to forgo his traditional customary obligations, the clan is bound to be left in total despair. Clearly, Yumbulul had no right to assign copyright by Galpu clan customary law, though he of course had such a right under the Copyrights Act. The Morning Star Pole was intergenerational clan heritage material, belonging to all the members of the Galpu Clan: present, past and future. The knowledge of how to carve the Pole was not his original creative work, but revealed to him through the initiation rites that he had gone through. If we do not want to repeat the Yumbulul situation in Papua New Guinea, we will have to provide, under copyright legislation (or such other IPR statute), specifically for a situation like this, such that authorisation must also be obtained from other members and not only from individual artists concerned. We will also have to consider equitable ways of benefit-sharing arrangements, for any monetary benefits. Otherwise, we might also have to consider whether material like these in the category of the Morning Star Pole should ever be allowed to be used outside their established contexts.

Secondly, the case falls into the category of those which deal with the reproduction of traditional cultural heritage material by individuals who are at once contemporary artists and are members of the respective clans.[8] Terry Yumbulul was authorised, at his last initiation, to carve the Morning Star Pole. One reason why he was authorised by his Galpu clan is that he possessed artistic skills: it was his role to use rather than to effect the design so as to enable and ensure the continuity of the Morning Star Pole tradition; to make him a custodian so that he could then pass that skill onto the next generation. So had Terry produced a derivative art work, not a reproduction but a work derived or inspired by the imagery and story behind the Morning Star Pole or the ancestral story of Djanda and the Sacred Waterhole, would this have offended the respective customs and traditions of their peoples? I think it would. And that is one of the main problems with copyright as well. As we know, copyright does not subsist in ideas; creativity inspired by existing ideas is exactly what copyright aims to encourage, promote and sustain economically. By copyright law, however, derivative works become the 'original' works of the contemporary artist – not of the clan or other such social group from which the artist 'appropriated' the idea or received the inspiration.

Should Papua New Guineans like to have individual artists who paint from clan-based heritage material have copyright over the work that they produce under such circumstances? What do PNG customary laws say about rights to artistic works depicting clan/group-based legends, ancestral stories, motifs, totems, and so forth? Take for example the 'Kambot Storyboard', a peculiar wood carving that depicts various life stories of the Kambot people, of the Lower Sepik area. This can be mass- produced by wood carvers in furniture workshops, generating an industry of its own, because what the furniture shop is producing are derivative works not reproductions. And, indeed, there is a furniture workshop in Lae, Morobe Province, doing exactly this. The majority of the carvers employed in this workshop are Sepik craftsmen and they produce 'story boards and religious plaques', based on designs originally from the Sepik, including the Kambot area (Stevenson 1999: 25–27). Imagine if the Kambot Storyboards were depicting sacred and culturally sensitive stories. No doubt the furniture produced from this workshop would have caused problems similar to those arising in the Yumbulul case. It is clear that we must find a way to deal with derivative works where the cultural material and related knowledge from which the work is inspired is of sensitive and sacred significance to the clan or such other social group concerned.

For there is an underlying issue. The Yumbulul case brings to the fore, on the one hand, the need to distinguish secret/sacred traditional cultural property and the associated traditional cultural knowledge that goes with the tangible cultural material from, on the other, practical traditional knowledge, and items falling under the first category but not treated as secret/sacred ('unclassified'). The main difference between these two lies in the mode of acquisition. For the former is acquired through a set cultural process such as an initiation or by offering sacrifice, whereas the latter is literally practical knowledge and therefore is usually acquired as general, and sometimes necessary, life skills. The secret/sacred material could then be regulated under a regime with particular emphasis on the protection and preservation of its integrity and continuity. The emphasis on the other category could be to regulate access with a view to facilitating economic exploitation, thereby protecting the economic interests of indigenous communities who might, say, want to trade in the use of the 'unclassified' traditional knowledge. So, if some sections of society wish to, they could be allowed to utilise 'unclassified' traditional knowledge and benefit economically, perhaps by asserting copyright over artistic work (carvings of various images etc.) under IPR laws. The 'Sepik carving trade', as in the case of the now popular 'Kambot Storyboard', or the 'Sepik basket trade', are examples where economic rights could be secured. IPR regimes would allow Sepik people to utilise their 'unclassified' traditional knowledge to trade with the wider Papua New Guinea society, and perhaps the world.

But before we too quickly adopt the idea of IPR as presenting an opportunity for the fair economic exploitation of indigenous intellectual and cultural property and related traditional knowledge, there may still be a question of who acquires the rights.

Sacred Flutes from New Guinea

A recent CD[9] features 'sacred flute music' from the villages of Boroi, Kaian, and Nubia-Sissimugum in the Bogia District of the far north coast of Madang; and the villages of Bo'da and Kuluguma on Manam Island Bogia District, Madang and Damaindeh-Bau, up on the Finisterre Ranges, Upper Ramu, Madang Province. The several tracks on this CD are accompanied by background explanatory notes, with precise dates of recording. Tracks 1 to 4 are from Bak hamlet in Boroi village; the background notes to track 4 explains that two Tika flutes (from Bak hamlet) 'are played by the brothers Magumbi and Porai, old men who said that they had learned these skills during their initiation into the men's cult'. Track 5 (two Noindeh flutes accompanied by two small garamut or slit gongs) is from Nubia-Sissimungum; tracks 6 and 7 are from the neighbouring Kaian ('Kaean') village, while tracks 8, 9 and 11 are from Bo'da village on Manam Island. The background notes to track 11 read: 'Gopu flutes are end-blown thin lengths of bamboo with one finger hole near the lower end of the flute. The flute played on this recording was made out of a length of aluminium pipe rather than the traditional bamboo. In contrast to the spirit cry flutes that are only ever played in ceremonial contexts, Gopu flutes are personal instruments on which men improvise. Men play their Gopu flutes to entice women.' Track 10 is from Kuluguma village on Manam Island. The final track, 12, is not from the Bogia District but from Damaindeh-Bau village, in the Finisterre Range, Upper Ramu. This (track 12) features three Mo-mo resonating tubes, explained thus:

> Mo-mos are end-blown lengths of bamboo (resonating tubes) with internodes knocked out approximately six to eight feet in length and open at each end. When played, the player rests one end on the ground and yodels down the other end. They are made and owned by individuals not by patrilineages. Mo-mos are some times played with garamuts which are still used in this area, but there were none in the village where this was recorded.

Male initiates were previously taught about the spirit cries of the Mo-mos during male initiation which has now been largely abandoned. Mo-mos are now played on village occasions, such as ceremonial exchanges, pig fertility festivals, funerals, marriages, births and other celebrations often accompanied by singsing [dance]. The songs sung vary with the occasions but the Mo-mos are capable of only one kind of cry. Rights to songs are sometimes purchased from the villages which own them.

The accompanying text thus offers detailed information on the nature of the material produced on the CD and lays out the contexts in which the material is performed in their respective societies. Indeed the text gives a graphic account of how the 'sacred flute music' is played – to the point of three coloured photographs demonstrating, revealing, to the whole world, how these flutes are blown and the correct positions the players of the flutes must take up when playing so that the sound or tunes are enhanced.

Now this sacred flute ritual ceremony is commonly found or widely practised through out the Sepik area, stretching through Madang and some of Morobe Province. The Manambu people of the Upper Sepik (consisting of the villages of Avatip, Malu and Yambon), of which I am a part, practise it too. Indeed in Avatip, it does exist to this day as the first level or stage of initiation for the adolescent male. The Haus Tambarans are fenced off with coconut or sago palm leaves, and these 'spirits' (we call them Daakul) are called with the beat of garamut (each 'Dakul' has its own and distinctive garamut beats) into the fenced Haus Tambarans. The 'Dakul' comes and 'cries' inside, and the adolescent male enters the fenced-off Haus Tambaran with a sacrifice (usually a live chicken or a big bunch of betelnut) in his hand and 'meets' the Dakul and gives 'it' the sacrifice. He is then initiated into this cult, where he is shown not only how to be 'involved' but also the rules and responsibilities that go with it. I was initiated into this in 1985. Most of what I saw and learnt then, is now presented on this CD! The accompanying notes also say:

> The flute sounds heard on this album 'are' the cries of spirits in the terms of ritual contexts in which they are played. In many parts of New Guinea one finds that wind sounds are associated with the supernatural – the sounds of bull-roarers are often attributed with spiritual properties, blowing through the mouth is an essential part of many magical spells ... The blowing of these flutes ... is to invoke the presence of the spirits with which they are associated, to make the powers associated with these spirits accessible to humans. The flutes are made, owned, played and kept secret by adult men. Women and children are forbidden to see the flutes and are told that the cries of the flutes are the voices of actual spirits.

And furthermore that:

> The playing of flutes is regulated by taboos and prohibitions. They may not be played outside the appropriate ceremonial contexts. Different pairs of flutes are blown on different occasions (for male initiations, inter-village

feasts, sago harvests, births, marriages, deaths, and celebrations). For sometime after a death there is a taboo against holding ceremonies involving flute blowing.

The producers of the CD thank the performers and people of the villages of Borai [Boroi], Bo'oda, Kaean [Kaian], Kuluguma, Nubia-Sissimungum and Damaindeh-Bau for making this record possible but the performance and copyright rights are with the record corporation.

Is it the lack of economic opportunity that is the issue here, or the lack of protection? One comment is in order that would apply to both derivations and reproductions. This is the topic of moral rights. The new copyright legislation has a part on moral rights. On the face of it, moral rights clauses seem to hold particular appeal and promise in terms of their potential to offer a regulatory regime, which would prevent misuse and debasement of indigenous intellectual and cultural property. Puri says: 'Moral rights are very significant for recognizing authorship and preventing debasement, mutilation or destruction of indigenous cultural works' (1999: 154). Article 6 bis of the Berne Convention recognises and accords two types of moral rights: paternity rights, i.e., the right of attribution to and author and creator of copyright work; and the moral right of integrity giving the author or the creator of copyright work the right to object to distortions, modifications or derogatory actions over the work. These rights exist independently of the author's economic rights and therefore may subsist even after the economic rights have been transferred to some one else.

Moral rights are, however, dependent on a copyright regime: they cannot exist without copyright. In essence, moral rights are aimed at protecting published or literary works – not unpublished indigenous intellectual and cultural property. Therefore, if moral rights are to be of some relevance, then moral rights clauses would have to be expanded to take in unpublished works such as indigenous intellectual and cultural property, possibly with a registration scheme invented to accommodate this.

Twin Objectives and the Law

I suggest that the object of preservation of indigenous culture and traditional knowledge, on the one hand, and the promulgation of an intellectual property rights regime for indigenous intellectual property rights and/or traditional knowledge on the other, are twin objectives: separate but related. These twin objectives can very well be likened to non-identical twins. Although being of the same parentage and living in the same house, they look different, act differently, and end up pursuing different paths – but always acknowledging that they come from the same household. The confusion is not in their appearance, but in their common origin.

Until very recently, I have been confused myself as to how best to deal with these twins. Perhaps I was not alone in this state of confusion. In

Papua New Guinea, I was in the company of notables, such as a former Chief Ombudsman (see n. 1) and the hierarchy of the National Cultural Commission (NCC) of Papua New Guinea. As we have seen, the former is reported to have said not only that our unique traditional music and dances 'must be recognised and accepted as such, encouraged and promoted, and above all must be protected', but called on the government to enact some form of copyright legislation 'to ensure that traditional music and dances belonging to a certain ethnic group are protected for their purposes' (*Post Courier*, 6 November 1997). Similarly, in a National Cultural Policy seminar (see n. 2), the NCC also advocated some form of IPR laws, particularly based on existing copyright models to be enacted to deal with the problem of inappropriate or improper use of indigenous cultural material, thus calling on IPR to address what is essentially an issue of the preservation of traditional culture!

I was in good anthropological company too. A similar state of confusion, or uneasiness, for want of a better expression, appears to exist in the debate internationally too. Here is the *Intellectual Property Rights for Indigenous Peoples: A Sourcebook* (Greaves 1994: ix):

> Intellectual property rights consist of efforts to assert access to, and control over, cultural knowledge and to things produced through its application. The most urgent reason to establish that control is to preserve meaning and due honour for elements of cultural knowledge and to insure that these traditional universes, and their peoples, maintain their vitality. Subsidiary intellectual property rights goals are to manage the degree and processes by which parts of that cultural knowledge are shared with outsiders and, in some instances, to be justly compensated for it.

I find the non-identical twins (of IPR and cultural preservation) appearing and disappearing in this same statement, where IPR is asked to take care of cultural preservation.

Perhaps, then, the endeavour of pursuing an intellectual property rights regime for indigenous intellectual property or traditional knowledge has to be approached separately, or, if not, with full cognizance of the differences, from the other closely related and equally important task of the wholesome preservation of indigenous cultural property (the heritage material), including related aspects of traditional knowledge. The drive towards intellectual property rights is to obtain monopolistic economic rights over a finite period of time with the use of indigenous intellectual property and/or traditional knowledge. By its very nature, IPR will bring into the public domain and commodify traditional knowledge and its creations or forms (with temporary protection in the creations only by bestowal of monopoly of use) with the aim of encouraging creativity and, hence, encouraging similar inventions or products. Consequently, if similar products are put out by other people from the idea or inspiration of existing (that is, in the public domain) indigenous cultural property, one cannot complain: that is fair game by the laws of IPR.

If there is a nexus between the issue of preservation of culture and IPR as a mechanism to preserve culture, to the extent that some seem to find an ally in IPR as a means of defence and conservation real or helpful, a traditional (as in indigenous) cultural preservation regime is still necessary on its own terms. It is required to facilitate continuity and/or reinvigoration and legitimacy, either of the continuity of contemporary traditional culture or of the reconstruction of traditional culture as a way of claiming or reclaiming lost heritage (in Weiner's sense [1998] with respect to peri-urban Aborigines). Furthermore, in so far as the preservation of a cultural base is necessary as a basis for the survival of traditional/indigenous societies, Article 8 of the CBD calls for national cultural preservation laws to maintain the 'knowledge and practices' of these communities.

The PNG National Cultural Commission is tasked with playing a leading role in the protection and promotion of the diverse traditional cultures of Papua New Guinea, no doubt to give effect to the Preamble to the National Constitution. If this is also the angle from which the NCC is coming, the aim of suitable legislation for the protection and preservation of tangible and intangible (intellectual) cultural property is actually different from that of IPR (particularly copyright) because:

> There is ... a significant difference in the scope of claims that can be made on behalf of a culture, and those that can be made on behalf of an individual author. Copyright laws enable individual authors not only to claim possession of their original works as discrete objects, but to claim possession and control over any and all reproductions of these works, or any substantial parts thereof, in any medium. Cultural property laws, however, enable proprietary claims to to be made only to original objects or authentic artifacts. (Coombe 1993: 264 footnotes omitted)

It is my contention that the debate over and the search for a suitable regulatory regime for indigenous cultural and intellectual property and traditional knowledge in Papua New Guinea, and perhaps the world, can be significantly enhanced if we separate out the issues, those non-identical twins – on the one hand, a regime for the preservation of culture and, on the other, IPR. In Papua New Guinea, the NCC should be encouraged to focus its attention on the issues of preservation of culture, but be vigilant for whatever dangers that IPR may pose for preservation of culture.

It was realising that existing IPR regimes, in particular the Universal Copyright Convention administered by WIPO, were ill suited for indigenous intellectual property that led the UNESCO/ WIPO Expert Committee many years ago, in 1982, to come up with Model Provisions for National Laws on the Protection of Expressions of Folklore Against Illicit Exploitation and Other Prejudicial Actions. The Model Provisions were meant to encourage nation states to enact national legislation to deal with matters of community heritage. These concerns culminated in the adoption of the *Draft Treaty on the International Protection of Expressions of Folklore against Illicit Exploitation and Other Prejudicial Actions* by the 25th Session of the UNESCO General Conference. This international consciousness and drive towards *sui generis* legislation appears to have weakened off in the last decade or so. Only a handful of African and Latin American countries appear to have enacted national laws based on or along the lines of the Model Provisions (Posey 1996: 86; Abada 1999: 128).

The suggested Model Provisions for a *sui generis* legislation do not, however, cover all aspects of indigenous intellectual property – or folklore, as the subject was then known. They are 'restricted to traditional artistic expressions which have been developed and perpetuated by communities or individuals in the country as the traditional artistic aspirations of that community. Therefore protection does not extend to traditional beliefs or scientific traditions, such as traditional cosmology or to legends, as well as purely practical traditions, if they do not take the form of a traditional artistic form of expression'(Abada 1999: 128). Perhaps another model can be developed to include the wider matters of indigenous intellectual and cultural property which are not included in the Model Provisions.

In the current context of developing *sui generis* forms of protection in the Pacific (*A Draft Model Law for the Pacific* [2001]), one of its architects, Kamal Puri, is very optimistic of the *sui generis* approach. But his plans go beyond the Model Provisions. He believes *sui generis* legislation giving indigenous people rights unknown to the common law 'is the most viable option for the future'(1999: 155). In principle, I concur. However, to make the *sui generis* effective, it requires concerted effort, not only at the national level, but also internationally through multilateral conventions, and such, so that there can be reciprocal arrangements between nation-states to recognise the new form of property rights. Without the necessary reciprocal arrangements, the *sui generis* approach may not mean much. So although something of the old Model Provisions have reappeared in PNG, this has not been to establish a special case but to bring domestic legislation in line with international requirements.

IPR for PNG?

As of November 2001, the IPO (Intellectual Property Office) PNG has been established physically; it exists as an office on its own, with the former Registrar of Trademarks as the Registrar of Trademarks and Patents and Industrial Designs. In the same month, the NIPRC was told that IPO PNG did not have the capacity to administer the Copyright and Neighbouring Rights Act 2000 and was therefore looking to offload the administration of that legislation onto another government institution. The Department of Attorney-General and the National Cultural Commission have been mentioned as the possible institutions to administer the copyrights legislation.

The future of the NIPRC is now in the balance. There is some thinking that since the necessary IPR legislation has been delivered, the NIPRC does not have any continuing role. Others hold the view that the NIPRC should be worked into the operational structure of the IPO PNG to act as an overarching policy formulation and coordination body. However, there is no statutory basis for the NIPRC to continue to exist – in the current set of IP legislation. So, what is this legislation? I briefly comment on the two new laws enacted in 2002, and on their implications for expressions of culture and traditional knowledge.

Patents and Industrial Designs Act 2000

The general aim of this legislation, as set out in the preamble to the Act, is to 'make provision for the protection of industrial property rights, namely patents, industrial designs and geographical indications and for related purposes'.[10] Are there any provisions in the Act that deal with traditional knowledge, setting out access arrangements and protection to that body of material? No; there are not. The only provision of some interest, from this standpoint, is Section 13, where it says that an invention would not pass the test of 'novelty' where it can be shown that such an invention is anticipated by 'prior art'. It then goes on to explain 'prior art' thus:

> For purposes of this section, prior art shall consist of everything disclosed to the public, anywhere in the world, by – (a) tangible form; or (b) oral disclosure; or (c) use; or (d) any other way, prior to the filing, or, where appropriate, the priority date of the application claiming the invention. (Subsection (2) of Section 13)

This provision offers some protection to traditional knowledge in the sense that an invention based on the use of traditional knowledge may not pass the novelty test as new.

It may be useful to note the approach that Vanuatu is taking in their draft Patents and Designs legislation. In the draft legislation, their National Cultural Council and their National Council of Chiefs are given roles to play, essentially as clearing/vetting agencies, concerning applications based on or derived from traditional knowledge. Either of these agencies is authorised to institute civil proceedings on behalf of indigenous people whose traditional knowledge has been illegally exploited. Under the Vanuatu proposals, patent applications involving traditional knowledge must also include an agreement between the applicant and the traditional/customary owners, setting out, inter alia, benefit-sharing arrangements. It is my respectful submission that such a clause is necessary and therefore must be instituted into the Papua New Guinea Patents and Industrial Designs Act 2000. Perhaps a benefit-sharing agreement must also be considered for copyright arising out of expressions of culture/folklore under Papua New Guinea's Copyright and Neighbouring Rights Act.

Copyright and Neighbouring Rights Act 2000

I take up two matters: protection of folklore and, more briefly, application of international treaties.[11]

Rather then using the more current language of traditional knowledge or expressions of culture, the Act uses the rather old phrase 'expression of folklore'. The phrase, 'expression of folklore', is defined for purposes of the Act under Section 2:

> a group-oriented and tradition-based creation of groups or individuals reflecting the expectations of the community as an adequate expression of its cultural and social identity, its standards and values as transmitted orally, by imitation or by other means, including – (a) folktales, folk poetry and folk riddles; and (b) folk songs and instrumental folk music; and (c) folk dances and folk plays; and (d) production of folk arts in particular drawings, paintings, carvings, sculptures, pottery, terra cotta, mosaic, woodwork, metal ware, jewelry, handicrafts, costumes and indigenous textiles.[12]

Whilst this definition is comprehensive and that is welcomed, there is no distinction between secret/sacred material/expressions of folklore and those which are not. This is a cause for concern for general protection purposes and for allowing access, including the current forms of transaction and transmission of various classes of expressions of folklore, either between generations or between neighbouring communities. A distinction must be made between secret/sacred expressions of folklore and those which are not so in order that appropriate levels of protection can be instituted: perhaps absolute protection for those secret/sacred materials and a lesser level of protection for those which do not fall under that category. As it is, Section 30 of the Act provides the same level of general protection:

> Expressions of folklore are protected against – (a) reproduction; and (b) communication to the public by performance, broadcasting, distribution by cable or by other means; and (c) adaptation, translation and other transformation when such uses are made either for commercial purposes or outside their traditional or customary context. (Section 30(1))[13]

Section 30(4) proposes to establish a 'competent authority' for purposes of giving 'authorization' and imposing 'terms and conditions of such authorization'. For any person who wishes to reproduce, perform, broadcast, distribute, adapt, translate or transform expressions of folklore as protected under Section 30(1), authorisation will have to be obtained from that authority. Implying that fees will be imposed for issuing authorisation, '[A]ll monies collected shall be used for purposes of cultural development', with ministerial approval and as the competent authority determines (Section 30(5)).

Ordinary indigenous Papua New Guineans whose expressions of folklore are 'authorised' to be used may not take kindly to the current arrangement under Section 30(5) of the Act. This is apparent from the current attitude of indigenous Papua New Guineans in matters relating to compensation and royalties for natural resources exploitation. In view of this, a new distribution mechanism for any monies collected by the 'competent authority' has to be worked out by immediately amending Section 30(5) of the Act. Such a distribution mechanism must involve indigenous communities whose traditional knowledge or expressions of culture are being exploited.

As to 'derivative works', Section 4(1)(b) of the Act identifies them as including:

(i) translations, adaptations, arrangements and other transformations or modifications of works; and (ii) collections of works and databases, whether in machines, readable or other forms; and (iv) collections of expressions of folklore provided that such collections are original by reason of the selection or arrangement of their contents.[14]

Clearly Section 4(1)(b)(iv) (see n. 13) must be a cause for concern for many reasons. First, this clause represents the greatest danger for the wholesome protection and preservation of traditional culture. Second, this clause allows for expressions of folklore to be mutilated and debased. Third, it allows just about anyone to use with impunity another cultural groups' expressions of folklore just by mere selection or arrangement of their contents. Fourth, it severely restricts/curtails the protection clauses of Section 30 of the Act. A solution to this problem is for the Act to distinguish between 'secret/sacred' expressions of folklore/traditional knowledge and those which are not, and then give absolute protection to the former, including the non-applicability of Section 4(1)(b)(iv) of the Act to that class of expressions of folklore/traditional knowledge and treat that as a matter of cultural protection rather than intellectual property. This is necessary to protect the integrity of that body of material so that it can continue to play its role in our indigenous communities. The other non-secret/sacred expressions of culture can then be made available for the kind of exploitation envisaged under this provision of the Act.

As to infringement of folklore, Section 31 of the Act addresses this by making it an offence for a person to obtain 'expression of folklore' without consent, the offence being framed not in relation to the indigenous peoples who collectively own the expressions of folklore but in relation to the 'competent authority'. Interestingly enough, there is no criminal penalty for this offence. Instead, the guilty person is 'liable to the competent authority for damages, injunctions and any other remedies as the Court may deem fit.' This provision does not offer much deterrence to would-be offenders. Deterrence should form the primary enforcement basis because damages paid in money (to the competent authority!) may not sufficiently compensate for the damage done (mutilation and debasement) to the expression of folklore/traditional knowledge.

These provisions have very strong resemblance to those found in the old Model Provisions for National Laws on the Protection of Expressions of Folklore Against Illicit Exploitation and Other Prejudicial Action 1982. As I foreshadowed, this reflects the level of influence that WIPO has had in the events leading up to the enactment of the legislation.

This reminds one of the question of the application of international treaties.

Section 32 of the Act addresses this. It says:

The provisions of any international treaty in respect of copyright and related rights to which Papua New Guinea is a party shall apply to matters dealt with under this Act and, in case of any conflict with a provision of this, the treaty shall prevail to the extent to any inconsistency.

This provision undoubtedly subjects the Act to PNG's international law obligations, such as TRIPS, WIPO and, I submit, the CBD, particularly in areas in which the Act purports to deal with traditional knowledge systems. This then poses an interesting question: in the event of conflict between TRIPS and WIPO on the one hand, and CBD on the other, who should decide which prevails over the other? This should really be a matter for PNG or individual nation-states to decide. Whilst Papua New Guinea has to date, taken steps to implement its international law obligations under the WTO and TRIPS, it has not taken any steps to do likewise for its international law obligations under the CBD. The CBD has of course come into force.

Concluding remarks: property or intellectual property?

Efforts are still continuing to put rather more imaginative provisions into place on a Pacific-wide basis where nation-states of the Pacific Island Countries (PIC) have been persuaded to adopt the Model Laws developed for the region. To date no PIC country has adopted the Model Laws. That not withstanding, in order to arrive at a conceptually and practically workable model, first we must recognise the differences in the non-identical twins, and find different ways to deal with them, for they are indeed different.

With regard to the existing options, I suggest that we have unfairly underestimated the potential of customary law and the common law, in particular, the tort of passing-off. This underestimation has caused us to search for options which, from a distance, appear to be appealing but, on a closer look, are found wanting. We really do not have to venture out into foreign territory and emulate concepts that are foreign, where those concepts have their own background, history and purpose. We must first search within. In many ways, Papua New Guinea is fortunate: we can learn from experiences from elsewhere, particularly the circumstances set out in the Australian Aborigine case of *Yumbulul v. The Reserve Bank of Australia*. One thing that is in our favour is that the PNG system recognises and sanctions customary law. We can perhaps do better than recreate the situation of despair that the various Aboriginal community leaders found themselves in.

Customary law in Papua New Guinea has great potential, particularly given its broad range of coverage and flexibility, not only in the sense of offering protection, but to in general regulating access to and use of indigenous cultural material and related traditional knowledge. In terms of the hierarchy of laws in Papua New Guinea, custom stands third in rank, after constitutional laws and other statutes. It applies as part of the unwritten body of law known as the 'underlying law' and is of course subject to all types of statute laws. The 'underlying law' is made up of, firstly, customs (of the indigenous peoples of Papua New Guinea) and, secondly, the common law of England as it stood on 16 September 1975, this being the date of Independence.

Custom 'is not created by the courts but is discovered as a matter of fact and adopted as law' (per Kapi J [now Chief Justice] in Supreme Court Reference No. 4 of 1980: Re Petition of M.T. Somare [1981] PNGLR 265 at 288). Any case studies of customs or customary transactions in or of dealings, either regulating the rights of access or use of indigenous cultural material and traditional knowledge, will certainly go a long way in assisting lawyers to plead custom in courts of Papua New Guinea and, as a result, develop the customary law in this particular area of our concern.

In my view, the use of the term 'property' rather than 'intellectual property' with particular reference to indigenous cultural material and related traditional knowledge may make the pleading of custom in this area much easier. It would not be necessary to plead custom with reference to indigenous intellectual property, for the reason that it may be conceptually conflicting and awkward for the courts to handle. For example, if I were to plead custom concerning rights over the ownership of a story or a spirit voice or design, claiming ownership would be 'akin to claiming the power of their source' because the creation is usually attributed to its situation or its place of origin rather than to individual creators of it (Leach 2000b: 19). Conceptually, then, I would be running a flawed argument if I were to plead intellectual property in the creation, because intellectual property concerns individual (including a corporate entity) rights in the thing itself, rather than its source or place of origin. Importing the concept of intellectual property (rather than simply property in traditional knowledge) would make the process of pleading custom over the ownership of such creations conceptually and logically difficult. In searching for a solution to the issue of (cultural) protection, perhaps we have also moved nearer to understanding what intellectual property is and is not all about.

Notes

An earlier version was presented to the WIPO Sub-Regional Workshop on Intellectual Property, Genetic Resources and Traditional Knowledge, Brisbane, 2001.

1. Sir Charles Maino, a Mekeo Chief himself, as reported in the *Post Courier* of 6 November 1997.
2. In a Cultural Policy Seminar held in Port Moresby in 1997, the NCC made it clear that, as part of the overall national cultural policy that it was working on, it advocated some form of IPR laws, particularly based on existing copyright law models, to deal with the kind of problem to which Sir Charles was referring.
3. Members, of which I was one, included representatives of the Department of Attorney-General and Justice, Department of Foreign Affairs, Department of

Trade and Industry, National Cultural Commission and Conservation Melanesia Inc., an NGO.
4. What this also means is that indigenous cultural and intellectual material performs significant social functions in contemporary indigenous communities. In Puri's (1997: 6) words:

> For Aboriginal people, folklore performs several important social functions. It helps them to release cultural tensions and ambivalence, and it provides amusement and education. It is a sort of 'social cement' that exists outside the formal or official structures. It strengthens social cohesiveness, raises the quality of life and assists in the development and articulation of cultural identity. Aboriginal people use folklore to reflect the past and make improvements for their future. Folklore gives them a chance of self expression through music, song, dance, speech, and many other avenues. Such cultural manifestations create an invisible bond among individuals and groups and forge social and spiritual contact.

5. Notwithstanding the fact that defining the sacred or secret is likely to elicit its own range of difficulties. I am grateful to the reader for this reminder.
6. Also see, at note 7, *Milpurrurru and others v. Indofurn Pty Ltd,* [1995] 30 IPR 209. Both cases are usefully discussed in Blakeney (1995: 442–45) (although the decision in the Milpurrurru case was handed down by von Doussa J on December 13 1994, it was only reported in 1995).
7. Or such other social group.
8. Another illustration is given by *Milpurrurru and others v Indofurn Pty Ltd* (1995) 30 IPR 209. This involves an action for breach of copyright by eight artists from three different Aboriginal tribes of the central Arnhem Land, whose art work was based on, inspired by or depicted traditional Aboriginal legends and imagery. Four of the Aboriginal artists had painted bark paintings based on legends of the peoples of Central Arnhem Land; while three, from the Central Australian western desert, painted Papunya style legends. The eighth, Mrs Makira (a lino cut artist) a member of Yalgnu clan, had painted imagery from a clan-based story of Djanda and the Sacred Waterhole; here the story is of Djang' Kawu, her ancestral creator, and his two sisters, the Wagilag sisters, ending their journey from Burralku to Yelangbara. 'Her right to use this imagery arose as an incident arising out of her membership of the Yalgnu Clan, the land owner group in the area' (Blakeney 1995: 443). All these paintings were then reproduced in portfolios of Aboriginal arts, either held by the Australian National Gallery or published by the Australian Government Printer for the Australian Information Service, mainly for purposes of educating the wider Australian community to understand and appreciate Aboriginal art. These institutions explained in publications containing these art works that they were based on stories of spiritual and sacred significance, that the images and symbols were strictly controlled by Aboriginal customary law, and 'that the right to create paintings and other art works depicting creations and dreaming stories and to use pre-existing designs and clan totems resided in the traditional custodians of the stories' (Blakeney 1995: 443 citing Ellinson 1994). But since the Australian Copyright Act did not recognise this aspect of Aboriginal customary law, the copyrights in all the paintings were found to be with the eight Aboriginal artists, individually. This was in the context of a court action brought by three of the living artists and the Public Trustee on behalf of the estates of the five deceased, against an Australian company that imported carpets which reproduced the artists' works on the carpets, and had written on their swing tags the words: 'Proudly designed in Australia by

Australian Aborigines – Made in Vietnam'. The Australian Federal Court found that the art works were used without licence from the owners of the copyright (the artists, not their clans) and, furthermore, found that the statements on their swing tags were false and misleading, and hence in breach of the Trade Practices Act. Damages were therefore awarded to the artists concerned.

9. A CD from Rounder Records Corporation 1999, Cambridge MA, USA http://www.rounder.com. I am indebted to Dr Melissa Demian for bringing this to my attention.
10. There are six parts to the Act: Part I deals with preliminary matters; Part II sets out the administrative arrangements, mainly by establishing the Office of the Registrar and vesting certain powers and functions on him/her; Part III deals with patents; Part IV deals with industrial designs; Part V takes up miscellaneous matters and Part VI makes provision for the subsequent promulgation of Regulations to the Act and for fees. As it is, there is no clause in the Act that deals with geographical indications, although it is mentioned in the preamble to be one of the purposes of the Act.
11. Part I deals with preliminary matters, mainly definitions of terms and phrases for purposes of the Act. Part II deals with copyrights whilst performers' rights are dealt with under Part III as neighbouring rights. Various enforcement measures both civil and criminal are set out under Part IV of the Act. Part V provides a protection mechanism for 'expressions of folklore'. Part VI is headed 'miscellaneous' and it deals with matters such as the scope of application of international treaties.
12. Original paragraphs not observed.
13. Subsection 2 reads: 'Subsection 1 shall not apply where acts referred to therein related to – (a) the use by a person exclusively for his own personal purposes; and (b) using short excerpts for reporting current events to the extent justified by the purpose of providing current information; and (c) the use solely for the purposes of face-to-face teaching or for scientific research.
14. There is no subsection (iii).

Chapter 3

Seeing, Knowing, Owning: Property Claims as Revelatory Acts

Melissa Demian

Should it be any wonder, then, that claims to property, those domineering pretensions to objective and lasting entitlement, should rely so heavily on a nontransacting, time-ignoring sense of vision? Should it be any wonder that property so deeply implicates an organ of perception that can treat the perceived thing as an object, and act as if the passage of time did not matter?   (Rose 1994c: 272)

The current men's house here, this is not a true men's house, it is a wind house [standalone 'veranda' for casual socialising]. The old one fell apart, and at the moment we don't have the pigs and everything that is needed to organise its reconstruction. This wind house is an image (*piksa*) of the men's house, a mark (*mak*) … It is our sisters' sons' turn now, they have to make the men's houses now. The one you see here, they built it in memory (*an tap*) of our brother who died. (Tanga Islander, New Ireland Province, Papua New Guinea, quoted in Holding n.d.: 11)

If you walk along one of the bush tracks that wind throughout the Suau Coast in the southeast of Papua New Guinea, it may be that you will come upon a fruiting tree, say a mango. The mango tree appears to have grown there of its own accord, like any of the other trees around it. In fact, the chances are very good that it was planted deliberately, especially if it appears alongside the track where it will be in plain view of anyone travelling past it. And if you are fortunate enough to be accompanied by a Suau person, she will probably be able to tell you not only the matrilineage of whose land the mango marks a boundary, but the name of the person who planted it twenty or thirty years ago. If she is especially knowledgeable about the history of this piece of land, she may also be able to tell you who has contested its ownership, or how the lineage that currently claims it came to do so. Perhaps their apical ancestress settled the land generations before the colonisation of Papua New Guinea. Perhaps their lineage was relocated there by the Australian administration, so they would be more accessible to government patrols. Or perhaps it was given to them as compensation by the lineage of a sorcerer who killed one of their kinsmen. Any of these cases may be common knowledge. The point is that what looks like just another tree to the foreign observer is, to a local one, an index not only to a land boundary but the history of one or more lineages who have resided upon that land.

This is a scenario which arguably could come from many parts of the world. Of interest is what it might have to offer discussions of the visual properties of property. I take as my starting point Rose's (1994c) essay on the subject, but my concern is with expanding her argument not only geographically but across different forms of property. The kinds of objects which now exercise both popular and academic imaginations are property in intangibles, which calls into question once again what it is we think we are looking at when we 'see' intellectual property, that is, conceive of its presence in a claimable form. 'Seeing' for Rose connotes the act of perception and, implicitly, recognition of property, but also the effects of property law on the physical world: 'property's visibility, in a sense, is especially attuned to letting people speak to each other, over time, about their relation to place' (1994c: 268). The following will be an experiment in asking whether the same can be said of property's effects on the world of intangible objects. It is to this area in particular that I think the property regimes of Melanesia may have salutary examples to offer, not only because Melanesian peoples conduct transactions in intangibles as readily as they do transactions in tangible objects,[1] but because the visual acknowledgement of property of all kinds in Melanesia carries with it entailments that oblige us to question at which moment the property actually comes into being. This is in turn a shorthand way of asking with whom an object is identified, how it came to be so identified, and to which other parties the identification 'points'. Whether such a relationship can be identified as one of 'property' underlies the question. When Papua New Guineans speak of 'belonging', whether in English, Tok Pisin or certain of the vernaculars,[2] they are as often as not referring to a relationship of identification rather than possession. An inquiry about a men's house, such as the one described above by Holding's Tangan informant, can unfold into a discourse on the history of an entire clan and its neighbours. The house is a 'mark' not only of the deceased men it commemorates, but also of the intentions of their sisters' sons to build a proper men's house some time in the future.

Is the visual appraisal of property always as 'time-ignoring' as Rose suggests it might be? She makes this suggestion because the sense of vision, unlike other forms of human perception, 'occurs with minimal reference to time, since the eye can capture a whole scene more or less synoptically and need not depend on memory of developments that only unfold over time' (1994c: 270). Furthermore, visual perception is generally only acknowledged as valid if the thing observed does not change under observation, or changes in ways that are predictable or follow a pattern (1994c: 271). It is because of these qualities that, as Rose observes,

> With respect to time, then, vision gives the impression that time does not matter, that the past will be like the future, that experience itself is logically irrelevant to the way events play out. This is because, in the visual metaphor of the 'real world', experience never transforms or changes anything. Events may indeed unfold in time, as when a stone drops to the ground, but they do so in ways that are in principle susceptible to prediction – precisely because they can be observed repeatedly. (1994c: 271)

These observations do not reflect Rose's own critique of vision, but her précis of endeavours in some quarters of the academic world to destabilise the 'scientific' model of vision and the principle of replicability as a foundation of scientific knowledge. The problem as she sees it is how to salvage the visual properties of property from sharing the same fate as other relationships which depend in whole or in part on visual appraisal, such as that between scientists and their objects of study. The problem for my purposes is the elucidation of visual manifestations of property which explicitly refer to a temporal register, as this in turn aids people in determining the form of property they are dealing with. Property claims are certainly most effective in tangible form, but the example of the Tangan men's house is not only a claim being made manifest. It may also be an anticipation of future claims, and a memorial to transactions conducted in the past. Rather than implying an 'endless present', some images of property may exist anywhere *but* the present.

Only Connect

My premise is that property claims are communication technologies. That is to say, something called 'property' exists only when people explicitly indicate to other people, whether by obtaining a title deed or planting a mango tree, that they have gathered to themselves a critical mass of rights to the thing claimed. A property claim communicates precisely because it is a rendering of relations in an informational form (Biersack 1982: 249–52): it allows people to know whether or not they are entitled access to the thing identified as property, and whether or not they are entitled to dispose of some or all of it. Property connects, then, even as it divides. A Suau person encountering an areca palm in the bush will not climb it or even gather the fallen nuts beneath it if there is a *katilipu*, a palm frond tied to the trunk signifying proprietorship. The *katilipu* indicates that the palm is not a generic palm but a specific one claimed by a specific lineage; that is to say, it has an 'identity'. The claim communicated by the *katilipu* therefore distinguishes a tree from other trees, just as it distinguishes a person or group of people from other persons or groups of people. A significant property of property, then, is the fact that it generates distinctions between things by means of distinctions between persons. Rose moves in this direction when she refers to the capacity of property to allow people to speak to each other. However, the connection implicit in the communicative aspect of property does not stop there, but goes on to instantiate a division. The term commonly used for the kind of division I have in mind is 'rights'.

Rights are of course simply placeholders for particular forms of action: exclusion, consumption, alteration or transmission, for example. To claim something is to claim the capacity to act upon it and the legitimacy of that action. But whatever we think property consists in, it matters not at all until we make our assumptions known to the world at large, and the most (but not the only) effective way to do this is by means of a visual indicator, something we can show other people that is sufficiently compelling for them to acknowledge that we have the rights we say we have. This is the point Rose makes in her meditation on the persuasive nature of property, which so often manifests in the visual domain. But, as she notes, depending on our eyes to tell us whether something is our own or others' property almost immediately gets us into trouble. Late twentieth-century objections to vision as arbiter of human knowledge about the world turn on the argument that a visual appraisal is an 'objectifying' one (1994c: 273). Rose's account of objectification in this instance suggests that it means an exclusive accumulation of agency to the observer, allowing none to the observed. Indeed, the forcefulness of the objectifying nature of property claims is precisely what has inspired the staking of claims in, say, airspace and the results of horse races.

In the first of these examples, twentieth-century case law has demonstrated that the immediate stratum of airspace over a parcel of land can be claimed, transacted, and even taxed as property together with *or separately from* the land itself (Gray 1991: 259). The 'upper stratum' of airspace remains poorly defined but nonetheless resolutely beyond the purview of property regimes (1991: 254), since aircraft are excluded from charges of trespass under most circumstances, even where they may compromise the privacy of a landowner.[3] But the 'lower stratum', the empty space between the surface of the land and the 'upper stratum', can be and is claimable as property. Its property status seems to be demonstrable on two grounds, both having to do with the introduction of other (tangible) objects into the airspace. Legitimate objects put in place by the landowner – fences, buildings, trees – very nearly require that the airspace be included in the fee simple estate. Whereas illegitimate objects – bullets, power lines – constitute trespass because they originate not from the landowner's intentions for his or her property, but from the unwelcome intentions of another. In other words, the legitimacy or illegitimacy of an object is determined by the action which (and the actor who) introduced it into a segment of airspace; the action in its turn is transformed into a reflection of particular 'rights' to act upon that space, thereby attributing to it the characteristics of property.

The second example is a celebrated Australian case, *Victoria Park Racing and Recreation Grounds Co. Ltd. v. Taylor*.[4] It involved the unsuccessful claim by the owners of a racecourse that the owner of an adjacent piece of land was not entitled to allow the use of his land for radio broadcasts of the neighbouring horse races and their results (Libling 1978: 106–7; Gray 1991: 264–69). The fame, or perhaps infamy, of this case appears to turn on the fact that the majority decision denied the possibility that property could be claimed in a spectacle (Gray 1991: 268), thereby depriving the plaintiffs of the primary ground for their case. Later comment on the case suggests that the majority decision failed to take into account the unfair appropriation of the profits that a spectacle has as its explicit object: '[I]t should have been recognised that they had no right to *so contrive their activities* that they appropriated the profits that could be made out of a spectacle' (Libling 1978: 106, emphasis added), since there was ample evidence that the radio broadcasts had a noticeable, and detrimental, effect on the racecourse's gate revenues. Again, it is the legitimacy or illegitimacy of action which appears to be the arguing point for the case. The plaintiffs lost, among other reasons, because they could not establish a proprietary right to information that was visible and audible to anyone capable of looking over the fence bounding the racecourse. While the majority in the case acknowledged that the defendants had acted ignobly, they could not agree with the plaintiffs that the exclusionary basis for a profit-making enterprise means that the spectacle produced by such enterprise ought to be categorised as property (Gray 1991: 268 n.2). The dissenting minority in the case also did not appear to accept the argument that the spectacle itself constituted a form of property, but held instead that a misappropriation of profits had occurred through illegitimate action. It would still seem, however, that in order for the defendants' actions to be deemed truly illegitimate, some sort of right on the part of the plaintiffs would have to be established. If not a property right, then a right of what sort?

In both of these instances, property claims to intangible objects transform those intangibles into resources yielding current or anticipated products by means of attaching them to persons – which may be, as Libling argues, the proper object of a claim rather than the intangible resource itself. Resources and their products whose identities as such originate in the imaginations of the claimants must be contested in court in order to be recognised as property at all.[5] But more importantly, their contestation is necessary in order for them to be recognised as distinct from tangible forms of property or from events ('spectacles') whose ownership itself may be contested. That it is possible to conceive as property, successfully or not, information gathered by watching the racecourse next door, is an indication of where the idea of property has been heading in Western thought throughout the twentieth century. Property emerges where someone can envision it, or more accurately persuade someone else of one's envisioning. This model has been so compelling that property even appears to emerge as a result of the misrecognition of an envisioning, such as the interpretation of Hawaiian taro gardens as evidence of private property regimes by European colonists (Rose 1994c: 295). Because the cultivation of land constituted a precondition for claiming the land as property – because, according to a Lockean model, labour had been added to it – the appearance of taro gardens suggested 'ownership' to the nineteenth-century European imagination. As it turned out, the gardens were both more and less than what the colonists took them for; they 'belonged' nominally to noble lineages but were cultivated and used primarily by commoners (cf. Strathern 1999a: ch. 7).

The risk, of course, is that enterprising souls are capable of imagining almost anything to be ownable, or at least imagining that it should be owned. As Maine remarked nearly a century and a half ago, the notion that occupancy is the ultimate source of property rights arises not from 'an instinctive bias towards the institution of Property, but a presumption arising out of the long continuance of that institution, that *everything ought to have an owner*' (Maine 2000: 151, emphasis in original). The implication was that any object deemed *res nullius* was not just fair game for anyone brazen enough to claim it, but that it was somehow morally repugnant, requiring a claim of ownership as a corrective to some error in the natural order of things. Maine then went on to anticipate the complaints of late twentieth-century property theorists in his observation that the problem with this picture of property's origins is that it not only presupposes the concept of *res nullius*, but that it also presupposes property relations to be conducted strictly between individual actors. In more recent times, there have been numerous exceptions made to such freewheeling application of the notion of occupancy. Gray (1991) notes that twentieth-century Anglophone courts have balked at permitting property to be claimed *everywhere* that its claimants propose it to exist. The resistance to such claims tends to emerge when the objects to be 'propertised' impinge too closely on notions of the common good, and are therefore 'non-excludable resources'. In Gray's view, this is because we still imagine there to be areas of human action which categorically must be preserved from the constraints implied by propertisation. Access to these forms of action and their products cannot be restricted if they are to exist in the first place, as in the emblematic example of a lighthouse beam (Gray 1991: 269), which, assuming it is turned on, is used by all ships within its area of operation whether or not they have any claim to the lighthouse itself.

I would add to his argument the suggestion that what Gray has identified as unpropertisable has this attribute at least in part because relationships between people with access to categorically non-excludable resources cannot be expressed by means of the property claim. Gray rightly notes that the commons are the commons because common resources possess this attribute of non-excludability. In turn, non-excludability might be definable as a form of 'broadcast' relationship, that is, a mode of communication which cannot be restricted to circulation between a limited number of parties. The beam of light from a lighthouse may have a single source, but its 'audience' is not restrictable through limited reception in the way that, say, the audience for a satellite television channel is. So in order to qualify as non-excludable, a resource must possess this 'broadcast' attribute; it must by its very nature be exploitable by a potentially unlimited number of interested parties. The property claim, initiated through legal or technological interventions (or both), can therefore count among its effects the transformation of an unlimited flow of relationships into one which is restricted to two or more – but always a finite number – parties.

My interest in shifting the emphasis from the thing-to-be-claimed to the interests of those staking claims stems from a desire to avoid the trap of scarcity-speak described by Pottage (1998a),[6] in which the finitude of resources rebounds upon the relationships they mediate, such that these relationships are also seen to be limited in their distribution – that is to say, they comprise a specific 'society'. But if the goal is to imagine a resource as universally non-excludable, then we must first acknowledge that its very identity as a resource is determined by the relationships between persons that it mediates. The constellation of interests around resources lend themselves more readily to the comparative agenda of anthropologists (Hann 1998b: 7) than do attempts to consider them as if they existed independently of such interests. When interests and other relationships are made the explicit object of focus, phenomena such as 'the enclosure of the commons' become a means of referring to the restriction of the kinds of relationships that can exist between the encloser-in and the enclosed-out, rather than a change of status solely for that which has been enclosed. Gudeman (1996), for instance, imagines the loss of the commons not as the degradation of tangible resources themselves, but rather as the loss of a domain of social activity he identifies as 'a human community whose relationships are expressed through and maintained by material resources' (1996: 106). The point is that the 'loss' here is not the disappearance of resources, but the effacing or enforced obsolescence of relationships which might lead to access to those resources. 'Community', like 'society', is a way of talking about a common repertoire of actions and intentions; it is in turn action which is constrained by means of the limitation of relationships.[7] Among matrilineal Suau, it is extremely difficult to make a formal land claim through a male ancestor, although people can and do claim use-rights to land and other resources through patrilateral ties. The division of a society into matrilineal lineages through whom most forms of property devolve presents one way to limit relationships, but the claims of maternal and paternal kin usually do not impinge on one another. Property is thus categorised according to the kinds of persons through whom it can and cannot flow. In contrast, the model of private property suggests a zero-sum game in which private possession invariably comes at the expense of public possession, one consequence of which is that property appears to generate categories of persons in the form of private owners versus users of the commons. Relationships between these categories of persons are thus delineated by their entitlement or lack of entitlement to particular property forms. What Gray documents – the refusal of courts to 'see' certain kinds of property – is in other words a refusal to allow the restriction of relationships in a given field of action.

But such a reduction is only possible in the first place if it is conceivable that an object, say a parcel of land, can start out associated with a number of relationships, some of which can then be privileged over others even at the expense of their continued existence. I have just described the condition of alienation of land from its putative prior users, but in this instance I would also invite consideration of the process which must precede alienation, that is, objectification. This is the moment at which, according to Rose's usage of the term,[8] the thing under observation is deprived of its agency, all of which accrues to the observer. Alienation is impossible unless there has been such an accumulation of agency, otherwise it is conceivable that not only other observing parties but the *thing itself* could contest the removal of relationships from the field of interests surrounding it. In a sense, the latter process is precisely the logical conclusion of alienation in a Marxian universe, where the objectification of persons proceeds from their division from each other and from the conditions of their humanity, that is, a continued identification with and control over the products of their labour (Ollman 1976: 139), and ultimately control over the disposal of their own capacities (1976: 142). Under these conditions, it is possible to imagine (as Marx did) that things possess agency at the expense of persons: 'With men taking themselves and others as appendages of their products, their own social relations will appear in the first instance as relations between things' (1976: 144). In this conception of social life under capitalism, the version of objectification described by Rose is turned on its head. It is as if persons were under the gaze of things, and as if property claims were a matter of things disputing amongst themselves by means of persons.

Is there evidence of such counter-objectifications? This is not as absurd as it sounds; it may even be seen to occur in a sense where courts are able to recognise and compensate for the loss of discrete objects with far more facility than they are able to contemplate the loss of wealth in general terms (Radin 1993: 63–65). This phenomenon is most visible in takings cases, where property owners may be compensated for the appropriation or curtailment of certain property rights in the interests of the state. Radin cites instances wherein 'six-figure losses imposed by zoning regulations will go uncompensated, while seizure of a one-acre plot of unused gravel patch will be compensated, though perhaps not much monetary loss can be measured' (1993: 64). She suggests that the inclination of courts to compensate more in takings cases for the loss of personal rather than, say, commercial property stems from an intuitive recognition of some kind of phenomenological coherence between a person, conceived as a subject experiencing 'a sense of continuity of self over time' (1993: 64), and the things which mediate this subject's relationship with his or her environment. The commercial value of a business, significant though it may be, is not apparently held to represent the same subject-defining relationship that a dwelling does. In which case, it appears that it is easier to discern a relationship between persons and things than it is to discern a relationship between persons and value in the abstract. As Radin observes, cases such as these point to an uneasy distinction between appropriate relations between persons and things, and inappropriate ones, in other words fetishism (Radin 1993: 43). The problem with 'fetishism' as an analytic is its own appropriation by Marx to describe one of the outcomes of alienation, namely the attribution of agency to things when the agency of persons has been displaced. In the cases Radin describes, it is unclear whether fetishism is an outcome of alienation or of extreme identification, as it tends to be in contemporary usage. For anthropologists working in societies which practise fetishism in the original sense of the term – the attribution of person-like capacities to talismanic objects – the problem now becomes one of distinguishing the practices of people in these societies from Marx's version of the concept (Graeber 2001: ch. 7). As one might imagine, both the activities and articulations of 'real' fetishists are far more sophisticated than Marx supposed. Users of fetish objects acknowledge that they don't work for everyone, that believing they work helps them to work, and that they work ultimately because people enable them to work (2001: 235–37). There does not seem to be much indication that fetish objects accumulate agency at the expense of their users' own agency. It seems easier, in fact, to find counter-objectification in American courtrooms than it does in the highlands of Madagascar, which arguably was Marx's whole point: that the true fetishists were actually to be found in Western capitalist societies.

Asking whether persons can be objectified by things is, for my purposes, simply another way of asking who is doing the looking in the regard implied by property claims, and what this might tell us about the effects of such a regard. Specifically, it is important to ask what sort of message is contained within the claim, and who is its intended recipient. Rose argues that objectification is not the inevitable effect of the visual appraisal or assertion of property, but one possible effect of several, some of which are constitutive of relationships rather than suppressing of them.[9] Instead, property's visible manifestation enables a limitation of some elements in the field of relations in order to make manageable what would otherwise be an unmanageable amount of information (Rose 1994c: 274–78). One of the majority judges in the *Victoria Park Racing* decision, for instance, suggested that it was not within the remit of the law to erect legal fences to substitute for or reinforce physical ones (Gray 1991: 265). The strength of the judge's fence analogy rested in no small part on the imagery deployed; a fence, whether explicit in the form of wooden posts or implicit in the form of an injunction, enables an observer to know where property begins and ends, and more importantly to know what forms of action are and are not permissible. This is commonly accomplished through vision and visual metaphors and devices (maps, photographs) because they take advantage of the cognitive strategies people employ on a daily basis: the ability to abstract parts from wholes, and conversely to educe wholes from parts. In other words, it is our imagination that rescues us from a world of abbreviated, inert things – and also perhaps from the counter-objectification lurking within alienation – because, even as we regard one thing, we are able to imagine the things it could become or the things to which it is connected. The imagination engenders, as well, the absent presence of things whose *anticipated appearance alone* can cause them to be 'invisibly foregrounded' (Battaglia 1994: 631), with the same or indeed more amplified effects than would be felt if they were 'really' there (1994: 638). It would appear that, in accordance with Rose's argument, if it is vision that delimits, then imagination is what removes those limits.

Imagining the Unimaginable

There is now a problem, however. Even assuming that Rose's solution to the objectification dilemma is satisfactory, there exists a form of property which calls even the liberating potential of imagination into question. Intellectual property is not only to do with ideas perceived to be behind the appearance of things and their apprehension, but is also to do with ideas and their replication. Anglophone legal discourse has so far denied the possibility of owning a disembodied idea (possibly the ultimate 'non-excludable resource'), but it is now taken for granted that one can own the right to control the form(s) in which an idea is replicated and disseminated. In this respect the term 'intellectual property' is a misnomer, but (the fact that we call it) what we call it is in itself instructive. It is received wisdom, however unjust, for specialists such as anthropologists and lawyers, that 'we' understand property is only really ever held in certain rights, not in things themselves; whereas 'they', people out there making property claims, actually think that what they own is land, cars, songs, or whatever. The case of intellectual property seems to bear up such an assumption, implying as it does a notion of ownership in ideas and often being described in this way (Garrity 1999: 1200). But the legal enforcement of intellectual property claims immediately gives the lie to such a notion, as what you are really claiming is a set of rights, and rather circumscribed ones at that, to receive compensation if someone else records your song or manufactures your drug. Even though the former depends on the mechanism of copyright and the latter on patent, both are assumed to protect 'creativity' and provide a system of reward for its products. Yet property rights are never actually granted to the ideas which brought the products into being in the first place.

So how do we account for the idea of *intellectual* property? Could it be the imaginative act that Rose says underlies all property claims, the capacity to 'see' relationships no one else sees, and then to persuade others of those relationships? If that is the case, then we have another conundrum. With intellectual property we are required to perform a double envisioning. Firstly, we must imagine the form an idea will take, which must be expressible to others. Then the task is to carry out the act of persuasion, to make others see what we see: that the form embodying our ideas somehow adheres to us as a property right adheres. This is not necessarily an obvious step. Kant (1998) saw the right of the author, for instance, as one of identity, not ownership, and the publication of a book distinct from the production of a work of art in that the former was the inalienable speech of a person – an action – while the latter was merely a work (*opus*), a thing which could be alienated. Publishers acted, in his estimation, almost literally as mouthpieces for authors: 'In a book, as a writing, the author *speaks* to his reader; and the one who has printed the book *speaks*, by his copy, not for himself but simply and solely in the author's name. He presents the author as speaking publicly and only mediates delivery of his speech to the public' (Kant 1998: 30, emphasis in original). The book was a medium for an author's actions in a way that a reproduced work of art was not, which enabled Kant to draw a distinction between the appropriateness of reproducing works of art without the artist's permission and the inappropriateness of reproducing books without the permission of the author:

> This, then, is the reason that all works of art of another may be copied for sale to the public whereas books that already have their appointed publisher may not be reprinted: the first are *works* (*opera*), whereas the second are *actions* (*operae*): the former can exist on their own, as things, whereas the latter can have their existence only in a person. Hence these latter belong exclusively to the person of the author, and the author has in them an inalienable right (*ius personalissimum*) always *himself* to speak through anyone else, the right, that is, that no one may deliver the same speech to the public other than in his (the author's) name. (Kant 1998: 34–35, emphasis in original)

In other words, Kant saw neither books nor works of art as the property of their originators – but for different reasons. A book was a kind of prosthesis, an extension of the author's person, and for this very reason could not qualify as 'property', conceived here as an alienable thing. A work of art was eminently alienable, so much so that it was too 'broadcast' in nature for the artist to enjoy exclusive rights to it. Elements of Kant's position can be found in contemporary intellectual property thinking, particularly the 'moral right' legally asserted by authors in the United Kingdom.[10] But the differing grounds on which Kant drew distinctions between different intellectual products points to the problem of the 'second envisioning' involved in intellectual property: the forms taken by the products of the intellect are so varied in nature that one cannot necessarily count on their being regarded as the same kind of property with similar 'rules' for distribution and restriction, or indeed as any kind of property at all.

Canonical forms have emerged to deal with this problem in part; copyright, trademark and patent each supply potential claim-stakers with mechanisms for the formal recognition of certain kinds of claims. But once the terms of intellectual property begin to be applied to other potential property in intangibles, such as 'cultural property', the limitations of these canonical forms begin to appear almost immediately. One of the more immediate problems is the notion of uniqueness, as it is conceived in order to claim authorship of a text or song or the patentability of an invention, and authenticity, which is the version of uniqueness that has emerged as most salient to cultural property claims (Brown 1998; Dombrowski 2001).[11] Both of these qualities are, at least on the face of it, resistors of imagination and innovation. The uniqueness of a thing is threatened if anyone at all can replicate it in their own name, as is its authenticity if it is appropriated by too many people, or rather by the wrong sorts of people who do not possess the identity prerequisite to the possession of the right to use a design, a plant, or even the name and ideas of a critical theorist (Coombe 1998: 242). The interesting thing about these problems is that they appear to stem from a Kantian postulate that what we are dealing with is not so much property as identity, or more specifically, the identity of a creative, and creating, subject.

Certainly the increasing number of foes of intellectual property, from the 'copyleft' movement to proponents of open source software (Kennedy 2001; Lambert 2001), would argue that in some of its latter-day manifestations intellectual property signals nothing less than the end of creativity as we know it (Vaidhyanathan 2001). Ownership may now literally be encoded into certain forms of electronic property to control access or replicability, which has in turn produced a controversy over whether or not machine code or its algorithms constitute 'free speech' and belong in the public domain (Foster 2001). Even some of the principles of fair use are seen to be under threat, not only from overly vigilant lawyers prepared to argue it out of existence (Negativland 1995) but from the refusal to recognise it ever existed on the World Wide Web, which is perceived in some quarters as a threat not only to creativity but to academic freedom and freedom of expression in general. This takes us back to Gray's point that property ends, in principle at least, where universal rights of access begin. Intellectual property is still so protean in appearance that it seems impossible to agree upon which universal rights it may or may not impinge. Just as one manages to make it appear, it disappears again at the boundaries of the canonical forms in which it has so far been established.

An oft-cited example is the *Tilted Arc* controversy of the 1980s (see e.g. Blake 1993; Rose 1994c: 293; Horowitz 1996; Senie 2002). *Tilted Arc* was a sculpture by Richard Serra, a 120' × 12' curving plane of steel, commissioned by the General Services Administration (GSA) for display in Federal Plaza, lower Manhattan. It was installed in 1981 but eventually dismantled in 1989, following a petition campaign and public hearings orchestrated by a GSA administrator, a media blitz, and a series of contestations in court by the artist.[12] In the first of these legal challenges[13] Serra sought to assert, among other things, that the threat to *Tilted Arc*'s continued presence in Federal Plaza was a violation of his rights under both copyright and trademark law and of his right to free speech under constitutional law. The court refused to recognise any property claim, intellectual or otherwise, asserted by Serra, citing the article in his contract with the GSA which stated unambiguously that the work produced under contract would be United States government property. It also did not agree that the sculpture represented 'speech' protectable under the First Amendment. It is important to note that in both of his claims, Serra was in essence asserting a moral right to *Tilted Arc*. He argued that moving the sculpture would constitute its 'destruction', because it was site-specific in nature, and because its relocation would express a *misrepresentation of his artistic intentions*. In other words, Serra produced a Kant-like argument that his identity and intentions were inalienably embedded in the sculpture, except that, contra Kant, he argued that a work of art was an action, a form of speech. His claims were unsuccessful in part because moral right does not have the status in American copyright law that it does in, for instance, British law. In essence, the court sided with Kant: it held that the GSA, in displaying *Tilted Arc* (and then in deciding to remove it), was not acting in Serra's name, but in its own right as proprietor of the sculpture. A challenge made on intellectual property grounds was bound to fail, since no form of intellectual property yet exists in the United States federal law which recognises the kind of 'right of identification' asserted by Serra, or indeed that such a right would override the contractual relinquishment of claims to a work of art.

The case of *Tilted Arc* illustrates the problems inherent in trying to elicit the public recognition of an intellectual property claim once it has been envisioned by a potential claimant. The consequence is that keeping in view precisely what it is one has just claimed seems to require constant vigilance of a kind that tangible forms of property never did.[14] The uneasiness of this position requires us to ask precisely who is doing the looking at intellectual property, and whose interests it reflects back. Such vigilance recalls again the question of objectification. Intellectual property depends for its existence on a literal objectification, that is, the appearance of something called property *because we say so*. Now, as Rose and Gray have argued in different ways, all property, tangible or intangible, has this characteristic. Intellectual property merely makes explicit what other forms of property suggest only implicitly: that there wasn't anything 'there' to lay claim to until someone made a convincing case that there was. Ever since Locke (1960: 311ff.) used the vast expanse of as-yet-unenclosed real estate that was the 'America' of the seventeenth-century European imagination for his rhetorical exemplar of the commons, it seems to have been necessary for us to imagine that the 'natural' or default state of things is to be unpropertised. In other words, it is possible for Euro-Americans to imagine that there are things which people cannot or should not use to mediate their relationships with one another. Or rather, that they have not yet contrived a way to do so, because everything is potentially property. Intellectual property, because it so flagrantly implicates the human imagination, appears to present a serious threat to the idea that there are yet things of this world which cannot be turned into property, whose agency cannot be placed in abeyance to that of the observer who has looked upon something and said, 'That belongs to me.' For while no court has yet recognised property in ideas themselves, a constant apprehension seems to be that such a recognition is only a matter of time.

Ritual (and) Appropriations

It is at this point that I reintroduce a Melanesian perspective on property forms and property claims. I opened with the example of a tree, precisely the sort of object which in a Lockean paradigm should not be property until someone claims it as such, and even then that claim has somehow to be made explicit and persuasive. The tree with which I began, like all land boundaries, also operates metonymically: the land that it demarcates belongs to a lineage because the tree was put there by a member of that lineage. You need to be from this part of Papua New Guinea, or informed by someone who is, in order to recognise the tree as property, but apart from the requirement of local semiotic knowledge there is nothing in this sort of signalling of property that a non-Papua New Guinean would have trouble recognising.

If for a moment we shift the focus away from property and towards ritual, however, other information must be taken on board. For decades, anthropologists working in Melanesia have documented the revelatory nature of ritual: that is, that no ritual is effective whose process or outcome is not publicly witnessed. Sometimes this witnessing is accomplished by a deliberately composed audience, as in Paiela boys' puberty rituals (Biersack 1982) and Kaluli seances (Schieffelin 1993); sometimes it is more a case of ritual production for the benefit of more or less anyone present, as in the case of Iatmul *naven* ceremonials (Bateson 1958) and the formal presentation of *malangan* mortuary carvings in New Ireland (Küchler 1992). The point was made some time ago by Strathern (1988: 280) that the revelatory nature of Melanesian public practice points always to its necessary but covert referent, the invisible processes (as of growth) within the actor or the things that are the focus of concealed or secretive processes.[15] The moment of revelation in ritual is the one at which not only esoteric knowledge, but the parts of persons which can only be grown or reproduced by such knowledge, are seen to have been successfully or appropriately achieved.

But the political effect epitomised by ritual protocols, that is to say the moment at which invisible processes are made deliberately and even spectacularly visible, is not necessarily restricted to reproduction by the same persons and their descendents. Ritual protocols can be transacted (Harrison 1992) and even stolen (Leach n.d.), the latter instance lending us some clue as to what kind of value these rituals may hold. Performed correctly by the correct people, they present the observers with an image of the world as it is ideally conceived: the relationships mediated through ritual, whether between moieties, men and women, young and old, or the living and the dead, have been replicated in a way that is desirable or satisfying. But a ritual design 'stolen', that is to say realised by the wrong persons or at the wrong time, may cause those who are obliged to witness it to ask whether it has been ruined, or worse, whether the people performing it have themselves been ruined by dint of subverting their own relationships with the owners of the ritual. It may be useful to recall here Radin's noting that American courts acknowledge *some* identification of persons with things as being perfectly acceptable, and are able to cope with it in their compensatory schemes, whereas 'too much' identification of persons with things carries the threat of perversion. Concerns about fetishism lie behind these distinctions in the context of which Radin writes, but do they not appear in Melanesia? Why is one group of people performing a ritual right and appropriate, while another group of people performing it a dangerous perversion?[16] The reason is that the distinction between ritual performed correctly and ritual performed incorrectly is as much a matter of who performs it, as it is a matter of the ancestrally derived 'script' for the ritual itself. There is more to it than this, however: those who observe an appropriated ritual are not so much monitoring the ritual itself for flaws, as they are monitoring the effects of the ritual on its performers, on themselves, on other parties who are witness to the appropriation. People may express dismay if a ritual is performed differently from how the original 'owners' would perform it, but their fundamental concern lies with the implications of the performance for their relations with the new performers (see Chapter 7). In other words, those witnessing a ritual are perfectly aware that the determination of its legitimacy and efficacy lies in relations between people, not between people and their ritual knowledge per se.

An example from the Suau Coast is the (probably, although not definitively) defunct practice of *udi*. Up until the mid-1980s, a man who intended to embark on any kind of activity which would require extraordinary powers of persuasion – from a request to affines for a single pig to the organisation of a *mata'asi* or large-scale competitive exchange feast – would *udi* beforehand. The practice encompasses a complex of restrictions designed to increase a man's capacity for *gigiboli*, literally 'heat', but in this case connoting personal authority, potency and charisma. A man with abundant *gigiboli* would be irresistible to those he asked to bring pigs to his feast, and so preparations for a feast would include the practice of *udi* by all of its principal sponsors. A *tau'udi* (*udi*-er) would either build a tiny, windowless structure in which to seclude himself next to the fire, or else cordon off a section of his house near the hearth and stop up any holes in the wall to prevent the inflow of cooling air. He could not wash or leave the house for any reason except elimination; he could drink only salt water or the liquid of green coconuts heated over the fire; he could eat no boiled foods but only dry tubers which had been roasted, and of this as little as possible; he could not sleep with his wife. These asceticisms would continue for as long as he could bear them, lasting anywhere from a few days to a month, and afterward he would be in a physically weakened but psychically or spiritually amplified condition. I was told variously that a *tau'udi* would be perceived as exceptionally trustworthy and persuasive, that people would give him anything he asked for (because they would 'lose their minds'), and that he had also achieved a more powerful state in which to perform magic. Serving the *tau'udi* in the capacity of *tau'aigabu* (food roaster) would be a young kinswoman who observed the same restrictions on eating, drinking, bathing and sex, but who could move about freely in a way that the *tau'udi* couldn't.[17] In the case of a major undertaking such as *mata'asi*, restrictions for both the *tau'udi* and the *tau'aigabu* continued until the conclusion of the feast, in order to ensure the satisfactory fulfilment of the proceedings. This is the point at which the relative success or failure of *udi* could be assessed, rather than in the practice itself, which after all took place almost entirely in seclusion.

Analogous values are found in the 'old-time' postpartum practices of Suau women, who would similarly observe a period of strictly enforced stillness and abstinence. This was expressed both externally in terms of the range of movement a woman was allowed, and internally in terms of the foods she was permitted to eat which were (and are) held to have a direct effect on the body fat and digestion of her neonate. After birth, the mother and baby could not wash or leave the house, but were required to stay near the hearth to keep warm until the mother had her first menstruation since pregnancy. Then, like the *tau'udi*, they would go and bathe, after which the mother drank coconut milk and then oily broth made from palm hearts or bush pig to make her baby grow fat. Foods she could not eat during her seclusion included a species of yam called *otea*, sago, cooking bananas, sugarcane, or any kind of meat or fish. These are all classified as 'hard' foods which will constipate a nursing baby. When the baby was fat and defecating properly at five to six months, the mother could eat the restricted foods again. She could not, however, have sexual relations with her husband while nursing because his semen would become mixed with her breast milk and poison the baby. And again like the assessments made of the proper ritual observances of *tau'udi*, the observances of a woman emerging from her seclusion would be assessed according to the health and size of her infant.

In both *udi* and women's postpartum restrictions, the emphasis was on 'stasis, continence and fasting versus mobility, excess and unrestrained appetite' (Young 1994: 270; see also Munn 1986: 49–73 for further elaboration of these oppositions). Young distils this set of virtues from the behaviour of *kaiwabu*, feast sponsors on Goodenough Island who remain seated and elevated on platforms above the festivities they have initiated, not partaking of the food they have distributed. There are obvious ideological homologies between this ritual behaviour and that of Suau *tau'udi*, but the principal difference between them is the point at which their efficacy is revealed or held to be most 'visible'. While the authority of *kaiwabu* is evidenced by their restrained conduct at festivals and exchange competitions, that of *tau'udi* is displayed when they emerge from their seclusion and begin to seek pigs for feasts yet to be held. Their period of severe self-abnegation has been 'hidden' – not primarily through secrecy, although the spells known to accomplished *tau'udi* were without question specialist knowledge – but through solitude and removal from the sight of others. The charisma and magnetism they accumulated by warming themselves, limiting their movements and the nature of what went into and out of their bodies, was potentised to the point where it could literally alter the intentions of others once it had been discharged into the world of relationships. The efficacy of *udi* lay in the fact that it entailed power achieved invisibly, but was only effective once exposed to a non-*udi*-ing 'audience'.

The desired effects of *udi* and postpartum restrictions differ in their ultimate manifestations: the attraction of pigs from kin and exchange partners on the one hand, and the health of a newborn baby on the other. However, the trajectory of 'cause' and 'effect' is almost identical in that both practices involve the imposition of ritual restrictions on oneself to produce a result in the person of someone else. This is what Young terms 'displaced agency' (1994: 271) and Strathern 'unmediated exchange' (1988: 178): it is the concealment or dislocation of social potency which renders in one person the outcome of an action initiated by another. Nobody I spoke to in Suau was under any illusions that *udi* was good for men practising it or that new mothers themselves benefited from the postpartum regime. Indeed, the arduousness of both is cited as one reason why they are no longer observed by most people. But Suau do still insist on the efficacy of these methods for affecting *someone else*. A desired outcome can be achieved in others by means of altering one's own psychic and somatic state by means of the appropriate ritual conventions. This is what I mean when I say that ritual knowledge only 'makes sense', that is, is demonstrated to be successful, when its effects on other people can be observed and gauged.

It is for this reason that the moment of revelation in ritual, or more specifically, the moment at which the effects of ritual practice are revealed, contains the bulk of ritual's moral and aesthetic value. For the negative counterpart to ritual, sorcery, is that which operates wholly in secret, whose effects are revealed by sickness and death if it is left unchecked, and whose protocols are only revealed to its designated inheritors. Revelation in ritual is not only an assertion of the success of knowledge and relationships, but an assertion of the success of the passage of time itself. Time and the form relationships can be demonstrated to have taken (for ritual revelation demands the acknowledgement of a *fait accompli*) are intimately implicated in one another. The power of secrecy, as Reed (1999) and Robbins (2001) have pointed out in the Melanesian contexts of incarceration and Christian millenarianism, respectively, is that it holds the future at bay. One does not know, because one cannot know, in what form relations will next appear. Sorcery, that most secretive of practices, is dangerously timeless in just this respect. Life cycle and other public rituals, by contrast, allow their participants the sense of being-in-the-world, of temporal efficacy. Ritual knowledge is an object which, deployed correctly, is an enabler of the movement of relationships through time. Used incorrectly, it throws up questions for people about the future of their relations with one another.

By now it should be clear what a discussion of ritual and sorcery is doing in an essay on property. It is not the transactibility of these two sets of practices that interests me – I take that more or less for granted – so much as how they come by the respective benefits they confer, which in turn affects how and even whether people can lay claim to them. Just as intellectual property simply makes explicit characteristics which are true of all forms of property, so the relational implications of ritual and sorcery are at their most 'visible' in ritual due to its literally spectacular nature, but they are in fact replicated across a whole range of non-ritual relations mediated by objects in Melanesia. When a Trobriand Islander takes over a *kula* partnership inherited from his mother's brother, or when a Highlander calls in enough debts and embarks on the initiation of new ones in order to compose a respectable bridewealth payment, what they are actually doing is making known to the world at large their intentions regarding relationships emanating from the past and projecting into the future. And when you are walking along the road with a young Suau woman who says, 'I planted that tree when I was a schoolgirl,' she is not just showing you a bit of arboricultural graffiti. Her planting the tree wasn't just 'I was here,' it was 'I will always be here, and my parents too because they sent me to school along this road, and every person who sees this tree will have to think of us.' Similarly, when 'Are'Are people in the Solomon Islands claim land because their tree is there, they are not referring simply to trees planted by apical ancestors, but all of a contemporary person's attainments in life, envisioned as a tree which is, both linguistically and cosmologically, inalienable from that person's being (de Coppet 1985; cf. Crook 1999; Gell 1999).

Inalienability, as the hallmark of things enjoying circulation in a 'gift economy', may seem to foreclose on analysis. What can one say, after all, what kind of history can one imagine, if the very precondition for human social dynamism, whether seen from a Lockean or a Marxist perspective, is taken out of the equation? Most property theory since the Enlightenment has assumed that some form of alienation and appropriation of resources, tangible or intangible, must take place in order for societies to *change*, technologically, socially, and of course economically. Here I would like to make a brief move away from Melanesia to New Zealand, where both Maori and Pakeha scholars have been debating for some time the principle of inalienability and its place in the negotiation of all sorts of relationships, from land claims to human rights. In an essay on the concept of *tangata whenua*, or people of the land, Pocock (1992) attempts nothing less than a description of Pakeha property thinking from a Maori, or Maori-informed, point of view:

> [T]he culture-specific assumptions of an economy based on agriculture and jurisdiction meant that Pakeha ideologies were very nearly incapable of imagining that property, which was their name for relationship, could be

vested in any tenants other than the individual heads of patriarchal families. The idea that it could reside in a tribe, a kin-group, a hapu, iwi, or any other such term it may be convenient to employ, was extraordinarily difficult for Pakeha jurists to accept, unless the kin-group could be represented as a corporation, which is to say a group of individuals supposed by metaphor and fiction to act as a single individual. (1992: 42)

Like Rose's essay which inspired my own consideration of the subject, Pocock's approach to property and property relations (among the peoples of New Zealand) is nothing less than an attempt to imagine how different peoples 'see' property, or in other words, how they bring it into being. Pocock's thought experiment ultimately winds up questioning the basis of claims to indigeneity itself, while at the same time acknowledging that some settlers have had a difficult time of recognising the property, that is to say the relationships, of earlier settlers (an observation also made by Rose). Melanesians, who for the most part have not had to use indigeneity as a basis for claiming restitution of alienated property, have only in recent years begun to cause their relationships to land and other resources to appear in the corporate forms so favoured by Western property law (Ernst 1999; Hirsch 2001). By forming clans in areas where no clans previously existed, 'councils of chiefs' among people who never had chiefs before, and 'land-owners' associations' in places where a 'land-owner' is an imported concept, Melanesians appear to have done nothing less than appropriate the Western ritual of property ownership. For if property claims are the point at which Westerners reveal their relations and intentions to one another, then these claims look like nothing so much as a ritual revelation obliging people to assess the transformed state of their relationships.

There is a crucial difference, however. Although both property and ritual are modes of communication, property appears to lend itself more to the Kantian model, the action performed by a 'speaking subject'. For Kant, the problem came down to determining who had the right essentially to assume someone else's identity by speaking in that person's name, and it is this model which still seems to inform the majority of property claims, particularly those involving intellectual property. The Melanesian model of communication, particularly ritual communication, is predicated instead on a transaction between the performers and 'receivers' or witnesses of the ritual (cf. Biersack 1982). Because a ritual is only effective if registered by an interested audience, the 'end' of its communicative strategy is already known as well as its 'beginning'. If property claims limit the potentially limitless number of interests in a thing by determining who can speak, then ritual limits them by determining who can hear, witness and respond.

If this is the case, then Melanesian ritual strategies offer important insights into the future of intellectual property, whether it is being considered 'here' or 'there'. As I mentioned earlier, there is a growing sentiment among Euro-Americans (particularly academics) that intellectual property claims have spun out of control, that copyright and patent are being stretched far beyond the purposes for which they were originally conceived, and that intangible resources which should be accessible to everyone are increasingly being cordoned off, particularly in digital form. But why is intellectual property suddenly so valuable and also so dangerous, when we have been invoking it in one form or another for a good 300 years or so? I would like to suggest that it is because our own fictions, which have sustained intellectual property claims for so long – that is, the way in which we made intellectual property appear to be concrete by asserting control over the forms in which it would be reproduced – are under threat. Because of the runaway effect of the imagination, of which the digital modality of reproduction is an example, resources converted to or created in this form appear to exist without any social or spatial referent, both of which may be 'recovered' by means of a property claim. A digital network is less like a plot of land than a pressing of compact discs is, for the reason that the number of CDs produced, like the boundaries of the land, is finite, whereas a network at least gives the *impression* of boundlessness and the absence of physical limitations. The opponents of extending intellectual property into the digital domain conceive it as a 'broadcast' form of communication, a virtual lighthouse beam. Those who would encode ownership in digital form are concerned with conceiving them instead as speech acts in the Kantian sense, restrictable, ironically enough, because they are not so much property as expressions of identity.

The ambiguous property status of digital reproduction, quintessentially invisible in its operations, apparently presents a profound threat to the legal mechanisms we have in place to safeguard the products of creativity. The form in which digital relations are conceived, that is, the network, is threatening precisely because it is perceived as potentially infinite in nature; it intimates the kind of willy-nilly reproduction of relationships property is supposed to limit. But we might want to consider the approach of people in parts of the world that have long experience in dealing with invisible forms of action. For Melanesians, relationships operating invisibly are rendered limitable and manageable, that is to say visible, through the social techniques of revelation and witnessing. For Westerners, it may yet be the case that we are very nearly incapable of imagining that networks, which is our new name for relationship, can safely be vested in any vehicles other than tangible ones. Fortunately perhaps for the future of property debates, there are alternative ways of seeing.

Acknowledgements

Versions of this chapter were presented at the 7th biennial EASA conference, 14–17 August 2002, Copenhagen, and at the AAA annual meetings, 20–24 November 2002, New Orleans. It benefited from discussion following both sessions, but special thanks are due to Katherine Verdery for her comments at the AAA session. I would also like to thank the students in my 'Intellectual and Cultural Property Rights' seminar during the spring 2002 semester at Bard College, whose enthusiasm for the subject challenged me to find cases that would make it 'appear' for them in concrete form. Lino Ribeiro is owed particular thanks for calling my attention to the IPR issues attendant upon the *Tilted Arc* case in the course of the class. Finally, I would like to recognise here the persisting inspiration of Debbora Battaglia's work on the aesthetics of sociality, whose intellectual imprint may be found throughout this chapter.

Notes

1. This is not to say that tangibles are transacted in the same way as intangibles, of course. There can be, and often are, different regimes for the transaction and devolution of different forms of property. Among the Suau speakers with whom I worked, for example, land is inherited matrilineally whereas sorcery knowledge is passed from fathers to sons. Important to note, however, is that these two forms of property are not primarily identified by their tangible/intangible status, but rather by their gendered trajectories of inheritance. Sometimes a tangible form can even carry with it, and depend upon, an intangible form, such as the lineage 'travelogues' which accompany any claim of ownership to land on the Suau Coast. Such a claim is validated primarily by the demonstration of accurate knowledge of the story relating how a lineage came to possess a piece of land.
2. Vernacular languages along the Austronesian 'fringe' of the country, for instance, often use different possessive forms to denote different spatial, temporal and substantive relationships between persons and persons, or persons and things. See Macintyre (1984) for a paradigmatic example.
3. Exceptions to this rule appear to turn on the intrusion of aircraft (and, by implication, their occupants) being 'innocent' in nature, and not a consequence of intrusive intentions, such as those of paparazzi seeking photographs of celebrities or narcotics officers seeking evidence of marijuana cultivation.
4. (1937) 58 C.L.R. 479.
5. This quality is by no means limited to intangible resources; see Verdery (1998: 170) for an example of the property status of land being resolvable only through litigation.
6. 'Where a sociological or social-theoretical perspective reveals a complex fabric of discursive roles and representations, property theory offers only a simple ontology of persons and things. This limitation might be traced to the deeply embedded assumption that property presupposes some naturalistic form of "scarcity"' (1998a: 337). Pottage goes on to lay much of the responsibility for this image of a world of scarce resources at Locke's feet, but what is of interest here is that he formulates the non-propertised world as one in which communication is the ontological default ('discursive roles and representations') while the standard image of life after propertisation is one in which communication is implicitly cut off because it cannot be conducted between 'persons and things'. Where Pottage confronts this image on the grounds of the myth of scarcity (as a condition, in turn, for an image of society), I am instead

concerned with confronting it on the grounds that property *does* entail communication, but that it is a restricted form of communication due to the limitations imposed by conventional images such as that of scarcity and their embodiment in law.
7. Gudeman appears to use 'community' as a synonym for what has elsewhere been called the 'subsistence' or 'gift' economy, contrasting it as he does to the 'market' model of conducting economic relationships (1996: 104–6). While I take his point that there are distinctions to be drawn between different economic regimes and their modes of negotiation for tangible and intangible forms of property, it seems unnecessary to press the concept of community into the service of standing for a kind of 'anti-market'. As anthropologists have documented for years, gift exchange and sharing regimes are attended by their own complex ideas about the restriction and granting of access to resources.
8. Rose unfortunately does not supply an explicit definition of objectification for the purposes of her argument. It appears that she intends a consequence of stereotypically 'scientific' detachment (1994c: 270), a rendering of specific forms into generic ones (1994c: 271), or the kind of agency-stealing effect I have chosen to privilege in my discussion (1994c: 273) because it potentially encompasses, or at least implicates, the other two.
9. Almost more significant than her argument against objectification is the fact that she feels compelled to compose it as if objectification were the most obvious objection to be made to the visual element of property claims in the first place. From an anthropological perspective, the 'obviousness' of objectification to a legal scholar seems more a primary effect of the property concept itself, rather than a secondary effect of property as if it existed externally to Euro-American definitions of it.
10. Moral rights, prevalent mainly in Europe and codified under the Berne Convention, are intended to safeguard the professional reputation of an artist or author by guaranteeing the correct attribution and integrity of the work produced. A book published in the United Kingdom, for example, can include assertions of both copyright and moral right on the page containing its publication information. In the United States, certain moral rights were recognised in some states but not others, until the passage of the Visual Artists Rights Act of 1990 (VARA), which was enacted upon the United States' becoming a signatory to the Berne Convention treaty.
11. It must be said that the preoccupation with authenticity underlying some cultural property debates bears more resemblance to 'appellation of origin' law than it does to patent law, in which the uniqueness requirement is most developed. But I maintain that the two concepts are linked, because both indicate a concern with distinguishing a thing from other potentially similar things on the grounds that there is nothing else quite like it in the world. For a patent this distinction is dependent upon the thing's novelty; for an appellation of origin it is dependent on its inalienable identification with a geographical location and/or the identity of the people living there.
12. The ostensible objections to the sculpture were that it was 'ugly', potentially 'dangerous', and in general an unforgiving intrusion into public space. I refer the reader to the large, and growing, literature on the case for extended discussion of the political and aesthetic implications of these objections and their successful prosecution in the New York City of the 1980s.
13. *Serra v. United States General Services Administration*, 664 F. Supp. 798 (S.D.N.Y. 1987). It is probably worth noting that had Serra prosecuted a similar

case after the passage of VARA in 1990, he might have met with more success.
14. The problem is not limited to 'fringe' claims such as Serra's. Even when intellectual property claims are legitimised by law, they are valid only for a limited period of time, e.g. the life of the author plus ninety years for a copyright, twenty years for a patent, and ten years for a trademark (renewable for successive ten year terms) in the United States. During the period in which a form of intellectual property is recognised, its owners and their lawyers are constantly on the lookout for possible infringements, for which royalties (and/or cease-and-desist orders) may be demanded.
15. By focusing on ritual as a particular mode of concealment and revelation I am referring to a specific instance of a more general phenomenon described by Strathern. I have chosen to do so in part because of the explicit nature of ritual revelations, and in part because ritual has of late been singled out as a form of 'intellectual property' of which Melanesians have long experience and interest in controlling. It can be no accident that ritual has begun to acquire intellectual property-like characteristics in contemporary anthropological and legal writing, for the very reason that I have singled it out here: its revelatory aesthetic 'looks like' similar strategies in property claims in other contexts.
16. See Harrison (1993) for a number of instances of the 'theft' of rituals in Melanesian societies. A characteristic of many of these is that once the theft had been rectified, usually by means of compensation paid in some form to the original 'owners' of a ritual complex, the appropriators of the complex took on other cultural characteristics of its originators, such as architectural, musical and horticultural techniques. What I have called the 'perversion' of people performing rituals to which they are not (yet) entitled is in other words an unseemly exhibition of sameness, an assertion that there is no essential distinction to be made between a group of ritual owners and a group of ritual appropriators. In a part of the world where exogamy is practised at some level of almost every society, some of the ramifications of such an assertion are clear. The elision of distinctions between kinds of people implied by the appropriation of a ritual complex presents potentially serious problems when it is the very maintenance of such distinctions that enables the conditions of reproduction.
17. One woman who had performed this service as an adolescent girl told me that the resulting 'heat' (*gigiboli*) from the ritual accounted for her sterility later in life. It was a privilege to serve as *tau'aigabu*, she said, but there were also risks involved.

Part II

Transactions

Chapter 4

TRANSACTIONS: AN ANALYTICAL FORAY

Marilyn Strathern

A document prepared for UNESCO deliberations on Intangible Cultural Heritage (Blake 2001), contains several reminders to the effect that tradition should be taken as living, evolving and linked to innovation.[1] Reiteration is necessary because the language appears unconvincing. 'Tradition' does not, in English, contain 'innovation' within it. Other concepts do fold into one another, notably the by now thoroughly accepted idea that if rights are at issue then they attach to tradition in a 'collective' or 'communal' manner. The implied contrast is with the individual rightholder of western-derived law, one of the stumbling blocks to endorsing IPR in this field in any straightforward manner.

This chapter is about practices folding into one another. It seeks theoretical justification for looking askance at the international vocabulary of 'collective' rights belonging to 'groups', and in the very societies where it might have most directly applied. Here it follows the lead of Jacob Simet (n.d.). Far more apposite in Papua New Guinea would be a model of multiple rights that allowed (contained) heterogeneity in different orders of claims, of which a group basis might be just one. Now it hardly requires a theory to say this. But we require some theorisation as to the way certain concepts refuse to adhere (tradition and change, say) while others (communal, collective, group interests) appear obvious, in ready-made bundles (Riles 2000). I offer a brief analytical foray. 'Transactions', on the periphery of international debate but at the heart of how people in Papua New Guinea negotiate claims, is the vehicle.

One experience of change comes through the kinds of transactions people there have with others. A tiny example: the perception that money is getting at once more ubiquitous and more scarce. Cash is needed for innumerable expenditures, including school fees, while population growth, lack of employment, pressure on land and national inflation all make it harder to generate income.[2] People feel they have no money, and seek stratagems to raise it. If they cannot increase the amount that comes into their network, in paying for services and enabling anyone to turn small trickles of cash into credit, at least it is possible to speed up its circulation among themselves. They invent ways to make money travel more quickly from hand to hand, and cajole others into participating. Paying 'parties' thus innovate on (re)distribution cycles, occasions which expressed the importance of 'thinking on' kinsfolk through the flow of food or valuables, and the attendant expectations of returns. Participants complain at the frequency of occasions when kin obligations are summoned in the constant re-creation of debts and credits. Elsewhere clans compete with one another, as in church fundraising that individuals also use to open and close debts with affines. Or pig exchanges escalate, so that the pigs circulate faster, thereby spreading the opportunities for making cash from them. People simultaneously feel that money is more important than ever and that they must work ever harder at extracting it from others. That they have a solution at all rests on their ability to turn things of all kinds into transactables.

An Analytical Foray

There was an arresting moment in the history of social anthropology when the construct 'transaction' emerged with some theoretical promise, and the critical collection edited by Kapferer (1976) looked back on several years of energetic debate. This was the time when the case study offered tools for analysis and game theory elucidated universal principles of interaction. 'Transactionalism' seemed to bridge general expectations of human behaviour and specific events. Rationality, calculation and self-interest were all part of the anthropological repertoire; above all transactionalism was hitched to what was known as 'exchange theory'. Exchange has continued to wink in and out of prominence. But at this historical moment, transactions seemed to offer the more fundamental insight into social processes. Certainly attractive about the construct was the slimmed-down effect of focusing on minute segments of interactions as keys to greater things.

Slimming down: on the surface nothing seems further from the intentions of Kapferer's book. Far from advocating reductionism, the contributors amplified the study of interchanges by supplying 'contexts' of all kinds.[3] They embedded transactions in communication praxis, symbolic behaviour, economic choice theory, in anything to give them 'meaning'. The essays criticised ongoing assumptions about maximisation and reciprocity. Yet it was precisely the focus on transactions as abstracted slices of (a larger) life which allowed the subsequent build-up of contexts. However, the reducing effect of transactions also holds other, rather different interests. For the moment, note that there is not much to add to the concept as such: most of what we might wish to claim for 'transactions' as an analytic was already there in the earlier thinking. What is open to us is a new working relationship with it.

One insight of the old transactionalism debate was that parties can come together in negotiation for quite different reasons. They do not have to see eye to eye, or even communicate in the same language: all that is required is that they recognise enough of the rules of the game to bring it to a conclusion. There are two elements here.

First, rendering values transactable. Transactionalists referred to the patterned transference of 'items'. What differentiates a transaction from other interactions is the view that the parties have on the value of those items for themselves.[4] A transaction entails both an acknowledgement that it is possible to substitute for one set of values another set and a process of computation whereby each party measures the values against one another.[5] This move encompasses emergent values[6] (values are not necessarily given in advance but may be created in the course of the transaction)[7] and emergent spheres of convertibility or substitution (people test out new possibilities, new resources). Transactions flow across situations which may seem inter-domain to one side but intra-domain to another. A classic cross-cultural case is the mixing of kinship, sentiment and money. Axiomatically equivocal in Euro-American thinking, that the value people have for one another converts into material resources is one of the major substitutions of Melanesian societies. As wealth can be transacted, so can relations be dealt with, that is, rendered transactable (iconographically miniaturised by a bride 'equated' with valuables, for example, or by an effigy of a corpse being made up of them). Wealth can thus be manipulated – cut up, distributed – where the body cannot. Such substitutions apply to resource extraction (mining, logging) when people demand compensation for loss of future potential value, so that the economics of present calculations are coloured by past and projected kinship relations (for a sceptical view, Filer 1997a).

Transactions enable the observer to focus on the process of substitution regardless of the items involved. This focus may or may not entail presumptions about ownership or sources of production. Items may be tangible or intangible, may enrol universal or specialised currency, can invoke conventional standards of worth or be idiosyncratic one-off agreements. The observer is not bound by prior classifications. This does not mean ignoring the information carried by those classifications. If it becomes acceptable in some regimes to sell human ova while in others such commercial activity is prohibited, then we learn about boundaries to values and convertibility across domains. Even theoretical presumptions may be held in suspense, as when one party is described as dealing with 'gifts' and the other with 'commodities'.[8] That a prestation received is not necessarily the prestation sent (Paine 1976: 65; Salisbury 1976: 41) obviates prior determination as to the nature of sociality: a transaction can appear to create its own rules of the game. So while many of Kapferer's contributors emphasise the importance of context (to establish 'meaning'), context can be built up from the transaction itself – what the parties' assumptions were, what they got from the interchange.

As to reducing effects, I confess that transactions had an appeal in relation to the gift-commodity debate. It promised to clear away the encumbrances of past theories.[9] Of course one throws out preconceived distinctions and dichotomies in order to allow others in, so while there is no freedom from encumbrance, there is some freedom to substitute one kind for another. But far from fulfilling this promise, the focus (on transactions) has in fact brought me back to this (gift–commodity) distinction. One reason will be that 'transactions' are in the end no substitute for a theory of exchange.

Second, a transaction is an event. The observer captures an interchange that the actors regard as in some sense finite.[10] To return to the Melanesian nexus of kinship and wealth: in homicide compensation those seeking recompense may never be satisfied with the values ('nothing can make up for the loss') but substitution is possible without equivalence (cf. Radin 1996: 118–20). The substitution simply blocks further action, displacing one act (revenge) by another (prestation).[11] At the same time, closure of communication is not necessarily the terminus of analysis. Blocking off further action may be what the actors want but that does not mean that the analytical object is closed – the event includes its truncation. For an event that brings parties together exists in social time. Demarcating a transaction as a unit of analysis may either embrace or occlude the history of relationships which enabled the interaction to take place; the point is that it gives information not on hypothetical alignments of values but on concrete occurrences when values were conferred. It both fixes moments of conversion and substitutes observation of what happens for what has happened in the past and is promised for the future. In short, actors or observers, or both, delimit and thereby objectify the encounter in terms of a specific social outcome.

It is not, however, necessary to make assumptions about people's prior interests – again, one can focus on interests created or recreated there and then.[12] This takes as axiomatic what Kapferer (1976: 16) felt he had to make explicit: to attend to the 'structure, form and content of social relationships produced through transactional activity'. Such activity gives insight into the subjects or agents which particular encounters engender. It reveals the way events dovetail into one another (transactions within transactions). It also allows social anthropologists their own 'transactions' – converting specific narratives and accounts into a currency for comparison and generalisation. The issue is not whether the actors occupy pre-determining positions, but how one can be open (hold a premise of doubt) as to what they might be.

I suggested that much we might wish to claim for 'transaction' is already in place – open to us are new ways of making the concept work. What might they be? Here I highlight its reducing effect. 'Transaction' is useful to deploy, as an analytic, provided we know that it cannot be elaborated upon. (It is not a theory.) Much as for actors so for the observer; it is an operation, not a model. It slices up data. It renders data into a form which will, at any scale, yield information about values across contexts. Riles's (2000; 2004) investigation of legal formalism is germane: one makes law by putting issues into the right form (makes them 'justiciable'). Similarly, actors search for the substitutions that make items 'transactable', and observers for what makes values 'observable'.

The genius of Papua New Guinean practice is that, by locking transactions into the values they have for social relationships, people are not constrained by the nature or materiality of the items themselves. Added to the formal (self-obviating) point, that anything can be rendered transactable if the conditions for a transaction are there, is an ethnographic one. Papua New Guineans tend to look first for (the appropriate) form in persons and their relations, with the result that exchange items, things, can indeed be 'anything'.[13]

Rights

Even if one wished to get away from theorising about gifts and commodities, these terms are constantly reinvented in their society (Euro-American) of origin, and to boundary-creating effect in debates over intellectual property. In order not to confuse this indigenous usage with a justification for pursuing such theorising to model the Melanesian case, I describe differences in transactional possibilities through two concepts that are in English neither pairs nor opposites: rights and debts.[14] Reasons for the choice will become apparent.

Scientific Authorship, Rights and Rewards

Interestingly enough, transactions figure in attempts to re-work 'the gift' in a climate of IPR interests which did not exist when Hagström (1965) first set out his gift model of scholarly interchange. I refer to a study of scientific exchange in genome research (Hilgartner 1997, citing Hilgartner and Brandt-Rauf 1994; in press). The different sorts of transactions in which scientists engage offer an approach to understanding evolving relations within scientific communities and between such communities and non-scientists. Free and open exchange[15] was how Merton (1942) originally characterised the normative ethos within – within the 'culture', we would probably say today. Hilgartner's reflections on the shortcomings of this formula lead him to consider transactions as social events. As against generalised ascriptions of behaviour, transactions draw attention to what happens and open up to observation the character of both value conversions and social interactions.

Hilgartner advocates paying attention to 'traffic patterns' in scientific exchange; the items transacted are data – findings, materials, techniques – and the issue is how these objects are rendered transactable. He borrows a data-stream perspective from Actor Network Theory (data, embedded in evolving assemblages, is only useful in combination with other data) but his central question could be a transactionalist one: how are portions of flowing streams (observably) turned (sliced) into entities which can enter into exchange relations? He asks about events. In addition to open publication which is so important in academic reward structures, data may, he says, be quietly given away to colleagues, transferred when visitors come to learn about novel techniques, privately released to corporate sponsors, and so forth. Diverse strategies, within and across laboratories, between individuals and different scientific communities, mobilise agents in ways that elude any simple reference to gift exchange.

Here gift exchange is not the classic familiar to anthropologists.[16] The name is given to a prestige-reward system through which scientists both ensure the circulation of information and gain recognition for doing so. Iconically, one gives publications to peers as a gift and receives credit as a counter-gift (Biagioli 2000: 85, quoting Hagström 1982). As in the Euro-American 'gift economy' (Cheal 1988), altruism towards the world at large often substitutes for reciprocity (see n. 5). But the flow is subject to interruption. To factor in Hilgartner's observations, we should also be interested in such strategies as delayed release of information and data-streams bound in ways difficult for others to build on. Intellectual property protection, in the form of demands from employers or sponsors, introduces a further dynamic – indeed, Biagioli (also see 1998; 2003) would argue that the logic of an intellectual property system is distinct from, even antithetical to, that of scientific reward.

There is more here than meets the eye. The individual supposedly shares findings with the scientific community at large so that knowledge taken out of a public domain is returned to it.[17] Biagioli sees this as a crucial distinction between the reward system and IPR. Unless scientific findings have circulated among co-researchers, they cannot be verified. Immediately in terms of personal reputation and ultimately in terms of the validity of data, the reason is that such findings are claimed to be truths about the world; they must become facts in the public domain.[18] Scientific findings build upon one another and, far from vaunting uniqueness, 'scientists buttress their new claims by connecting them as much as possible to the body of previous scientific literature' (2000: 88).[19] Contributions take many forms, but there is a sense of moral community with individuals each carrying responsibility for what they contribute. Biagioli (2000:104) concludes that 'scientific responsibility is not a legal category, but a set of relations among colleagues'.

However, the primary focus of these relations are things, the data for which people are responsible. Verification by the scientific community means that it matters what the 'facts' are, and how the scientist's effort is embodied in them. This need only be a step away from the demand that intellectual effort must be embodied in a 'product' or 'work' to be the subject of legal claims. Equivocally, it seems in practice that 'gift exchange' among scientists can refer either to the circulation of gift and counter-gift among peers, an explicitly non-property relation, or to the overall mechanisms through which scientific data flows 'freely', where property protection may be regarded – especially in the USA (McSherry 2001) – as an ultimate adjunct to academic freedom.

McSherry examines the wider ideologies. The twentieth-century development of the research university as the primary producer of science was originally most useful to commerce and government in its apparent uselessness, that is, in its independence from them. Its role, to validate the autonomy of scientific facts, finds a social form in an autonomous community – where it becomes 'inappropriate to identify one's creations as private property' (2001: 74–75).[20] Yet, as she points out, any division between the market with its commodities and the community with its gifts is compromised by increasing pressure to bring intellectual protection into the reward system, even as universities turn themselves into corporations. This is the hybrid situation that Hilgartner (2000: 7) addresses: these days one needs to understand 'the processes that shape what gets made public, what is kept private, and what is deployed in transactions that fall between these extremes'. 'These extremes' define a sociality which assimilates private appropriations to individual (personal or corporate) property rights and public freedoms to common (including human) rights. That 'rights' can be claimed for public and private ends alike betrays what McSherry would call their boundary status, and assists the conflation of the two kinds of reward (counter-gift/profit).

From this we can appreciate some of the present debates in IPR over limits to transactions, such as objections to gene patenting on the grounds of inappropriate transactability.[21] Arguments are focused on the things, on the kinds of items (data) at stake. So the very nature of the genetic material – whether 'genes' have value for the way human beings think about themselves that cannot be appropriated or whether gene sequencing fails the technical criteria of a work of invention – leads to queries about the propriety of creating rights in this area, or to objections that any benefit should be public not private.[22] 'The challenge is to find the right balance between commercial and public interests' (BMA 2001: 3). Presaged in the controversy surrounding the decoding of the human genome, and conflict between what should be publicly available by contrast with being tied up in property rights, this is widely interpreted as the difference between free and restricted access to scientific information.

Trying to conserve a distinction between what can and cannot be commodified (see especially Pottage 1998b) is also a matter of conserving certain kinds of relations among scientists.[23] For individual effort could be aligned equally with promoting the commons or with private profit. As McSherry (2001; 2003) observes, the concept of reward is open to both gift and commodity readings. A comparison suggests itself.

Culture: New Property, New Commons

What things qualify as cultural productions? What rights do these things compel people to seek? While the international cultural property debate is global in scope, many of its concerns echo the property/commons nexus found in Euro-American discourse on scientific knowledge. Crudely, knowledge belongs to (can be claimed by) communities near and far: the near one of scientists and the far one of a universal beneficiary, 'mankind'; both ordinarily lie beyond property. Similarly, cultural products belong both to their culture of origin and to world heritage, here as a kind of nonexclusive, distributable resource.[24] Resources of 'near' communities only become commodifiable if they are turned into items outsiders will value (tourist art, patentable inventions); but anything can be a potential resource for these 'far' ones. In either case, would property rights assist their protection or should they be protected from property rights? ('Protection' works as another boundary concept.)

It does not take much to see the uses served industrial nations by the notion of open-access culture. Resources existing in some kind of public domain, if not *terra nullius* then outside prior property claims, are seemingly available to all (e.g., Brush 1999: 540). Beside this, the perceived autonomy of 'traditional culture' puts a certain political if not neocolonial stamp on developing countries or ethnic minorities. Of course, few these days would admit to such extreme views. However, I suggest (and see Chapter 1) that they linger in the way that peoples with cultures, especially 'indigenous', 'third world', 'first nations' peoples, are imagined as collective or communal entities.

A statement on benefit sharing from the Human Genome Organisation (HUGO 2000) addresses rewards of a kind. It is concerned about the involvement of private companies in genetic research against the double fact, first, that 'the human genome is part of the common heritage of humanity',[25] and second, that one must respect 'the values, traditions, culture, and integrity of the participants', they being the general public, families, communities of all kinds, whether (in their words) defined by region, tribe or disease group. It anticipates a search for genes that will advance medical knowledge but which has to enlist specific populations, and these need recognition, even recompense. The scheme bypasses any determination of property; but the need – even duty – to offer material compensation is created by the same climate of private investment as affects academia, in which researchers and institutions increasingly demand shares in monetary benefits. Compare this with the claim, also apropos the human genome, that because 'the building blocks of intangible work – knowledge – is a social product', no individual should have exclusive rights in what is already shared (Moore 2000: 113).

It is widely regarded as possible to draw up generalised characterisations of indigenous heritage, including the nature of knowledge systems. To get 'indigenous heritage' on the international table was a major achievement at the time (Daes 1993; also 1997; see Preface), and the formulations still adhere, hold together as a bundle. Today's international consensus translates roughly as follows. Practices of transmission mean that information taken out of the public domain is invariably returned to it, as when people act as its stewards, a responsibility which often brings prestige: in anticipation of their 'gifts' to society, knowledge-holders are accorded respect. Additionally, the engagement of others is crucial to verification. Indigenous knowledge – whether of soil types, plant species or ancestral songs – has value as truths about the world, and such truths build upon one another. Indeed far from vaunting uniqueness, new claims are often buttressed by connecting them as strongly as possible to the body of tradition. This creates a moral community where individuals carry responsibility for what they know, including keeping information in circulation. Responsibility, after Biagioli, is not a legal category but a set of relations among people. Yet – I would add – at the very point where culture might seem least property-like, it can take on that appearance.

The HUGO statement appeals to benefit-sharing as a principle generally accepted in the area of biodiversity in (for example) food and agriculture; there is no suggestion that anyone is after cultural knowledge *as culture* – they are after genes, plant products, disease genealogies, or simple readiness in the HUGO case to participate in research. The rights at issue concern control over various kinds of resources, and culture as such has no utility. But the basis of the HUGO recommendation about compensation entails 'the private domain of indigenous and other traditional communities' (cf. Blake 2001: 52), and thus precisely what people know as their own particular heritage (their 'culture'). The rights at issue concern control of identity.[26] They are exclusive (phrased in terms of rights to protection, meaning that only right-holders may also enjoy, use, exploit its products). And claims to the protection of culture, through its products, are claims to protect the community itself. Whereas communities of scientists focus on whatever data concerns them, what is being protected in people's rights to cultural determination is the very construct ('culture') that makes them a social entity ('people'). It is a short step from here to imagining that the culture is, if not like data, like an assemblage or datastream.

One mechanism that keeps the assemblage together, makes culture an item, is that a 'community' of people can be summoned as a 'collectivity'. Conversely, their rights in it are invariably described as communal or collective. So we find that the language of 'collective' rights can be mobilised either for the protection of non-propertised heritage or for the protection of identity through property rights such as trademarks (Coombe 1998).

At the same time, a collective justification is also the point at which attempts to develop a thoroughgoing IPR system predictably falter. International agencies aiming at an equitable distribution of benefits seek other transactional possibilities. Culture is rendered transactable through entities such as 'heritage, 'tradition', 'indigenous knowledge', and local practices of knowledge-holding have prompted NGOs and others to imagine alternatives to IPR.[27] Drahos (2000), for instance, outlines a possible benefit-sharing scheme, vested in a private global organisation which would bypass the politics of international treaties. A global collecting society[28] would have the IPR aim of stimulating both 'corporations' and 'indigenous groups' (his terms) to put traditional knowledge to productive use without the IPR constraints of property laws. Recognition (that people have rights to their knowledge) and recompense could both follow. I add that it would set up a transactional context that would not have to specify interests in advance but should be open to any form of social involvement in the knowledge sharing.

International rhetoric, then, may lead people to think that they can turn an abstract asset, such as know-how, into something of economic value (realised for themselves or protected from general use). Much is anticipated. For rights can be imagined before intangibles are embodied in any particular item.[29] This is made possible by the fact that they are already embodied in another entity. When the target of potential claims is 'traditional knowledge' or 'cultural property', only secondarily may these be assumed to refer to specific items such as plants or carvings.[30] Rather, knowledge can be envisaged as an abstract resource which already 'belongs' to a people as a whole because it is embodied in another abstraction, their 'culture'.

Negative Rights and Positive Duties

I have been drawing a parallel between two contexts in which transactions are coloured by the possibility of turning intangible assets into property, contexts where, in the conventional view, they first circulate within a community of persons. Scientific knowledge passes in a non-property form between peers who have an interest in it – whether or not their transactions are gift-like – before it enters the market. Cultural knowledge gives identity to the people to whom it belongs in an essentially noncommodifiable mode, commodification being taken as sign of transactions with outsiders. The concept of 'rights' is canonically attached to property, but when noncommodifiable rewards or prestige touch on questions of equal recognition or equitable distributions of benefit the language of 'rights' may not be far behind there too. To show how these constructs adhere to one another, including the regularity of the way in which property, and its transactional form, the commodity, works against a domain from which it is (ideally) excluded, I have taken the examples from Euro-American/international debate.

A concurrent theme is that the domains are not as discrete as they were once imagined to be, specifically that ever more things are becoming propertisable. There is a greater visibility to the kinds of transactions property makes possible – possibly even 'more' transactions. As McSherry (2001: 24) notes, both academia and IPR are represented as in crisis. It not just that the boundaries are blurred, or that a public domain is being eroded or autonomy undermined, or even that the new propertisation offends. It is that things are transactable, fungible, can be made profitable, to what are perceived to be new levels. Inflation follows when the level of activity is not accompanied by a concomitant rise in a sense of overall benefit.

It was an increase in *non*propertisable transactions that gave Biagioli (2000: 92) his starting point, the emergent conventions by which scientific periodicals try to recognise 'everyone' involved in a piece of research while avoiding being swamped by multi-authorship citatations, an 'inflation of authorship credit'. We could even talk of inflation in cultural rights if peoples are required to list, register, specify ever more closely the things to which rights attach; rights become devalued when there are too many rights (that is, claims) and too few realisations of them (that is, implementations) (cf. Winthrop 2002b: 178; also Cowan et al. 2001).

Liabilities and Accountabilities

But should we be content to keep rights, property and assets in a bundle? I turn briefly to two other accounts. The first unfolding of this particular bundle comes from Verdery's (n.d.; see also 2003) critique of models of property relations prevalent in anthropology. An exclusively rights-based approach to property is (she argues) inadequate as an interpretative tool for understanding current realities in postsocialist Europe. Consider the liabilities. The privatisation of land in Romania is a case in point. Devolving property rights privatises liabilities more than assets: privatisation creates new arenas of economic responsibility and jural persons who bear not just rights but risks. 'Decollectivization is *about* making land a carrier of liabilities' (n.d.: 4, original emphasis). Owners (who have the property right) are liable to upkeep the land in order to make a profit, itself a tax liability, and get into debt to do so. In short, people become legally 'responsible for land (through the obligation to cultivate it) without their having most of the remaining factors of production necessary to act effectively as owners, [and] all had the problem of securing those other factors – labor and capital inputs' (n.d.: 10, emphasis removed). The rewards are hard to see. Property (here, land) turns into a potentially negative economic cost.

What fuels inflation, and indeed may (as in this case) sit alongside monetary inflation,[31] can also settle into inertia. This is to follow Brennan's (2000) conception of inertia as the binding of energy at fixed points in ways which drive up the real cost of production.[32] We see something like inertia in forms of auditing which turn responsibilities into accountabilities: the duty to be responsible (with others in mind) becomes the liability to be accountable (to report to these others). One example, my second case, is political auditing in Palestine, a kind of analogue to claiming cultural rights (Jean-Klein 2002).[33] Western observers are encouraged to come and see the Palestinian struggle for themselves, urged to send their 'independent' accounts back home. While witnessing gives their narratives authenticity, the observers' autonomy is crucial to the process. But that can become subject to inertia. As is true elsewhere, accountability procedures can run away with themselves – liability being at once increasingly easy to implement (routinised in audit systems) and increasingly difficult to discharge (more elaborate systems of audit), with the result that satisfaction with the accounting process becomes harder to sustain. In short, as more energy becomes tied up in the routinisation of procedures, less becomes available for spending on 'real' accountability. In the political audit which Jean-Klein describes, autonomy requires effort to sustain. For the more expert the witnesses become, the more skill they acquire in the observation, then the more they become party to, or prey to, already existing accounts. Whether on the Palestinian or the international side, the observers' accounts become bound to local narratives.

I take the two situations for the concepts, 'liability' and 'accountability', with which their ethnographers would complexify any analysis of transactions. Unalike as they are, these instances of new propertisation and of cultural self-presentation both contain ingredients that lie beyond Euro-American or internationalist discourses; both also raise questions about indebtedness. Let me substantiate this last point.

First, trouble was taken by the Palestinian activists to give Western tourists, including student visitors, 'fact finding' tours. Local students would remind their international counterparts that, when they returned home, they 'had a responsibility to tell'. The former may have regarded themselves as acting out of duty; their efforts to communicate were intended to create a sense of obligation, a debt to be discharged, on the part of the latter.[34] Second, with reference to Maurer (1999), Verdery explicitly uses 'debt' and 'obligation' as well as 'liability' to describe the negative effects of property ownership in Romania. Debt refers principally to financial transactions. In the same way as she queries the axiomatic connections between rights, property and assets, perhaps we should query any axiomatic connection between money and credit – axiomatic, that is, for Euro-Americans who (as productive consumers) tend to think of money in terms of spending power. Possession gives the possessor market opportunities and opens up a world of choice. The other side (debt) becomes choice which has been preempted. But are there are situations where the possession of money itself signals a debt, that is, possession is also dispossession? One answer has been given: when money itself generates something akin to liability. The situation is familiar to anyone liable to taxation – a portion of income is already owned by the state – or responsive to the anonymous obligation of charity giving. In drawing on the language of liability to characterise debt (money already, so to speak, spent), we could also say that money in credit confers a right of a sorts (to spend as one chooses). The negative and positive values seem evident, as Verdery intended.

Money plays a major role in contemporary Melanesian transactions. While it passes between parties in interchanges that may also have non-monetary dimensions, far beyond Euro-American experience virtually anything that is transactable is also monetisable (cf. Abramson 1999). However, whether the increase of transactional activity noted at the beginning of the chapter turns out to be inflation or inertia will be a matter of analysis. Interestingly, the indigenous perception of there being both more money and less money around resonates with recent descriptions from postsocialist regimes other than Romania:[35] more money because with everything privatised everything also has a price, and less because, among other reasons, currency starts disappearing. 'In sharp contrast to the late Soviet situation where collective farms had money but very few commodities on their shelves, money started to disappear in daily transactions at the same time ... as goods became available for purchase' (Ssorin-Chaikov 2000: 345).

Debts

With its emphasis on creativity as a resource, IPR throws up a radical difference between innovatory and noninnovatory regimes of production.[36] This may be epitomised in the contrast between inventiveness, characteristic of technology-rich economies, and its obverse, conserving convention. In counterpoint, indigenous activists make convention itself, in terms of 'tradition', 'heritage' and so forth, carry new freight. The contrast dovetails into preoccupations over the profit-generating exclusiveness of private claims as against access to a public domain, over rewards for personal effort being pitched against benefits for all, and above all over an opposition between individual property rights and collective community-based, even humanity-based, interests. The more international debate proliferates, the more it seems locked into ready-make bundles of concepts. Inertia renders the contrasts prone to exaggeration.

The entire web of categorical distinctions and oppositions has the global reach of liberal economy. It is the language of all kinds of NGOs, international agencies, local bureaucracies and aspirant developers. In the new nation of Papua New Guinea we would search for its absence in vain. The whole lot – innovation, private ownership, property rights and individual appropriation *along with* their alternatives in collective authorship, moral communities and preexisting conventions and traditions – appears to contain the terms of debate within itself.[37] Precisely: communal and collective ownership is a long-standing Euro-American, and now ubiquitous internationalist, alternative to private property, a necessary foil to its workings. The 'alternative' alternatives we might find Papua New Guineans entertaining in other parts of their lives are not obvious. They require analysis.

Embodiment and Disembodiment

International activists concerned with traditional knowledge find many intangibles, such as pervasive ancestral power or information about the seasons or stars, or the inside names of things, rendered nontransactable by both law and commerce: they lie outside any product or process that could realise their legal status or economic potential. As we have seen, one solution has been to go the other way, to imagine knowledge as an abstract resource 'belonging' to people as part of their 'culture'. People are in turn imagined as having collective interests in these resources. In short, one set of abstractions ('TK') is embodied inside another ('culture')! This view contributes to the salience of culture as a powerful construct in the politics of identity. Following Harrison (2000), we can see the legacies of nation-state nationalism here (the imagined sharing of a common culture as the moral basis of nationhood).[38] At the end of her critique of rights based on appeals to historical deprivation, Weatherall (2001: 230) comments how 'the reasoning tends ineluctably to return to the underlying rationale of protecting culture, as it is only this aspect which distinguishes the claims of indigenous peoples from any other groups who may be economically harmed by some public domain activity and "appropriation"'.

One consequence is that the claims of political entities, such as first nations or ethnic minorities, as they circulate within the international community, slide seamlessly into the claims that indigenous people may put forward as 'a people' who feel they have been violated or whose powers have been infringed. The further consequence is that this concreteness seems already taken care of in, bundled up in, the notion of specific, named 'cultures'. What gets fudged is the standing of different groups, political or otherwise. When culture is glossed as a communal or collective entity as against individuals, 'groups' may be unthinkingly assimilated to the communal end of the spectrum.[39] What disappears is the specificity of knowledge held by individual groups *as against* public knowledge (Simet 2000: 74–75). What also disappears is the significance of the people in the population. Let me point to one way in which this is true.

Neither construct ('cultures'/'peoples') finds it easy to gain purchase against the dominant legal structures of capitalism such as, under WTO, compelled the adoption of standard copyright and patent laws among developing countries.[40] And that is because, as we have seen, law and commerce require embodiment of a specific order. IPR may presume an intangible input into an artefact, e.g., form of expression, modification of nature, original inventive step, and so forth, all of which are abstract attributes. But the right to use or profit derived from this intangible intellectual effort is held in relation to the concrete artefact embodying it (cf. Küchler 1999).[41] There always has to be an embodiment in a *res* (a thing in law). This is both a tangible item that is evidence of the intangible capacity, and an item that is commodifiable or exploitable because the rights in it must have a value that can be realised by the owner.[42]

To some degree this resonates with what we know from PNG transactions. On the one hand, information about the medicinal values of plants or about the landscape, which one person 'shows' another, looks like heritage that is intangible. On the other hand, as Chapters 3 and 7 of this volume in make particularly clear, items such as sculptures or dance routines embody such powers or knowledge about the world in forms that are tangible or perceptible. Products and performances are at once evidence of a general capacity and transactable in relations with others. Here it seems to be transactable concrete 'things' (*res*) which mark out intellectual effort or power. Nonetheless, at a point of apparent similarity we encounter a temporal sequence foreign to the expectations embedded in IPR, and foreign to the nexus of concepts in which it nestles. Those tangible things are not the end result of embodiment – they merely convey it. For such capacities are *already* embodied in being embodied in persons. And their destiny is reembodiment in others.[43]

This means that when such items are rendered transactable they are in effect being disembodied, brought out, transferred from one person to another. And persons, whether individuals or groups, are activated in the course of this process as specific concrete agents of extraction and absorption. Without their relationship there would be no object of transaction.[44] I cannot make the case here, but such disembodiment may be regarded as a (re-)empowerment (the stripping away of extraneous identity), as well as a moment of loss for one party and gain for another.

In sum, the two sides of the Euro-American international debate over private property and public commons in IPR, and its relevance to scientific rewards or cultural rights, can be rewritten as two loci for embodiment. On the one hand, the law (and commerce) demands that evidence of intellectual effort is identifiable in a thing; on the other hand are those who assert that intellectual capacity primordially lies in a culture or community. In each case, and what renders both these views part of a single nexus, transactions can only take place once the idea or invention has been embodied. They (the transactions) then compute the value of the thing or verify the cultural origin of the intellectual product. Now it would seem that either position can be translated into Melanesian preoccupations with wealth and group activity, and indeed do appear thus in international discourse on the same. Yet, I have insisted, neither touches on the quite distinct configuration through which many Melanesian transactions work.

When capacities are regarded as embodied in persons (not 'things') and in people (not their 'culture'), then transactions take the distinct trajectory of disembodiment and reembodiment. The anthropologist should not be surprised if concepts adhere in unfamiliar combinations.

A Transactional Solution

We have already encountered a term for one aspect of this trajectory – indebtedness. It affects the modes of inflation and inertia. Escalating prices have their origins in domestic financial policy, as well in the World Bank and global trading conditions outside Papua New Guinea. This is familiar monetary inflation. But what is one to make of escalating transactions in the situations with which the chapter opened? Inflation in an arena of commodity exchanges oriented towards productive consumption, where what is at issue is spending power (accumulating credit), implies a readjustment in the ratio of goods and money (too much money after too few goods).[45] One answer to the question (Strathern 1999a: 105) of what inflation would look like in regimes oriented to consumptive production[46] is to point to changes in the rate by which relationships are reproduced, that is, an increase in the quantity of items, goods or money against the capacity of relations to absorb them. One would expect a heightened intensity of interaction as a result, not necessarily more relationships but more occasions on which existing relationships are summoned for the circulation of things, so that the demands people make on one another appear to increase. Demands multiply. Yet, as we saw, this may be done in the context not of too many items in circulation but, at least as far as money is concerned, of too few.

Scarcity reminds us of the Romanian farmers, and the comparison is helpful. There, privatisation has reinvented a separation of property/commodity relations from 'community'. Rising costs of maintaining the land undermines their social capital of mutual assistance; in turn the need to purchase equipment, such as pesticides, further forces them 'to substitute money for social relations,' and 'Devaluation therefore occurred on two intersecting planes, as abstract money obligations overwhelmed social ones' (Verdery, n.d.: 5).[47] Social and monetary obligations compete with one another. By contrast, in the kinds of Papua New Guinean cases we have been considering, social and monetary obligations frequently run together. When either can be construed as investment in others (not always the case), there may be little difference between meeting social obligations and meeting financial ones. Wealth is stored when debts are created: a debt is money once in the hand but now held by others for returns in the future. Money presently in hand, by contrast, can make one prey to one's creditors.[48] While we may call them debts, these transactional entailments carry very different resonances from the postsocialist case. Money certainly generates something akin to liability: whether as cash or transformed into pigs and purchases, it is bound to be absorbed by social relations. But this does not turn it into a negative asset. The value signs can appear round the other way. Debt relations can be counted as positive assets.[49]

If inflation is too many items (including too much money) after too little relationship[50] to absorb them, conditions of scarcity seem to be creating not an opposite but a parallel movement. (Both may, of course, be going on at the same time.) Far from demand slackening, it can increase, that is, one response to less money is an increase in the velocity of exchange. Now there seems too much relationship after too little money. In other words, regardless of whether money increases or decreases, the speed and number of transactions may increase. In so far as transactions derive their momentum from the relationships they fuel, relationships become subject to elaboration and (re-)invention.

Precisely because such possibilities feed into the continuous reevaluation of relationships, change in the quantity of money in either direction may lead people to increase their expectations about what relationships can do. Scarcity particularly affects the way in which relationships can *bind* money. It is locked up in internal circulation.[51] Is one effect to make even scarcer the money available for commodity exchange? That is, does scarcity increase the extent to which the same relationships are called on time and again, reinforcing the preexisting web of debts and obligations? These would seem to be conditions for inertia.

As far as the reproduction of relationships is concerned in PNG, cost (debt) is regarded as a general sign of expansiveness. I suspect this conceals the inertia effect which preexisting claims have on assets. Expectations on the increase bind more and more assets to themselves into obligations to be discharged.[52] When they are tied to persons (relationship) rather than products (things), and when transactions tend to mobilise the same pool of people, inflation and inertia have similar effect – more transactions. More pigs for the same transactions, and more transactions in which the same items (pigs) can figure: both result in a rising cost of relationship.[53] Yet cost is written into relationships from the outset. They do not require any other form of auditing, to remind ourselves of the Palestinian case. The recognition of a debt contains its own responsibility for discharging it – nothing more need be said.

We can revisit transactions as an analytic, with its two sides. One side consists in parties rendering an item transactable by expressing sets of values in terms of one another, while the other side consists of observable, specific events at which conversions have taken place. Analysis can work them together, like the two sides of a Massim canoe.[54] Or that would be the view from the outside. The Melanesians we know have outboard motors as well. It is relationships that render items transactable and present conversions have past relationships built into them. Here transactions mobilise the power of indebtedness. (Debt is at once a source of and a drag on energy, as anyone who has started a petrol motor by hand knows.) But where debt becomes the operational analogue of transactions, the concept of transaction becomes redundant. One only needs it when translating back into the language of regimes that have to work hard at making concrete things and abstract categories do the work of relations.

Postscript

'Right is the form that the relation takes in a commodity economy. What would be the equivalent ... in the gift economy?' The question comes from a conversation between Vivieros de Castro and Fausto (Strathern 1999b), which Fausto later answers: 'gift is to *debt* as commodity is to right'.[55] A commodity is of course already a relation (between use value and exchange value) so what did the question mean? Perhaps it is that commodities, that is, things which compel exchange by their own nature, mobilise people through the rights that their transfers confer. Debts? By filtering the question through transactions, I have filtered it through an analytic that presupposes the mobilisation of persons in interchanges with one another. What has it yielded?

When contributors to scientific papers do not hold equal status, McSherry (2001: 90) remarks, 'two senses of origination may come into play' – the creator of the idea behind the paper (its author) and the provider of the conditions which supported its realisation (head of a team, employer, investor). Both senses may justify persons claiming 'rights' in respect of the outcome. While it would be perfectly possible to talk of 'debts' in this context, that is not how actions tend to be framed; rather, rights are likely to be asserted on the basis of the nature of the enterprise (the scientific project) and the characteristics of the person.[56] What occasionally surfaces in Euro-American contexts, however, is routine in Melanesian computations of ownership (Kalinoe and Leach 2001). The past efforts of specific persons are constructed as debts incurred in the course of interactions with them.

Now rights can enhance the owners of them without being put to specific test; the possibility of future claims is already an asset. Rights, we may say, anticipate transactions. Debts, on the other hand, presuppose them.[57] The logic of the debt implies an existing state of negotiation between debtor and creditor: multiple claims are written into things because of the specificity of past events. This can be put another way. Transactions also entail the substitution of values, but where the substitutions have already taken place, there are no rights to claim because the parties *have already benefited*. Indeed Papua New Guineans might pay for someone else's song or dance in order to put themselves into the position of 'having benefited' from the transaction, that is, from the origination of these items in someone else.[58] Out of this nexus, if anything needs protection it is the perpetual reminder of sources in others.

We begin to see why multiple claims of this kind could never be the equivalent of collective or communal interests in property-based regimes. Property-based regimes construct a sphere of social life that lies 'beyond' individual claims. In this beyond, commmunal rights may be imagined as inalienable, in opposition to the alienable rights of property or commodity, and thereby seen to divide gift giving from commercial transactions. By contrast, in a situation of the kind encountered in those Papua New Guinean practices where anything is amenable to transaction, and where debts presuppose enchainment to others (and the reverse), one does not have to specify the conditions under which things are alienable or inalienable. What has to be endlessly, infinitely, specified are the conditions of relationship, for relationships are not of equal weight or value. This is another kind of infinity.

Notes

1. WIPO's 1998/9 fact-finding missions, to investigate the application of intellectual property law to the protection of traditional knowledge, took as their remit 'traditional knowledge, innovations and creativity' (Blake 2001: 58). Further, while traditional indigenous knowledge 'is community generated and usually held collectively', what applies to it also applies to the traditional knowledge of nonindigenous societies: 'It is dynamic and is based on innovation, adaptation and experimentation' (2001: 48, after Dutfield). Simpson (1997: 18) takes intellectual and cultural property to refer to 'indigenous works, practices, innovations, knowledge, ideas'. 'Knowledge, innovations and practices' appears in the Convention on Biodiversity (8j); on the inclusion of 'ideas', see Brown (1998).
2. I do not give individual attributions to ideas or material which have come from PTC colleagues. Examples here are based on instances cited in a paper, 'Money appearing and disappearing', given to the 3rd PTC Colloquim (*The Commodity*

and its Alternatives: Old Money, New Money, No Money, Girton College, Cambridge, 2001); they could be replicated in many contexts. James Carrier's contribution to the colloquium was a particular stimulus; on the specific phenomenon of monetisation, see Akin and Robbins (1999).

3. The contributors were heirs to an intense concern with how in the description of social life one could get from structure to process. Amazingly, in retrospect, none dealt with transactions beyond national boundaries or with global actants such as multinational companies or development agencies. (What lay ahead was the emergence of a diverse international community, NGOs, human rights movements, and world attention on environmental resources, as well as the expansion of the life sciences, and further apostasisations of 'technology'.)

4. One sees the other getting *a* while it gets *b*, whether through exchange (e.g., a purchase), distribution (each takes its share) or recognition of reward, and whether the parties are individual agents or – from the perspective of one agent – involve on the other side imagined communities. As in Titmuss's (1970) famous study of blood donation, and see Konrad (1998), Euro-Americans may imagine themselves transacting with an abstract community 'out there', such as the general public.

5. Practices of computation became a preoccupation of the transactionalists. In formal terms there has to be some reckoning of mutuality, e.g., equivalence and reciprocity in people's actions, but there need be no substantive measure of comparable worth.

6. I borrow from Kapferer's (1976: 15–16) discussion, after Nadel and Blau, of 'emergent properties', a point also taken up by Parkin (1976: 167).

7. I do not distinguish between kinds of values here. In barter, Joachim Görlich (pers. comm., 2002; cf. 1998) points out that while the exchange value can be negotiable, actors may have weighed up the use value of the items in advance. Compare Callon 1998: 8–9: 'In the social network ... the agents' identities, interests and objectives, in short everything which might stabilize their descriptions and their being, are variable outcomes which fluctuate with the form and dynamics of relations between these agents'.

8. See for example Ssorin-Chaikov (2000: 358), citing the works of Taussig and Appadurai; Gregory (1997); Goddard (2000); also Strathern (1985).

9. Rather as Goddard (2000: 148) suggests that 'a focus on praxis in relation to exchange' will obviate some of the grosser misunderstandings, for example the notion that one could ever find *in exchange itself* the distinction between gift and commodity. His own starting point is the primary condition of the commodity as one of alienation, defining the gift as the unalienated object. This is a description not of a society or an economy, but of the intentions and projections of those who engage in the exchange. In Cohen and Comaroff's (1976: 103) analysis of certain Tshidi marriages, whether the spouse is regarded as a patrilateral or matrilateral cousin will depend on the meanings which the parties manage to impose on it.

10. As Paine (1976: 64) argues, 'exchanges are themselves events that explain – that is, people "use" their exchanges to render life experiences more intelligible'.

11. The sense in which we might understand Breton's (2000; and see Clark 1991) comment on shell money in Wodani, Western Highlands of Irian Jaya: 'It is said of a shell that is the object of a transaction – whether given or received – that it is eaten and that it dies on this occasion ... but the death is only relative

to the transaction in question.' By contrast, where debts are outstanding and the transaction thus incomplete, the shells are still alive.

12. Dwyer (2000: 232) returns to game theory as offering a focus on strategy, or on the logical structure of situations, without making assumptions about intentions.
13. So the appropriate form of things as items in exchange is largely governed by the relationships involved. Several comparative exemplifications are thus to be found in the essays edited by Akin and Robbins (1999).
14. Pairs would be: right with duty, debt with credit. An initial version of this chapter, which tried to steer clear of gifts and commodities altogether, was strongly criticised by Joachim Görlich (pers. comm.) to whom I am grateful for a set of extremely detailed comments. I fear I have not taken sufficient advantage of them, nor of his elucidation of continuing issues in game theory. Mosko (e.g., 1999, 2001, 2002), who compellingly takes insights from the gift–commodity model into the analysis of historical transformation, has no truck with faintheartedness on this score either.
15. An ethos not of course exclusive to science (see Born 1996 on IRCAM, a computer music institute).
16. And definitively is not comparable to the gift side of the anthropologists' gift/commodity antinomy.
17. 'While the production of value in liberal economy involves a movement between two complementary categories, from generic public domain to specific private property, in science the movement is within the same category (the public domain) and it goes from "unspecified" to "specified truth"' (Biagioli 2000: 88–89).
18. For a caustic critique of what (and when) in academia counts as public domain, see McSherry (2001: ch. 2), and more generally Rose (1994b: ch. 5).
19. Copyright, by contrast, is about original expression, a veritable distraction to truth claims, especially when 'originality' is read into 'origin', while patents are about utility, an irrelevancy as far as their factual status is concerned. IPR is inimical, in his view, to the workings of the scientific reward system. Biagioli (2003: 274) goes so far as to suggest that 'authorship' is a misnomer in science.
20. Specifically: 'intellectual property is defined in contradistinction to a conceptual space, namely, the public domain, that is anchored in the United States by the research university' (McSherry 2001: 27). The market traditionally thrived on the production of information authenticated by being produced independently of it (the commodity creates a 'non-commodity' sphere).
21. For example Drahos (1999), BMA (2001). Of interest to the anthropologist is the active cultural interpretation that the very notion of intellectual property generates. Here the concern with appropriateness ('limits') resonates with cultural anxieties over limits in assisted conception debates.
22. E.g., 'the private appropriation of the genetic commons', discussed in Nuffield Council on Bioethics (2002: ch. 3). Patents confer the right to prevent commercial exploitation by others without license; the patent holder can sell his ownership rights in the patent. The correlative duty is to disclose the details of the product, and thus keep information flowing (hence the argument that intellectual property protects freedom of disclosure, so it is without penalty to the primary information-holder).
23. Similar distinctions are repeated in other contexts. The issue of public funding is one (e.g., Eisenberg 1996). Discussions of health policy in developing countries set property protection to pharmaceutical companies (seeking the private

means to develop products) against world-wide access (IGH 2001). And the very notion of property ownership in environmental resources attracts protest in terms of private property versus public stewardship: 'a contradiction between the inflexibility of property relations in land and the urgency of stewarding the boundless Environment emerges as one of the defining tensions of modern Western culture' (Abramson 2000: 27). Separately, the reader's attention is drawn to the 'crisis' in IPR of which many speak; Pottage and McSherry would both regard the effort to uphold such distinctions – as in the 'balance' to which the BMA (above) appeals – as symptomatic attempts to 'fix' a crisis in foundational assumptions.

24. In 2001 the General Conference of UNESCO adopted a Universal Declaration on Cultural Diversity, 'a comprehensive standard-setting instrument, elevating cultural diversity to the rank of "common heritage of humanity"', urging that 'While ensuring the free circulation of ideas and works, cultural policies must create conditions conducive to the production and dissemination of diversified cultural goods and services' – it cannot just be left to 'market forces' (from press statement http://www.unesco.org/confgen/press_rel/021101_clt_diversity.shtml).

25. From the same document: 'While not respected by all nations, the concept of common heritage also resonates under international law ...[For] beyond the individual, the family or the population, there is a common shared interest in the genetic heritage of mankind. Therefore, the Human Genome Project should benefit all humanity.' More generally it may be argued that enjoying the benefits of scientific progress is indivisibly part of human rights. The UN Sub-Commission for the Promotion and Protection of Human Rights, pointing to 'apparent conflicts between the intellectual property rights regime embodied in the TRIPS Agreement, on the one hand, and international human rights law, on the other', declared in 2000 that 'the implementation of the TRIPS agreement does not adequately reflect the fundamental nature and indivisibility of all human rights, *including the right of everyone to enjoy the benefits of scientific progress and its applications*, the right to health, the right to food ...' (Press release, Institute for Agriculture and Trade Policy, USA, 22 viii 00, on a declaration from the Commission's 52nd session; my emphasis).

26. Though based on international discourse, the antithesis to resources is only for the sake of present argument. On tropes of possession in the making of nationhood in a Pacific context, see Foster (1995: 18–19).

27. Simpson (1997: 59), and for examples, Posey (1996), Posey and Dutfield (1996), Dutfield (1999a). Drahos argues that IPR as it stands will not do, although there is always the possibility of developing *sui generis* (special purpose) intellectual property rights in local knowledge, as plant breeders and semiconductor chip manufacturers have done.

28. His concern here is with ethnobotanical knowledge; the collecting would be for plant specimens of possible pharmaceutical application. The transactional context is imagined as one where corporations on the one hand and indigenous groups on the other can apparently interact without having to be embedded in a particular society or culture. For a survey of benefit-sharing practices, see King et al. 1996, and for an ethnography, Hayden 2004.

29. As in the desire to develop protection regimes for natural resources in advance of potential bioprospecting forays (Blakeney 1999c).

30. Much is omitted here from the argument. What is of interest is the rhetoric of claims which elaborates on possibilities precisely when, under present legal

and commercial protocols, they are not embodied in a product or in some thing which could realise its own commercial potential.
31. South-Central Transylvania 1994–2000: fifteen- to forty-fold increase in production costs/three- to five-fold increase in land value (Verdery n.d.; 2003). It becomes ever more costly to keep land productive.
32. She applies it to the circulation of commodities. Whereas inflation refers to a ratio of costs and values, inertia refers to the quantum of drag (extra resource input) on keeping an activity going – the effect of running harder to stay in the same place. One example is the way in which the cost of commodities is only kept down because of the ever-increasing applications of technology in production and marketing, applications (such as pesticides and fertilisers) which then become perpetually bound to the productive operation (Brennan 2000: 11).
33. My comparison. Jean-Klein calls organised political observation 'audit' in order to draw attention to, among other things, asymmetries in the relationship between Palestinian activists and observer-tourists.
34. Activists could not expect the tourists to acquire duties towards the Palestinian state; they could expect their own actions to have fostered some sense of debt to themselves as hosts.
35. From a Wenner Gren symposium on property relations organised by Caroline Humphrey and Katherine Verdery in 2000 (also see Alexander n.d.; Sneath n.d.; Humphrey 2000a, 2000b). I appreciate permission to cite the unpublished papers, and particularly thank Katherine Verdery for our conversations.
36. On innovative and noninnovative practices within the same regime, see Whitehouse on the Mali Baining, East New Britain (1996: 177, 190). Some magical rites, like spells, are regarded as conventional, nonauthored, do not summon the spirits with any experiential depth: the spirits are objects manipulable through appropriate techniques. By contrast, he describes a religious movement as both heavily authored (named mediums) and innovative (restoration of old practices, fresh imposition of taboos, newly dreamed ceremonies).
37. One hallmark of liberal government is that it must embrace 'opposition', i.e. views counter to itself.
38. Using the language of property ownership, Harrison (2000) describes Melanesian societies as though they had long been involved in trading artefacts that signify 'culture'. Whether or not one would agree, and I follow Mosko's (2002) and Hirsch's (pers. comm.) hesitations, it is important that he distinguishes *two forms of* cultural property. One is associated with Western nationalism which 'models cultural property after the concepts of private property characteristic of capitalism, in acordance with the logic of "possessive individualism"'; the other is found in earlier Melanesian forms of 'property' grounded in trading and gift-exchange systems, where 'quasi-objects [were] capable of being used to establish relationships between groups'. See Mosko (2002, n. 3), on this point.
39. For example Garrity (1999: 1198–99) argues, first, that Maori rights of possession are not accorded on an individual basis; second, that 'traditional society was organised communally'; third, that 'the group as a whole' had such rights, and finally that by contrast with rights of exclusive possession held by individuals in English law, Maori have a 'holistic' approach to resources. The individual–communal antinomy, repeated in terms of the Maori regime

being 'collective' in character and encouraging 'communal' ownership as against the 'individualistic' approach of Western IPR (1999: 1205), sits uneasily with the exclusive character of the ancestral groups (tribe and subtribe) also mentioned here. The *corporate* nature of exclusive group holdings in PNG has been thoroughly elucidated by Kalinoe (1999) with respect to water resources; and Foster's observations on the 'collective individual' (1995) remain germane.

40. Other agencies and conventions such as CBD, UNESCO, and recently WIPO, have all searched for just such a purchase.
41. This simplification ignores those aspects of IPR that deal with the protection of reputation and goodwill. Bainbridge's textbook (1999: 45, 317) is unequivocal: 'the method used by copyright law is to require that the work has some tangible form'; an invention on which a patent is sought may refer to a product or a process but in any event 'must be capable of industrial application'. Küchler's point is to offer a contrast with Melanesian practices. In clearing away confusions over the concept of alienability in gift/commodity debates, Küchler elsewhere (1997: 42) draws attention to the possibilities of artefacts being 'alienated' as material objects (destroyed, sold as commodities) while their image remains 'unalienated' and can be reproduced. The issue of alienation aside, for *image* one could almost read *debt*: when pigs or other valuables are given away we could say that the items are consumed, the debt (the virtual presence of the pig) remains.
42. Minimally the ability to exclude others from enjoyment of it, e.g. Gray (1991). Sherman and Bently (1999: ch. 2) give a brief history of 'The Mentality of Intangible Property'. Thanks to Lawrence Kalinoe and Alain Pottage for these references.
43. Here Maori material is suggestive. *Taonga* ('property') can manifest itself in both physical objects and intangibles such as language or ideas; the physical objects listed include land, forests, weapons – and people (Garrity 1999: 1195).
44. The point is not just that transactions require transactions, which would hold anywhere, but that the nature of and desire for the object is relative to the relationship. Melanesianists will find many simplifications in this account. To take just one example: Nihill (1996: 108) discusses debt and 'body logics', where he contrasts situations in which transactors are the focal point and those in which the focus is on the body of the person (such as a corpse) for which wealth substitutes; his observation that men's autonomy 'is constrained by the significance of others' would hold for either.
45. But see Gregory's caveats against the quantity view of inflation (1997: ch. 7).
46. It would be disingenuous not to note that the contrast was originally in terms of 'commodity economy' and 'gift economy'.
47. And also leached some of the economic significance out of social relations.
48. One could also say that it makes visible the ability to call one's own debts in. But transactions may be accompanied by the stated preference to have assets held by others which can be called up as debts at some future date. A parallel iconography exists in many areas, especially in the Massim and along the southern PNG coast, concerning food. People would rather have empty stomachs and full gardens than the reverse.
49. Tactics of delay and uncertainties of return mean that people can become quite dependent on those who owe them things (waiting for debts to be made good), while in turn to owe can put one into a position of power. One effect

of rendering kinship relationships visible through material transactions is the explicit dependency it generates: for example, maternal kin with an expectation of payments from sisters' children are dependent both on being recognised and on the gifts being made good.

50. In commonsense terms this would be more intelligibly written as 'too few relationships', but – as explained – relationships can also expand in the rate at which they absorb items.
51. The social networks necessary to underpin barter in present-day Russia have their 'cost', that is, divert a percentage of the transaction to network maintenance (Humphrey 2000a). So the goods have to be over-valued. In the words of one businessman: 'I have to pay about 2 per cent for the acquaintanceship' (ibid: 80). This remark follows Humphrey's comparison with Melanesian exchange partnerships and the over-valuing that comes from the fact that partnerships are valued for themselves.
52. Relations between the generations sometimes take on this cast – each may regard the other as locked into its own value system (see especially Chapter 6).
53. I am very grateful to Christopher Gregory for his commentary on this point.
54. Muyuw [Woodlark Island] canoes are asymmetrical (the hull's two sides are distinctly pitched and curved; one side also has an outrigger). The result is that a craft meets on-coming waves on one side differently from the way it cuts the water on the other – tacking from side to side, as well as up and down (through the motions of a rudder plunged into the sea and lifted out again) and pitching in the water from stern to prow. Occupying space in three directions all at once, it is the ability to keep those tensions in play which give it movement. (Frederick Damon, seminar paper, Cambridge, 2001).
55. Omitted from the published version. If one were to give a thorough-going answer one would need to translate all these terms, e.g., one would be looking at debt as the *phenomenal* form of gift, since relationisim is preempted in the gift. Gregory (1982: 19) anticipated the answer: 'The gift economy ... is a debt economy.'
56. Including corporate persons. The division between rights and debts is, of course, a heuristic to point to different systemic emphases in computations of ownership. 'Debts' in a commodity economy, if the term is permitted, with the emphasis on entitlement given by the nature of the product or equally by the nature of the person, may be dischargeable in the form of acknowledgement. 'Rights' in a gift economy, where obligations are built up through and inhere in transactions, may be a good translation for the background rationale (e.g., what is 'owed' to specific kin by virtue of one's own kinship standing) but the question of how the obligation has already been discharged to date is likely to be the starting point of claims. In the second case, I also note that the transactions may be cross-generational, as in the nuance Simet (n.d.) puts on this point: in rejecting the concept of 'rights', he argues that the issue is not the inherent value of items as such, but how the holder's responsibility is properly discharged in passing them on to heirs, who in turn acquire the same responsibility.
57. In parallel to this we may note that rights and debts both depend on being recognised, but whereas pursuing one's rights requires legitimation through an authority (typically the framework of a national legal system, the sanctions of 'customary law' etc.), debts that arise in the course of transactions can be settled in the course of more transactions.

58. And thus point to an embodiment that has already happened and is part of the way the world is, which comes out looking 'traditional', except this is not modernity's tradition – it is necessary to actively perpetuate the future conditions of reproduction.

Chapter 5

TRANSACTIONS IN PERPETUAL MOTION

Tony Crook

... to subject the civil order to rational enquiry unavoidably turns it into a mechanism. (M. Oakeshott, 'Introduction', in T. Hobbes, *Leviathan*, p. 1946: xxi)

Transactions in Sustainability

In 1999, Broken Hill Proprietary (BHP), the majority shareholder in Ok Tedi Mining Limited (OTML), signalled an intention to exit the Ok Tedi project in PNG – described as a 'social and environmental disaster' (Hyndman 1988: 24; 1994). It has long attracted more negative attention for its publicised environmental effects than positive attention for its economic development effects. BHP had already been called to the Victoria Supreme Court in Australia by a consortium of Lower Ok Tedi and Fly River plaintiffs to defend the project in the mid-1990s – and to settle out of court – through what became known retrospectively as the 'downstream compensation debate' (see Kirsch 1997a and this volume (Chapter 1); Banks and Ballard 1997). This defining moment in 1999 accompanied a change of government led by Sir Mekere Morouta, which promised an end to financial waste, corruption and 'merry-go-round politics'. The moment exposed the rationale for the enterprise to intense domestic and international scrutiny, and focused attention on its engineering a balance between competing aims.

Global corporate citizenship and environmental responsibility were forceful issues on the international agenda at the Seattle WTO trade talks later that year, and prompted US President Clinton to call for 'globalisation with a human face'.[1] BHP was responding to the challenge across the board: BHP Minerals' President noted at the time that 'responsible companies can create for themselves a competitive advantage through responsible management of environmental issues' (McNeilly 1999: 5); he highlighted 'the added value of a synergistic approach' (ibid: 6), and promised 'to be sensitive to the cultural values wherever we operate around the world' (ibid: 6). The company's 'success in getting steel fully accredited as a "green" building material' for the 2000 Sydney Olympics indicated the possibilities of these new combinations (ibid: 5). BHP was not alone in perceiving exceptional prospects in this millennial moment: under the heading 'The Myth of Mineral Scarcity', Rio Tinto's Chief Economist declared that:

> Over time, technology has served to reduce the costs of extracting and recovering mineral raw materials, more than offsetting the cost-increasing effects of declining ore grades ... Far from becoming *less* abundant, minerals have for most practical purposes become *more* abundant, rendering their classification as 'non-renewable' unhelpful at best and misleading at worst. (Humphreys 2000: 1, original emphasis)

The notion here is that, as test beds for improving technology, mines effectively make more materials available than those exhausted in the process – a 'win-win' scenario if ever there was one! The eagerness to display 'green' credentials and participation in the new rhetorics of sustainability culminated in the claim that '[a]pplying the Bruntland rule to the subject, and asking whether the interests of future generations are being compromised by our rate of mining today, the answer has to be an emphatic *no*' (Humphreys 2000: 1, original emphasis). Of course, this utopian vision becomes possible by misrecognising the slippage between the general and the specific. But enthusiasm for such alchemy, and the sheer willingness to believe the possibility, are indicative of the moment in which the events that follow were conceived and played out. (And with these events now past, my account retains the ethnographic present of July 1999–April 2001, and analyses how these moves were framed during that period).

The Ok Tedi Mine Continuation Agreement (MCA) was proposed as an ambitious attempt to find a solution to resolve the question of balancing social and environmental effects *once and for all*.[2] This was to be an unprecedented transaction (as was evident in OTML's transformed rhetoric, 'this is not compensation, this is sustainable development'), in seeming to separate out monetary from humanitarian motivations for *all* 'stakeholders', and in the sheer ambitious scale of the vision: the sustainable development equivalent of settling every possible compensation claim in advance *once and for all*. There was a strong sense of there being nothing beyond this totalising transaction. The MCA then, was to finally reconcile a balance between the social and environmental domains, set in motion a regime of sustainable development recompense and an uninterrupted regime of resource extraction requiring no further legal or monetary inputs.

BHP's move in turn set in motion a series of knock-on separations, accomplished by reorganising internal divisions. Both 'collectives' and 'individuals' were apprehended as though they constituted 'social units', and with the faith that particular elements could be isolated into compartments. One aim was to create a new set of working relationships in which self-interest was separated out. As such, the designs imagined for this unprecedented new social contract are helpful in thinking about anthropological assumptions of how transactions, social agency and resources are conceived and analytically figured.

In *Transaction and Meaning* (Kapferer 1976) transactionalism is portrayed as a movement exemplified by Barth's *Models of Social Organization* (1966). This questioned the structural functionalist paradigm's 'models of static equilibrium' by pointing to the importance of social process, variation and change, and by looking to individual 'transactional behaviour' and formal strategies. (Having worked in the Ok Tedi area amongst the nearby Baktaman, in a study that exemplified his transactionalism and the 'generative model' [1975; 1987], Barth co-wrote a thoughtful and undeservedly neglected cultural impact study of the project [Barth and Wikan 1982]). Transactionalism debated the strategies through which values were negotiated, and revealed a shared concern to maintain a certain symmetry – combining individual and collective, agency and structure, rationality and culture – rather than allow any one factor to predominate. Rationalised within these parameters, the differences revealed by comparative case studies appeared simply as variety amongst limited combinations. Kapferer perceived these limits in 'Barth's distinction between relationships built on transactions in which individuals pursue self interest, and relationships in which individuals pursue benefits for the group' (1976: 7), which ultimately 'reveals a mechanism for the maintenance of political equilibrium' (ibid: 6). This same conclusion was reached by Asad (1972: 91) whose critique framed Barth's model as a 'logically closed system' (ibid: 90), and looked to the history of these ideas to suggest that, genealogically speaking:

> [a] simple connection might be made between Barth's picture of Swat and Hobbes' model by noticing that each landlord-chief and his following forms an island of authority. (1972: 81)

These perceptions of a mechanism producing and sustaining social process by reconciling 'individualistic' and 'collectivistic' forces (Kapferer 1976: 2) are intriguing.

The following discussion suggests a genealogy for these contractual notions of reciprocity, and their achievement of a certain symmetry. The reorganisations motivated by the MCA are analysed and historically placed in Ok Tedi's overall development; this leads to a genealogy, placing transactionalism within a tradition of social thinking that historically borrows resources from the parallel development of a mechanised worldpicture. The Ok Tedi MCA subsequently appears as an exemplary enactment of the models imagined by this tradition. However, the discussion begins here with three examples that together suggest a genealogy for noncontractual notions of reciprocity, in which asymmetry is emphasised. In juxtaposing these genealogies, other limits to transactionalist assumptions subsequently appear.

'Half' a Transactor

The first example derives from the work of Wopkaimin artist, Bob Kain, which is ubiquitous around the Ok Tedi mine project. His bright murals of fauna, flora, traditional costumes and scenes of industrial operations cover the walls of the company mess halls at Tabubil and Bige, the golf clubs in Tabubil and Kiunga, and a 'Keep Tabubil Tidy' campaign, whilst his caricatures of managers adorn safety notices painted directly onto parts of the factory structures. The references are local: a waterfall depicts *kutim fon* (lit. early morning waterfall), a powerful spirit site (*awem tem*) from which the *fom wok* stream (lit. stream of the rotting dead) now flows below the concrete, underneath a quarter of Tabubil town that the artist meticulously avoids. These colourful and animated murals (admitting of shock and nostalgia) were developed after Kain was warned at art college to 'leave the politics out' of his work after graduating – as if it were that easy to detach a domain of concerns from one's self. *Cross-Cut* (1993) formed part of the degree portfolio: two horizontal bands of dark rock are separated by a middle slice in the orange of sodium lighting, and depict the enlargement and electrification of a natural tunnel now used as an access route for machinery. As one becomes accustomed to the colouring, a pair of spirit eyes appear out of the darkness, as if looking into the new light. Such effects are intended.

Lives in River (1993) is a deeply scored collograph in heavy charcoal, a blotchy image having an irregular side joining together another three straight sides. Although finished, the work is deliberately incomplete, as Kain explained: 'I don't want to give the whole story away, I want people to finish it for themselves, to make up the story which the painting is trying to tell'. In determining a selling price, Kain reaches his valuations by effect: measuring how much a painting and a prospective buyer get involved in each other. Guided (by the artist) to turn *Lives in River* on its side, a glimpse of river life appeared (to the viewer) amongst the impressions: plants, mussels, prawns, eels, turtles and fish below a sailing canoe. Told that the idea came from having photographed the raised bed of an unloading dump truck in the mine pit from a rear three-quarters position, the straight edges appeared to be joined by the silhouette of tyres and driver's cab. Shown how this irregular side also held the profile of a face inspecting the scene from outside, another image was elicited – equally joining and displacing the others, in much the way that Kain saw the raised dump truck as joining its load of mine wastes with the river life, and displacing it in the river system also.

The aesthetics here, of connecting juxtaposed images (the over-burden, the habitat into which it is tipped) and eliciting further perceptions (the witness) that simultaneously complete and make incomplete anew (is it, the dwelling 'lives', or the 'lives' at stake?) – these were all familiar to me from the knowledge practices of the neighbouring Angkaiyakmin people of Bolivip village (Crook 1999). These provide a second example. In much the way a person might come and sit silently in a house, presenting a figure for others to think on – 'how can we satisfy this person?; maybe they are hungry and came; maybe they have some concern and want my help' – so people often elicit others to complete their thoughts. Such respectful and sorrowful feelings for others (*kiinkiin*; lit. 'eye-eye') elicits reciprocity and sociality. Whereas a person might voice their request for help respectfully to an affine by speaking in their earshot but to someone else, they are likely to voice a request to closer kin more directly: using 'straight talk' (*weng turon*) indicates closeness. This kind of talk is also the medium for an exchange whereby younger men and women 'look after the skin' by respecting and caring for an older person, and in return receive advice, names, stories and techniques which are all regarded as 'skin'. Although the talk in such knowledge transactions is straight, and phrased in language the other can understand, it is also deliberately incomplete. A person will give only 'half' (*mari*), and leave the other person to add the other 'half' themselves with their own thinking. One old man became fond of telling me that our skin had gone on to each other, and that we were now 'one skin'.

As a bodily substance kept especially in the thigh muscles, such knowledge is known as *lamlam* – this refers to the shiny membrane covering muscle; to advice and knowledge; and to the shining effects of these when manifested in the world: strong and healthy plants, people and pigs all have a shine to their skin. Often conceived as a kind of bodily liquid (*wok*), this circulates in these exchanges of skin, passes into children, plants and pigs by caring and playing with them (another man suggested that '*wok* is another word for love'), and passes into plants, forest birds and fruit trees, marsupials and cassowaries by means of the smoke released in ritual from the *yolam* cult house. A skilled and knowledgeable cult leader who has learnt in return for having cared for another person's skin by 'leaving the eyes following straight' will be able to follow the 'ancestor paths' (*kukup leip*) straight in their ritual performances. This results in the liquid-laden smoke going in a straight line out of the cult house and, for example, into the gardens where the taro plants – newly planted on an angle – will stand up and grow straight. Without these circulations of respect and care, advice and knowledge, paths and liquid, nothing grows with strength or abundance, and the skin of plants, birds, animals and people is not as it should be. Rather than a lively and active village life conducted on ground so hot and dry that the children pretend it is sago flour in their hands, the ground is saturated and cold, people do not go round the village, forest or gardens, and a dark green slippery moss (*sesol*) encroaches upon the *yolam* cult house. Landscapes here are malleable; animated by peoples' relations and activities, by their respect and care, and by their bodily substances and ancestral spirits. Having once asked about the coming of the government, the Catholic missionaries and the Ok Tedi mine, I was handed something to think on: a small shrivelled taro corm with bad skin. Nothing was said.

Thirdly, as Burton has shown (1997: 41ff.), reports of poor crops, bad-tasting water and stories of an ancestral connection with the Mt. Fubilan mine-site have been reported by people in the Ningerum area since early 1984. OTML receives a steady flow of letters claiming compensation for similar environmental effects from places all over Western Province, and often far removed from the river systems carrying the mine sediments. In September 2000, a new generation presented a petition on behalf of the West Ningerum Pressure Association (WNPA: 2000), claiming for damages to the Ok Tarim and Ok Birim rivers, which flow south (overground at least) from a ridge overlooked by Mt. Fubilan and join the Ok Tedi river below Ningerum government station. The document had very carefully screened out any traces of customary explanation, and presented the case as if a manifest of poor crops, unfruitful trees, poor water, sparse river life, dried-out foliage, and rocks now slippery with moss were the measurable effects of the mine wastes believed to be entering their river systems from underground (Crook 2000a). A series of company and government tests and samples have failed to pick up any traces of mine-derived wastes in the two rivers above the meeting with the main Ok Tedi River drainage. The petition left out any trace of a tunnel used by spirits and the people who would trade with them to move between places in the Ningerum area and Mt. Fubilan, where their creation being and a huge spirit-python still dwell, and left out any trace of the means by which important stones were able to release a fecund liquid (called *okakana*), which appears to have effects akin to the Angkaiyakmin *wok*.

One WNPA leader described how – although WNPA had no belief in it themselves – the (mainly Australian) managers of the mine believed in the ability of 'science' to measure everything real in the world. Accordingly, although premised on a set of cosmological connections, the petition left out all references to them. Instead, it is as if the WNPA were relying on the authorities to reciprocate the thought and respect they (the WNPA) had shown in deliberately phrasing their concerns in language the company could understand: 'even if they do not believe our stories, we want them to look at this and at least give us half of the money we are claiming'. The leader also explained how he assumed it was enough to present a figure displaying plight and rely on the authorities to feel sorrow and think how they might satisfy the people he represented. Whenever he tried this posture, though, rather than half a transactor, so to speak, the other side took this as no transaction at all. And yet, when he once put his claim into the confrontational language of demands that he took to be expected of him, this immediately ended the meeting and he was told that his statements were 'a threat to the Independent State of Papua New Guinea'. Since before the mine began production, then, an unwillingness to reveal extremely important stories, whose efficacy derives from keeping them hidden, has been matched by an unwillingness to take such stories seriously. These Ningerum claims to ownership rights in Mt. Fubilan have never been recognised. Subsequently, they, their cosmology and all such local explanations remain outside of the totalising MCA transaction.

In these three examples from around Tabubil, transactions are perceived to become possible precisely by establishing an asymmetry between the transactors (by not giving the whole thing away, by eliciting completion). Their difference becomes the cause for social action: paintings elicit involvement, knowledge elicits additional thoughts, and silent figures elicit sorrow. In the example of the old man who becomes 'one skin' through his knowledge transactions, it is as if a social agent here amounts to only 'half' a transactor. Rather than perceiving equality only in the symmetry of roles and social agents, and anticipating that a transaction produces social agents as equal parties to it – as equally 'half' of a transaction, so to speak – the examples here suggest different perceptions at work.

Dividing a Transactor in Half

Another of Kain's paintings, *First Gold at Ok Tedi* (late 1990s)[3] works by anticipating what different viewers might bring to complete the image. On the left a tiny nugget of shining yellow gold is held betwixt the index finger and thumb of a brown hand (as if also making an 'OK' signal). Behind this image a dark bare mountain ridge is capped on the right by clouds, below which fall the long streaks of orange-red earth from dumped mine waste. One either chooses to see a celebration of first fruits from a wilderness, or that so much effort and destruction was deemed a worthwhile measure of that first gold nugget. Both Polier (1994) and Burton (1997) have commented on the continuing rhetorics of 'discovery' which, like the Hagahai (Chapter 1), have portrayed Ok Tedi as remote and primitively developed, whose inhabitants were only contacted in 1963: this discounts a series of encounters since 1922 (Burton 1997: 31), suggests that the people and ore deposit were more or less dually discovered, and ignores the speedily established connections with metropolitan centres. Such a 'discovery paradigm' depicts the local population surviving as human nature reduced to its bare essentials, emphasises the technological and civilising improvements available to them in terms of health, nutrition and life expectancy, and narrates a drama of dual first contact through which the 'discoverers become "culture heroes" who wander across usually hostile landscapes until they reach their goal' (Burton 1997: 28; see Schieffelin and Crittenden 1991). 'Remoteness from Civilization' – geographically and socially – is the key metaphor that enables a fantasy of isolation where life is a matter of survival: hard enough even for those with a few technological advantages, let alone those without.

Burton describes the discovered land around Ok Tedi as *terra nugax*: 'land that, not being used for anything else or having "trifling other uses", is a promising candidate for industrial use through mineral extraction' (1997: 29), with the aim of bringing civilising and life-enhancing advances. Cronon shows how a view of Nature 'as capable of perpetuating itself forever unless something interfered with its natural balance' (1995: 24) was part of a portrayal of indigenous lands as similarly untouched (and see Ingold 1993). Burton further suggests that 'the political connections of land treated as *terra nugax* are believed "trifling, of no consequence, nugatory" and that decisions can happily be made about it with few repercussions' (1997: 30), and analyses how this framed attitudes that resulted in weak enforcement of social and environmental obligations even before production started in 1984. As 'politically invisible' (1997: 29) then, *terra nugax* refers to little-used and isolated land lying beyond the horizons of metropolitan society. Indeed, and as if to emphasise the perception, the initial geological survey work on the steep cloud-forest slopes of Mt. Fubilan itself was carried out via an archipelago of tiny makeshift camps which dotted the mountain, which were only accessible by helicopter – and were named after the likes of Edinburgh, Hong Kong and Townsville to where the inhabitants longed for deliverance. These conceptions of *terra nugax* appear to describe the kind of place only inhabitable by some kind of Robinson Crusoe figure.

The day 20 February 2001 was a particularly fine one for the OTML Consultation and Communication team to be flying over the rain forest. (This team was involved in negotiating the MCA, and I had joined them for the day as an observer [Crook 2001b]). Whilst dropping down from the notoriously cloud-bound mountains around Tabubil, and throughout the hour-long journey to a meeting with the 'Lower Ok Tedi land-owners' at the golf club in Kiunga, the helicopter afforded an exciting viewing platform. At one point, as we followed the Ok Tedi River down towards its meeting with the Fly river in the lowlands, it seemed possible to see in one sweep the entire Ok Tedi operation as a mechanised landscape. Immediately south of Tabubil lies the Ok Ma valley, the site of a once-planned massive capacity dam designed to hold the waste tailings (a grey liquid of fine materials and reagent chemicals), abandoned before production began after a landslide halted work on the foundations. Looking backwards one could see the range containing the Mt. Fubilan copper deposit extending away over the border with Indonesia, and looking forwards one could see the urban development of Kiunga, the furthest navigable point on the Fly river for the barges which bring supplies hundreds of kilometres upstream from the south coast and return downstream with loads of dried copper concentrate. Below us ran the muddy water and gravel banks of the Ok Tedi River, and the gravel-surfaced Highway which runs 135 km connecting Kiunga and Tabubil. On this dry-season morning, each conduit stood out, twisting a way through the forested mountains and meandering alongside lowland wooded ridges. Dust clouds on the Highway indicated the passing of a supply convoy of more than a dozen articulated trucks, or a tarpaulin-covered passenger bus, or a company four-wheel-drive pickup. Elsewhere we could see work crews grading the road surface. A maintenance crew was attending to the copper slurry pipe which is buried by the roadside and which connects the Folomian Mill (where the copper ore is ground and processed) high on Mt. Fubilan's shoulder with a drying facility on the wharfside at Kiunga in the lowlands.

These connected parts of the 'mining, milling and shipping copper' operation seemed one vast machine system (Crook 2000b; forthcoming). The vantage point was such that even whilst we were passing the stark brown stands of poisoned 'forest die-back' trees around the floodplain in the lower Ok Tedi (a catchment point where flooding now deposits mine waste instead of nutrients on top of garden sites), it seemed possible to also keep the scar of the Southern Waste Dump at the edge of the mine pit in view. This dump together with its northern counterpart are where waste rock and uneconomic ore are dumped and washed down by extremely heavy rainfall into the river system designated (since the initial 1970s engineering design) for its storage. The river's upper reaches are now filled and choked by the mine wastes. Together with the small waterfall on Mt. Fubilan's south side, which now releases the mill waste tailings directly into the river system, these dumps – in continuous use round the clock since production started – were factors contributing to the negotiations to which we were flying that sunny morning.

As part the MCA consultation process, this meeting considered a proposal for one of the reorganisational knock-on effects – one that would be separated out from any involvement with the negative environmental mine-impact side of the Ok Tedi project:[4]

> The [Ok Tedi Development Foundation], while new as an institution, would be a means of formalizing and externalizing OTML's long-term commitment, working out, through programs and projects, innovative strategies for long-term sustainable development – food security, economic development, capacity building, and infrastructure development. (Wissink 2000: 1)

The OTML team told the meeting that 'at the moment we can't focus on development because we have to deal with compensation', and described their need to 'pull the Foundation away from the company' in order to be recognised as a credible partner to development donor agencies[5] (and described elsewhere in these terms):

> In the remaining life of the mine, the Ok Tedi Development Foundation, working in partnership with the communities, governments and other stakeholders, will provide the skills to convert substantial benefit streams into coordinated social infrastructure thus leaving a positive legacy from the Ok Tedi mine, contributing to a sustainable future, and a better life for the people of Western Province and Telefomin District. (Wissink 2000: 1)

Eventually, the Foundation's role in the MCA would be to implement a basket of sustainable development projects[6] in return for the affected landowners giving their consent for the mine to enjoy unfettered and continuous production through to 2009.

A paramount challenge for the Foundation in effecting this separation was to balance tight controls and decision-making capacity with representation satisfactory to both land owners and potential donor partners. This appeared especially important as the Foundation would be implementing 'development programs' as some kind of 'compensation' for mine impacts, and yet having to present a separate enough entity for donor partnerships. Questions at the meeting addressed the sources of funding, whether the government would have to pay their share, and whether the funding (both income and expenditure) would be 'politician-proof'. Consequently, one of the most debated issues concerned another knock-on separation, namely the representation and governance of the Foundation itself.[7]

Within the MCA's nominal grouping together of communities up and down the river system into six regional units comprising many different (and even rival) ethnicities, the concern here was that communities were not put into a position of disadvantage (in lieu of an advantageous one). The importance attached to establishing this kind of symmetry amongst transacting parties was evident in courses offered in preparation for the negotiation process: 'Personal Skills' and 'Conflict Resolution' gave Papua New Guineans the model of a person in three parts – Parent, Adult, Child – with which to categorise the motivations of people in a series of text-book examples. One manager, acknowledging an ethnocentric origin for the courses, gave a shrug and commented: 'we know we are treating people as if they are globalised consumptive individuals, but hey...'. A newly acquired gadget that scanned and printed out what had been written on a whiteboard ('so that we can all see what we agreed') was hailed as a further improvement to establishing symmetry amongst the transactors. And so it seemed the OTML delegation readily understood why the Lower Ok Tedi participants should be so concerned about representation, and explained that they had designed the Foundation's organisational machinery with these dangers in mind by placing great emphasis on having a small Board to keep consensus on decision making more easily achievable:[8]

> Obviously we can't have representatives from every community. Having even ten people and having them to be unanimous is very difficult, so we want to keep the Board small so they can make decisions.

Importance was placed on the role of 'advisers' regarded as free of self-interest, working within the Foundation's regulatory framework, who would check any tendency there might be to favour projects, tenders and contracts on any basis other than individual merit: 'We can have advisers – and they might be community representatives – but they give advice about the programs, the implementation etc.'.

The proposal for the Board, then, was to have the actual decision-making machinery operated by social agents who were themselves free of self-interested social claims. Furthermore, and given that the part of themselves that was susceptible to social claims had been isolated by the design, they could only operate the organisational machinery as intended. The fine upstanding citizens envisioned as 'Board members' – possibly drawn from the wider PNG society beyond Western Province – were perceived to be rather more immune to social claims than their counterpart 'advisers' drawn from the communities' representatives. For their part, the Lower Ok Tedi participants repeatedly asked about having representation on the Board, in order to ensure that projects were accepted and contracts handed out fairly, and to make sure funds were used correctly. Despite the repeated explanations about the structure and operation of the Foundation (funds coming in, the management of projects), this issue was evidently also one of the motivations for the Lower Ok Tedi people repeatedly asking to have their own representative on the Board. The meeting closed with their insistence on knowing 'who will actually be doing the work and making the decisions?' still hanging in the air.

Now, if the perception of Ok Tedi as *terra nugax* – politically invisible land with only trifling improvements on show – provided the perfect rationale for the mining company on its way into the project, it was as if the process were now being played out in reverse and providing the perfect rationale for the mining company on its way out. Much of the rhetoric informing the consultation process portrayed the achievements towards development as amounting to relatively little of consequence, and warned of the difficulties the local population would face if this landscape were simply abandoned with the haste with which it was first discovered:

> Since the mine commenced operations in 1982, it is calculated that some K200 million in mine-related benefits have been distributed by the National Government to the Western Provincial Government. Because of inadequate planning and implementation capacity, as well as poor levels of accountability, much of this money was spent with no substantive benefit for the province. In the remaining life of the mine, and beyond, the [Ok Tedi Development Foundation] could provide the skills to convert these cashflows into useful social infrastructure to support economic growth. (Wissink 2000: 6)

These notions of the slate remaining relatively clean accompanied comments making previous efforts and actions redundant, and lent a spirit of a fresh start to the discussions. For example, a letter – entitled 'Close Ok Tedi mine now' – to a daily newspaper, *The National* (21st June 2000), was pinned on the OTML Community Relations notice-board:

> Why all of a sudden is [the Managing Director of the OTML] saying that a solution has to be found now? Why didn't they find the solution during the feasibility study of the entire mining area when the environment was still intact and in its natural form is a question best left to him to answer.

Similarly, the architect of the proposed Foundation was equally blunt:

> We might just tear up all the agreements and start again, renegotiate the whole project!... OK, so we know the river is stuffed – we can't change that now – what can we do in the remaining years to make sure that there are some long-term benefits left behind?

And the imagery of 'inadequate capacities' here reveals yet another symmetry with earlier phases of the project. Filer's analysis of the Ok Tedi out-of-court settlement in 1996 suggests that:

> [t]he origins of the social relationship between the plaintiffs [lower Ok Tedi landowners] and the defendants [BHP] in the case brought before the Victorian Supreme Court can be traced back to the night of 7 January 1984, when a landslide halted work on the construction of the Ok Ma tailings dam. This 'helping hand from Mother Nature' provided the mining company's executives with a timely opportunity to pursue their long-term goal of persuading the government to waive its requirement for a tailings dam to be completed before the mine could begin. (1997: 58, note and reference omitted)

Following the damage caused to the dam's foundations by the earthquake (or the writhing of a huge spirit-python in several Ningerum accounts), the mine wastes were released directly into the streams flowing from Mt. Fubilan. Due to shaky foundations, then, the arrangements to contain these waste streams had failed. Filer goes on to reveal a history of subsequent events that put off, delayed and prevented the construction of a stable waste-storage facility with sufficient capacity to contain the issuances of the mine. And now, through a version of *terra nugax* thinking, the mining company was advancing a proposal for a new type of Foundation – an organisation that would be more successful in capturing and containing the benefit streams due to flow from Mt. Fublian over the remaining years of production, rather than allowing these issuances to be wasted by the provincial and national governments. As configured in the negotiations towards the 'mine continuation agreement' then, it is as if two substances have been overspilling their appropriate channels since 1984: mine waste and tailings now flow freely into the river systems, and mine-derived benefits have been 'wasted' by a planning and regulatory regime in Western Province with inadequate institutional capacity to contain them.

These arguments were backed up by the efforts being made through the OTML-driven Western Province Capacity Building Program (2000–2), which was training local and provincial government officers to enhance their ability to manage projects, and designing systems capable of containing funds within the appropriate channels. Whereas the Foundation proposed to work by reengineering the existing organisational machinery so as to enable social agents to operate in new ways, the Capacity Building Program proposed to focus on reengineering the social agents more directly.[9]

Compared to what might have been accomplished to date then, and compared to what might yet be accomplished if the mine continued production, the development infrastructures appeared trifling or nugatory. Here, it is as if the area still remains relatively unaffected by the insufficient reaches of Papua New Guinean metropolitan society, and – unless the mine continued production – would remain the kind of place only inhabitable by some kind of Robinson Crusoe figure.

Set in motion by BHP's move to make its environmental values evident by exiting the project and separating itself from OTML, the subsequent series of reorganised internal divisions were characterised by similar concerns about managing responsibility and representation. These other separations – the Foundation; the Board; the decision makers; their self-interests – each enacted a version of the division between monetary self-interest and environmental-cum-humanitarian collective interests. What grabs my attention here is that these transactions each have a particular image of a social agent at their centre, one able to compartmentalise individual self-interest from responsibilities to collective society precisely because these were imagined to be the constituent components. Such a model carries with it assumptions about a social agent's capacity to entirely separate off self-interest and the claims of social relationships from their own individual social motivations and actions. As the Lower Ok Tedi participants' response made evident, the very idea of a social agent able to act without interest and free from social claims made upon them was met with utter disbelief. Their consternation suggests that a particular genealogy is behind the resiliant figure of social agency as imagined by the mining company.

Transactions in a Mechanised World Picture

In drawing Robinson Crusoe into his discussions of motivated action in social life, Weber was following a long tradition of using Defoe's (1719) fictional shipwrecked mariner as an exemplary measure of human nature reduced to its bare essentials. Crusoe has long been thought to be modelled on Alexander Selkirk, 'an undisciplined Scot' from Largo in Fife (Ross 1985: 301), who marooned himself on Juan Fernandez island off the coast of Chile from 1704 to 1709. Making a brief appearance as an 'isolated economic man' in 'Protestant Asceticism and the Spirit of Capitalism' (Weber 1989a: 166), Crusoe's solitude and island survival features in 'The Concept of "Following a Rule"' (Weber 1989b) as an illustration *both* of an individual freed and separated from society, and of his rule-governed purposive action (by which he husbands his salvage of tools and goods, and resources of crops, goats and raisins). As such, Defoe's literary myth of individual freedom under an overarching governance (here, divine providence) acts out a dichotomy at the centre of a thought experiment that has enchanted and exercised a tradition of social theorists, and around which contemporary debates continue to revolve. A genealogy of the stimulus Crusoe provides to this tradition of social thinking is briefly rehearsed here, before the discussion moves on to survey an historical borrowing of resources from the parallel development of a mechanised world picture.

Rather than exploring the limits of a subject's freedom entailed in, so to speak, a 'divine-contract' of the sort that Defoe has his dabbling-Christian hero caught up in, Rousseau introduces Crusoe as an example,[10] alongside Adam, of a 'sole-inhabitant' in a world beyond the need for a 'social-contract'.[11] The influence that Rousseau's ideas had on Kant are evident in a piece entitled *Perpetual Peace* (1915[1795]), which regards a state of peaceful coexistence (he had expansive European colonisers in mind) as an inevitability:

> This guarantee is given by no less a power than the great artist nature ... in whose mechanical course is clearly exhibited a predetermined design to make harmony spring from human discord, even against the will of man. (1915: 145)

Much as Rousseau perceived Crusoe's island to have provided him with all the needs of mankind, Kant gives the example of currents in the Pacific delivering a supply of driftwood to Eskimos on arctic shores to illustrate the equalising poise of nature: 'she does it herself, whether we will or not' (1915: 152). Kant's own formulation of the predicament requiring a social contract relies on a similar idea to Rousseau's in having to manufacture such a balance:

> 'Given a multitude of rational beings who, in a body, require general laws for their own preservation, but each of whom, as an individual, is secretly inclined to exempt himself from this restraint: how are we to order their affairs and how to establish for them a constitution such that, although their private dispositions may really be antagonistic, they may yet so act as a check upon one another, that, in their public relations, the effect is the same as if they had no such evil sentiments.' Such a problem must be capable of solution. (1915: 154)

Now, whilst Bentham was initially working out his Utilitarian method for calculating 'the greatest good for the greatest number' – and indeed, publishing his own thoughts on 'perpetual peace' – he was also engaged in finalising his plans for the *Panopticon* (1791), the penitentiary machine that lends Foucault his theory of 'perpetual observation' (1977: 304), and that operated by ensuring the greatest observation of the greatest number. By means of a circular building with cleverly arranged cells around a central observation tower, the prisoners could not see the inspector, or each other, a feature that Bentham chose to convey by drawing upon the popularity of the Robinson Crusoe myth: 'Each Cell is an island: the inhabitants, shipwrecked mariners ...' (1791, Postscript I: 35). Bentham was already used to making the claim that 'My prison is transparent: my management, no less so' (Milne 1981: 229, Letter 738), but another feature of the Panopticon was that it was entirely independent of the quality of human resources brought in to operate it.[12] When Marx brings Crusoe's experiences into his discussion of commodities (1896 [1867]), he condemns what had become 'a favourite theme with political economists':

> The individual and isolated hunter and fisherman, with whom Smith and Ricardo begin, belongs to the unimaginative conceits of the eighteenth-century Robinsonades .... (Cited in Freudenthal 1986: 161)

He also shows how Crusoe, 'like a true-born Briton', kept a set of books to mark the labour time he divided between tasks, which served Marx as a model means of both production and distribution.

When Weber places Defoe's character at the centre of a discussion of rule-governed action, he deploys the island setting's affordance of laboratory-like scientific measurement somewhat as a foil:

> We could ask, for instance, what Robinson Crusoe's 'economic' behaviour would 'have to be' like, if it were pushed to its ultimate logical 'consequences'. That is what the theory of marginal utility does. And we could then 'measure' his empirical behaviour against the standard thus worked out by pure reason. (Weber 1989: 107)

And it is as a contemporary manifestation of these attempts to account of a mechanism whereby individual decision making produces the perpetuation of social life that 'transactionalism' became a focus of anthropological debate in the 1960s and 1970s. Several of the contributors to *Transaction and Meaning* engage transactionalism's models of rational decision making by referring to 'the maximization-of-value principle' (Kapferer 1976: 8), and 'utility maximization' (Heath 1976: 26), and thereby draw upon versions of Bentham's utilitarianism doctrine. Asad argues that Barth has, based on 'individual, contractual maximizing behaviour' (1972: 79), generated a 'Hobbesian model of Swat' (1972: 92), and cites a passage from *Leviathan*: 'So that in the first place, I put for a general inclination of all mankind, a perpetual and restless desire of Power after power, that ceaseth only in Death' (1972: 80). In his monograph, Barth argues that individuals have freedom of choice to whom they give their political affiliation, and uses a familiar metaphor in suggesting that:

> the landowner faced with a sea of politically undifferentiated villagers proceeds to organize a central island of authority, and from this island he attempts to exercise authority over the surrounding sea. (1959: 69)

Kapferer's own concerns about Barth's model are that it goes too far towards the individualistic pole: 'the separation of actor's value scales from the social relationships produced by transactional behaviour is problematic' (1976: 7). In these formulations it is as if the perpetuation of social life is the result of a contracted equilibrium between individuals and society. Of course, when it's put this way, 'Society' itself appears as some kind of device for perpetual motion.

In his recent re-evaluation of Actor Network Theory (ANT), Latour has argued that:

> It is not exactly true that social sciences have always alternated between actor and system, or agency and structure. It might be more productive to say that they have alternated between two types of equally powerful *dissatisfactions* ... ANT might have hit on one of the very phenomena of the social order: maybe the social possesses the bizarre property of not being made of

agency and structure at all, but rather of being a *circulating* entity. (1999: 16, 17, original emphasis)

And when he sums up these seemingly endless movements between agent and structure – 'Social scientists soon realize that the local situation is exactly as abstract...and they now want to leave it again for what holds the situation together. And so on *ad infinitum*' (1999: 17) – then Latour's phrasing makes social science itself appear as some kind of device for perpetual motion. We might wonder here just how far social science has managed to escape from all those images of individual Robinson Crusoes whose motions are balanced by some mechanism of overarching governance, and whose cooperation produces something more than the sum of their parts.

*

The conditions anticipating Robinson Crusoe's appearance in 1719 had, of course, already been prepared in the previous century. In *The Politics of Motion* (1973), Spragens argues that for Hobbes, 'conceptual patterns and models developed to deal with natural phenomena became prisms through which he perceived human and political phenomena' (1973: 7; and see e.g. Brandt 1927).[13] Having become familiar with the intellectual field of mathematics and geometry, and been introduced to some of the leading practitioners – among them Galileo in Florence – Hobbes developed a systematic civil philosophy of reconciliation, embodied in the figure of his *Leviathan* (1651). Hobbes was designing a figure to overcome what he regarded as the fundamental predicament of mankind: man is by nature a solitary animal whose freedom is brought into collision with the freedom of others.[14] Hobbes's famous description of man in a state of nature approximates the predicament Defoe chooses for his hero, and provides a manifest of Crusoe's subsequent anxieties on the island, which – from the footprints and cannibal-meal bones he finds – evidently has occasional inhabitants, even if their use of the place amounted to little of consequence:

> In such condition, there is no place for industry; because the fruit thereof is uncertain: and consequently no culture of the earth; no navigation, nor use of the commodities that may be imported by sea; no commodious building; no instruments of building, and removing, such things as require much force; no knowledge of the face of the earth; no account of time; no arts; no letters; no society; and which is worst of all, continual fear, and danger of violent death; and the life of man, solitary, nasty, brutish, and short. (1946 [1651]: 82)

Motion plays a central role for Hobbes. Indeed, when illustrating the terms of the predicament of freedom, he draws on contemporary theories of motion – 'When a body is in motion, it moveth, unless something else hinder it, eternally' (1946: 9) – Hobbes might equally have used the words of Galileo:

> For if its motion is not contrary to nature, it seems that it should move perpetually; but if its motion is not according to nature, it seems that it should finally come to rest. (Drabkin 1960: 73)

Or the words of Newton's Axiom 1:

> Every body continues in its state of rest, or of uniform motion in a right line, unless it is compelled to change that state by forces impressed upon it. (Quoted in Dijksterhuis 1961: 466)

Hobbes found his resolution to the predicament in a contract by which 'A multitude of men, are made *one* person, when they are by one man represented; so that it be done with the consent of every one of that multitude in particular' (1946: 107). Composed in a moment when civil war was in the offing throughout England, the terms of Hobbes's design treated all men as equal (thereby affording a reconciliation of competing forces, such as feudal and bourgeois, abroad at the time), and symmetrical parts of the Leviathan: 'an artificial man; though of greater stature and strength than the natural, for whose protection and defence it was intended; and in which the *sovereignty* is an artificial *soul*, as giving life and motion to the whole body' (1946: 5).

The historian of science Freudenthal has analysed the 'mediated dependency of Newton's theory of space on social relations' (1986: 172), and identifies a 'specifically bourgeois conception of human freedom as the undetermined arbitrary will of an isolated Robinson Crusoe, which Newton shared' (ibid: 212), in order to describe the mutual influence of:

> Newton's assumption that essential properties would belong to a single particle upon the assumption of social philosophy that essential properties would be attributable to a single individual. (1986: 172)

Freudenthal demonstrates how the governance of motion became a central problem for both natural science and social philosophy.[15] Now, Newton's lasting achievement is to have reconciled, within a single explanatory calculus, the organising forces sustaining individual planetary motion around the central Sun with those forces drawing objects to the centre of the Earth. Newton's formulation of the mathematical terms for this 'natural contract', so to speak, was accompanied by a number of early attempts – notably by Locke and Hobbes – to formulate the rational terms of a 'social contract' for mankind whereby individual motion came under governance. Although these social theorists, and those following, begin from different premises, the notion of an instrument to reconcile opposed or contradictory forces is a common theme. These manifestations of the governance of motion – the motions of the heavens, the motions of machines, and the motions of social agents – served as intellectual resources to social theorists in the age of Newton grappling with the possibilities of emerging natural and social orders.[16] Dijksterhuis traces the historical development of this vision, concluding that:

> A mechanized world-picture is ... a conception according to which the physical universe is seen as a great machine, which, once it is set in motion,

by virtue of its construction performs the work for which it was called into existence. (Dijksterhuis 1961: 495 and see Mayr 1986) [17]

What I would add is that this mechanised world picture also informed a tradition of social thinking. Governance could be described in terms of the same capacities that were attributed to the momentum of machines. Rousseau's descriptions of the 'astonishing properties of the body politic by which it reconciles apparently contradictory operations' (1997: 117) are indicative:

> Now, since men cannot engender new forces, but only unite and direct those that exist, they are left with no other means of self-preservation than to form, by aggregation, a sum of forces that might prevail over those obstacles' resistance, to set them in motion by a single impetus, and make them act in concert. (1997: 49)

And this brings to mind another description of the Development Foundation, produced as an outcome of the Mine Continuation Agreement that was designed to keep the Ok Tedi mine running around the clock through to 2009:

> In the firm belief that only autonomous development can prove to be sustainable, the Foundation's principal purpose would be to lend support to the efforts that the communities and government themselves undertake to meet their basic needs up to the point where they are able to carry on the momentum on their own initiative. (Wissink 2000: 2)

Transactions in Perpetual Motion

Having been impressed by the Ok Tedi process of negotiating a novel *once-and-for-all* social contract designed to guarantee the continuous operation of the machine-system without added inputs of compensation, and struck by the way that machine-thinking was providing the metaphors by which the mining company fashioned a series of equivalences with the new organisational mechanisms, it seems all the more instructive to trace the social counterparts which have accompanied this genealogy of the mechanised world picture. The premises and ambitions of this long-running thought experiment were being acted out in these attempts towards the MCA to formulate a mechanism that would produce the continuous smooth operation of the Ok Tedi machine-system. The discussion has suggested that a nexus of individualist (Robinson Crusoe) and mechanical (perpetual motion) metaphors has an enduring charm for a social imaginary manifested in transactionalism and the Ok Tedi MCA.

A social agency with a particular history is at work in these mechanisms, which operate by reducing possible frictions amongst the parties through establishing a certain symmetry amongst the agents. These aspirations triggered the separating out of self-interest – as each move created an asymmetry, a further move redressed the symmetry. The mechanism here correlates with the designs Hobbes and Rousseau imagined for a means of guaranteeing individual motions and ensuring societal continuity respectively: in each case, there is a notion of trying to balance symmetrical elements (a fair contract for everyone) through a mechanism able to screen off what differentiates them – so BHP jettison an environmental and commercial liability, aid donors prefer independent Foundations, decisions are more easily reached with fewer disagree-ers, projects are more likely to succeed when they are judged on merits rather than social connections. In treating social agents as if they were undifferentiated in their symmetry (crassly put as 'globalized consumptive individuals'), and treating a social contract transaction as if it were the means and guarantor, such mechanisms find no place for the kinds of beliefs and interpersonal practices that the Papua New Guineans described above were aware differentiated them. A different age might have deduced an attempt to reproduce the celestial motions in the form of a perpetual motion machine. But in this millennial moment, the conceit of a 'win-win' scenario (the language holds the transacting agents in symmetry even if the 'wins' prove asymmetrical) could be projected out on a massive scale.

This is such an enchanting idea – of a mechanism that once set in motion is able to sustain its own momentum without further inputs of energy, and one that relies only on the conversion of contradictory forces into a product that is greater than the sum of its parts – this miraculous machine that produces and perpetuates social life.

Acknowledgements

In addition to doctoral work in 1994–96, and postdoctoral work in 1997, the field research for this chapter was carried out over three months in 1999, and seven months in 2000–1. I was based at Edinburgh University at the time, and enjoyed the support of the British Academy as a postdoctoral fellow, and the ESRC-funded PTC project as Research Associate. The paper was written once I had joined St Andrews University. Members of PTC provided invaluable stimulus and support, and the editors gave rare levels of encouragement. Versions of the paper were given in Edinburgh, New Orleans, Manchester, Oxford and Aberdeen and the paper benefited from the discussions on each occasion, as it did from Colin Filer's and Nigel Rapport's comments on an earlier draft. Many 'local tourists' and 'village ex-pats' from Bolivip, Wangbin and Tabubil made me feel at home, and amongst those to whom I owe my understanding are Paulus Banimeng, Martin Bongfakoyeng, Lawrence Christian, Alex Dalsep, Angella Dalsep, Ray Kisol Tamal, Ken Kongkalaneng, Leslie Mamnak, George Paulus, Dominicus Sulumeng, Cathy Tobias and Petro Warumasal. Amongst the collaborators on the 'Case Studies from the Ok Tedi Area' project, Tekela Waine, Libo Tatias and Bronya Kumulgo-Kain's work and assistance greatly helped my own research. Bronya and Bob Kain, and

Andrew and Colleen Nickson gave me friendship and hospitality when I needed it most. I am mindful of my debt to Boka Kondra. I am grateful to the OTML personnel who facilitated my research, most notably Martin Paining and Julie Moide, and to OTML for giving me what support they could afford up to the point where my interest in the West Ningerum Pressure Association case appeared to them politically motivated, and to be raising a difficult issue at a time they preferred to perceive as one in which 'there are no more stories about Ok Tedi'.

Notes

1. Rehearsing these issues as far as OTML was concerned, a workshop in July 1999 heard that:

   > These [indicators, aspirations] are worthy goals [...] A high level of success will leave Ok Tedi Mining in good stead, will enhance the reputation of its shareholders as responsible international corporate citizens [...] Outcomes such as these would in fact justify the decisions to develop Ok Tedi in the first place, and justify its life as a national project in PNG. [...] Conversely, significant failure to achieve these goals will leave the Ok Tedi project, and others like it by implication, exposed as inappropriate exploiters and fodder for a ready band of international critics and lawyers. (Ok Tedi Mining Ltd. 1999: 12)

2. The consultation process leading to the MCA aimed to inform communities living along the affected rivers about the predicted future mine impacts, about a World Bank recommendation that the mine be closed as soon as an alternative viable economic future could be ensured, and about the various options, which ranged from immediate closure to a planned closure in 2009. The rhetoric of the consultation process that followed was to allow Western Province villagers to decide the fate of the mine, which has long provided a significant contribution to PNG's gross domestic product and foreign exchange earnings, and which – the touted figures showed – had yet to release 69 percent of the potential total value of the twenty-five year project in the remaining eight years. In OTML circles, Mt. Fubilan ore-body was described as a 'cash cow', and a 'mountain of money'.
3. The photograph on which it is based appeared in Browne et al. (1983).
4. The issue here was to create the Foundation as an independent entity dealing solely with sustainable development issues, and although it would be the same OTML Community Relations department, the same staff and buildings, it was to be more than simply rebadging the staff and renaming their offices.
5. '[E]xternal groups such as NGOs and aid donors who might normally reject partnerships with OTML out of political correctness may find it easier to partner with the OTDF' (Wissink 2000: 8).
6. Perhaps it is no coincidence that around the same time that BHP's announcement posed the question of finding a balance once again, OTML began to engage the principles of 'sustainable development' which had grown over the previous five years, and held a workshop to agree a definition which posits 'a relationship between *current* and *future* generations'; 'requires an *institutional framework* for governance so that facilities and programs can persist; and 'assumes both *socio-economic* and *environmental* improvements, on-going after mine life' (OTML:1999, emphasis added).

The workshop was attended exclusively by OTML, BHP and GoPNG officers, and a handful of consultants and advisers. However, by the following month, '[t]he diverse group of people who gathered for the workshop [and who] were united in their concern' now curiously included 'the community'. Moreover, come November, they had also been joined by 'landowner representatives'!

7. The issue was evidently a preoccupation for the OTML delegation: the Lower Ok Tedi people were asked to form an Executive or Working Committee to make the negotiations more manageable, and to ensure for themselves that everyone was included and represented appropriately. These comments were directed towards a 'leader' (as the OTML delegation perceived him) who nonetheless repeatedly expressed his concern that he was unrealistically being taken as a representative.
8. 'It is envisaged that the OTDF would have a small board nominated by OTML, one or two Non-Government Organizations (NGOs) of high standing and a relevant government agency' (Wissink 2000: 5).
9. The Foundation's position outlined in December 2000 suggested that benefits would flow to all the communities in the wider Preferred Area (which encompasses many separate river drainages, including those over a mountain range in West Sepik Province). By February 2001, however, through a proposal to pull elements of mine equity, tax credit schemes and special support grants (some of which were 'for the benefit of the people of Western Province') over to the Foundation, the recipient area had narrowed to those who, living along the Ok Tedi and Fly Rivers, were signatories to the MCA. Increasingly identified with the flow of streams carrying the mine waste and pollution, it is as though the new 'benefit streams' were designed to deposit sustainable development in the places and to the extent that mine wastes had left deposits. Money released from the mine would flow into a new Foundation built with better holding capacities. The resulting allegory also imagined money covering the waste mud that covers the gardens – as if these were attempts to make up for the absent dam in a double manner.
10. In the same year, Rousseau also published *Émile*, in which he recommends *The Life and Strange Surprizing Adventures of Robinson Crusoe, of York* (1719) as 'the happiest introduction to natural education' for a growing boy, and in which 'all the needs of mankind are vividly displayed … and in which the means to supply these needs are presented' (in Rogers 1972: 52)
11. Rousseau first formulated the premises for his own social pact in the *'Geneva Manuscript'*:

    …let us conceive of mankind as a moral person having both a sentiment of common existence which endows it with individuality and constitutes it as one, and a universal motivation which makes every part act for the sake of an end related to the whole. Let us conceive of this common sentiment as that of humanity, and of the natural law as the active principle of the entire machine. (1997: 155)

12. In other words, it could *only* be operated by anyone – for example, the inspector's family and visitors – who has nothing else to look at and nothing else to do but look (Bentham 1791: 26).
13. Hobbes boldly introduces his mechanical analogies for the *Leviathan* at the very start:

    Nature, the art whereby God hath made and governs the world, is by the *art* of man, as in many other things, so in this also imitated, that it can make an artificial animal. For seeing life is but a motion of the limbs, the beginning whereof is in some principal part within; why may we not say, that all *automata* (engines that move themselves by springs and wheels as doth a watch) have an artificial life? For what is the *heart*, but a *spring*; and the *nerves*, but so many *strings*; and the *joints* but so many *wheels*, giving motion to the whole body, such as was intended by the artificer. *Art* goes yet further, imitating that rational and most excellent work of nature, *man*. (1946 [1651]: 5)

14. Oakeshott describes the dichotomy in the following terms: 'There is a radical conflict between the nature of man and the natural condition of mankind: what the one urges with the hope of achievement, the other makes impossible. Man is solitary; would that he were alone. For the sweetness of all he may come by through the efforts of others, is made bitter by the price he must pay for it. And it is neither sin nor depravity that creates the predicament; nature itself is the author of his ruin' (1946: xxxv).
15. Building on Freudenthal's work, Hadden (1994) suggests that the mechanical model was mutually constituted by parallel developments in the mathematical solutions provided to merchant traders for calculating the exchange value of various products:

    mathematical mechanics, received its calculable object from a group of mathematical practitioners whose initial concern was the reckoning up of value on behalf of mercantile interests that employed them. The calculation of value in the context of growing commodity exchange helped produce a particularly western mathematics; a concept of 'general magnitude' emerged which formalized the techniques of calculating 'incommensurables', a concept applicable thereafter to mechanics. Calculation of value of dissimilar commodities allowed the projection of similar techniques onto nature; observable phenomena were interpreted as resulting from the motion of bodies, motion which could be calculated as well in terms of the notion of general magnitude. (1994: xiv)

    Grossman (1987[1935]: 167–80) has argued that, as much as particular relations of production, any explanation must equally consider the example provided by particular types of machine – specifically, firearms, clockwork, lifting and water mechanisms.
16. One consequence of mechanical and labour specialisation, then, was a set of social relations whereby capabilities could be effectively isolated. In other words, they provided a mechanism for conceiving the division of persons and their capacities – both in terms of divisions between each other as autarchic individuals, and of activating (and de-activating) particular motions within a person. These new possibilities raised a set of appropriate social questions: how to make social equivalences between the conflicting freedoms of individuals, how to make political equivalences between members of society who occupied different productive roles, and how to make economic equivalences between the products of a manufacturing process.
17. The enduring influence of such a vision is evident in the long-standing and renewed interest in the origins of this worldpicture – analysts have variously argued that the epistemology was modelled on machines, modelled on pure ideas, modelled on exchange relations, modelled on physiology of the passions and sympathies, modelled on God's harmony, or modelled on the heavens.

Chapter 6

NEGOTIATING INTERESTS IN CULTURE

Karen Sykes

The Interesting Thing about Transactions …

In Chapter 4, Strathern proposes a departure for the study of the escalation of claims being made in cultural property by examining how practices unfold into each other. I am inspired by the possibility of understanding the wider processes at work in a world where money seems hard to find, where people innovate by drawing upon their relationships, and where conventionally recognised forms of private property, such as land, become liabilities when the moral claim to ownership turns on the person's ability to fulfil an obligation to develop it. Her search for a 'theoretical justification for looking askance at the international vocabulary of "collective rights"'[1] motivates my own interrogations of the concept of private interest.

My chapter will address itself to only one aspect of her analytical foray: the argument that culture and its values becomes 'the new commons' under current international regimes of deliberation over Cultural Heritage that emphasise the evolving, living character of tradition (Blake 2001). If culture is the new commons, then anthropologists need better understanding of the transactions through which people negotiate the work of 'enhousing' their traditions. Matter-of-fact efforts to 'enhouse', that is to make arrangements for the protection of the material forms of culture in museums, have been a matter of intense debate almost everywhere where indigenous peoples, their advocates, NGOs, and different levels of government make claims on one another for repatriation, or for enshrinement of their material culture. In such circumstances, the negotiations break down over different persons' claims on material culture, and threaten to stumble over each other, stopping the flow and reducing claims to matters of private interest. The circumstances of such debate suggest much for enhancing anthropological concerns with how people 'enhouse' culture more generally as a process of the materialisation of lifeways.

It is often assumed that individuals naturally hold interests; however, the odd thing regarding 'interest', which we might notice in most discussions of cultural property, must be the rapidity by which the interest appears as a material value in bids for ownership. Clifford (1997) captures a fine example of this in his description of Northwest Coast Museums as 'contact zones', in which reciprocity comes to be defined as asymmetrical commodity exchange between curators and indigenous artists. I would clear a space away from such tournaments of value (in which transactions determine the value of material forms as an escalating monetary value). Instead, I analyse 'interest' itself. This paper will discuss how private interest is constituted *as an effect of* negotiating the enhousement of material culture. In describing such negotiations I aim to illuminate processes that transform ontological (a concern with how to live meaningfully) to epistemological claims (a matter of how to express experience truly). This distinction between cultural processes can enable a fuller analysis of social change in Melanesia, to respond to what is felt widely and deeply by most people there.

I will address practices of revelation, as in the work of making a Malanggan display in New Ireland. Malanggan is renowned both for the beauty of its complex composite images and for the disturbing convention whereby makers destroy its form after display (Lewis 1969; Lincoln 1987; Derlon 1997; Forty and Küchler 1999; Küchler 2002). The sculptural form has since become an example in cultural property debates (Harvey et al. 1998).[2] Now the striking thing that comes to view when an anthropologist studies transactions in Malanggan must be the fact that processes that otherwise might be implicit, complex or mystifying come into visibility for the actors and fascinate them as versions of their own history, returning in feverish dreams, as the German ethnographer Kraemer reported (1925). Possibly too, anthropologists fascinate themselves by 'seeing' the concept of culture revealed in action, and thereby confirm their judicious interest in 'it' as the subject of ethnography while staking their own claim in 'its' description. When anthropologists analyse negotiations as transactions, it is as if people exposed themselves in much the same way that people reveal hidden ritual objects suddenly in places of public display. This description of negotiating interests can contribute to a better understanding of the substantivisation of human relations in an era that finds culture to be the new commons.

One kind of revelation brings interest into view through transactions as a process transforming relations into substantive forms. Such turns of understanding have been documented in the ethnography of the Min (Jorgensen 1990; Crook 1999), but bear out just as well with reference to the cognitive problems raised by the display of Malanggan ceremonies in New Ireland (Küchler 2002), where people told me that the after-images remain etched on the back of the eye, causing one to desire the opportunity to create the sculpture, yet again. Following the dynamics entailed in revealing the Malanggan sculpture, I would like to turn the world upside down in order to describe an example of the constitution of interest. Not an example of misattributions or a case of its mutual expression in the act of negotiation, rather this is a case where individuals come to believe that they possess interests. They come to this by seeing the result of their transactions with each other.

New Ireland ethnography, which I develop here, teaches that there is much to be risked by exposing the work of human transactions in material culture. As early as 1933, Hortense Powdermaker recorded the sadness of Notsi carvers that the Malanggan sculpture being taken away by collectors to European museums would fail to inspire museum visitors because 'they would not recognize the work' entailed in their manufacture (Powdermaker 1933: 276). There is much at risk in revealing social relations in material form; at most, the possibility that whoever sees that form might fail to recognizse its power and suffer malaise and injury as a result. This is aptly demonstrated in the angst expressed in the debate over the building of a local museum to house Malanggan sculptures on the Lelet Plateau, in central New Ireland. On the one hand, younger men concern themselves with revelation as an epistemological problem. They consider what forms of expression and communication of culture best share the experience of Malanggan with others who might visit. On the other hand, older men worry over the ontological dimensions of Malanggan's meanings through acting out their own place in respect of the different 'tourists', and the many categories of material culture known across the area.

Negotiating Interests/Enhousing Malanggan

A discussion of a negotiation at the village level in Papua New Guinea turns attention to what Papua New Guineans say about each other's interests in cultural expression and thereby helps to delimit the scope of the concept (interest). In this case, the differences exist between the interests of the senior and younger generations as they appeared in discussions about the constructions of a local museum.

People spoke of the plans to build the museum on the Lelet Plateau during my very first visit in 1990 to the five villages spotting the high series of valleys, but even by 1999 no museum or 'haus touris' had been erected. Their consternation that artefacts from the plateau should be properly housed arose at the time that national politicians planning the opening of new airport terminal in the New Ireland provincial capital of Kavieng proudly erected a series of carved house posts, embellished with the Malanggan images from carvers across the province. The politician who commissioned them failed to let the carvers properly negotiate the extended network of social relations sustaining the work. Making his plans in ignorance, he rushed the completion of the carvings. Some carvers refused the invitation to display their skills, expressing deep regard for the Malanggan ceremonies and the dangers of exposing, as public art, images on sculptures that should be viewed under restrictions. An insult against a senior man's dignity might be phrased as 'you've never seen a Malanggan', and the privilege of enjoying the Malanggan aesthetic remained as deeply embedded with the ethics of personal conduct as prohibitions on specific forms of sexual relationships. For many people the broadly public display suggested a failure to attend to the ethos of social relations across the province, rather than a prideful display of shared culture.

For those New Irelanders who welcomed changing times as much as they welcomed the manufacture and display of ritual sculpture as public art, there remained the disturbing recognition that by 1999 all of the carvers whose work created the posts at the terminal had died prematurely, unpleasantly and mysteriously. Commitees of Kavieng bureaucrats admitted their concerns, while advocating new plans for increasing tourism to the province. They wondered aloud whether the ancestral spirits had taken their due measure of respect with the deaths of the six master carvers. This unanswered question perplexed the people of the Lelet Plateau (as it did many New Irelanders) as they discussed the plans to build their own local museum. The high stakes could not be dismissed, yet the plans could not be dropped until the question of how to house the artefacts was resolved. Although everyone felt that something must be done to care for the objects, most people avoided the decision about building the museum until a better course of action appeared.[3]

Had New Irelanders finally put the past of Malanggan ceremonies behind them with the turn of the millennium and the final revelation of the Malanggans as public art in the provincial capital? In 2000 some excitement arose with anticipation of a visit from a group of eight Australian youths that precipitated new discussion and raised the levels of concern about the issues. A mini-coach would carry the young winners of the Duke of Edinburgh Award for personal excellence along the east coast highway of New Ireland Province to ascend the three-quarter-mile long road of hairpin turns up the 3,000 feet to the plateau in order to view 'sacred sites of the area'. The visit to the Lelet was an option, and residents feared that the youth would choose to disembark from the bus at Konos Station and travel by speedboat to Tabar Island, where they could see Malanggan carvers producing objects for tourist trade in Kavieng and abroad. If the Lelets wanted to draw the youth into a visit to the plateau, they needed the museum plan to be in order. They realised that it would take very little work to raise the traditional materials house, once the decision to build it had been made.

The discussion emerged more powerfully than ever and it seemed that the actual work of putting up walls soon would begin. But it never did. An intense debate developed over the location of the building, with the current Member of Local Level Government offering his garden land, a large plot on his own clan grounds, as the ideal site for a museum because it was easily accessed by tourists, with lovely views to the valleys below. The museum could not be so easily built on the Member's land as he had hoped because he needed to satisfy the largest part of the community that the site and its museum, known in the Tok Pisin of the area as a Haus Touris, would belong to all of residents of the plateau. Given that the region provided the means for a livelihood for about 1,000 people, from which they needed to prepare ceremonial feasts as a major event of the year and for smaller market-garden projects grown on the old gardens, this undertaking demanded a great deal of expertise in negotiation and persuasion.

From amongst the men two interest groups emerged, giving the debate two sides, each distinguished from the other by their ages as elder and junior men. Keeping a list of who belonged with which collective would not make an accurate record of the composition of the groups. Indeed, the Member, a distinguished 45-year-old retiree from the Papua New Guinean Defence Force, identified himself with the shared interests of the younger men. Customarily, he found himself drawn towards the younger generation's concern for the well-being of the community at large. The younger group made clear that the museum should house the wealth of the plateau that belonged to everybody, and not just the prize items of one clan, also a sensible position for the Member of Local Level Government to hold. Nonetheless, on alternative days and occasions he joined his voice to the concerns of the elder men, who argued that only one clan had the right to host or manage the museum. The elders expressed concern that the younger men would become lackadaisical in their custodial work and defame the objects by not caring for them. Could a museum that did not attend to the peculiar needs of the objects displayed also house properly such marvellous things as Malanggans?

The public display of the intricacies of the famous carvings of the region raised concerns and widened eyes across the region. Simply at the thought of revealing these objects (which senior men normally controlled display and access to when they appeared at a feast) changed everyone's appreciation of the enormity of the events that were about to unfold. An apt comparison drawn with the carvings on public display in the terminal at Kavieng Airport suggested a warning. Those carvers who had put their skills to the test in the creation of several pieces of public art in 1992 died mysteriously. If the ancestors had their due from specific clans with the untimely deaths of the delinquent carvers who had worked for money in Kavieng, the problem of the exposed features and images would not be easily forgotten. Some argued that the problems associated with the display of Malanggan objects no longer held sway over the decisions of the moment. All the secrets were known and the images visible. Some elders argued that the great Malanggan tradition had ended, so it became possible to display the masks and carvings as they wished.

It became increasingly clear to me that the membership of each interest group and the identities of the individuals making the arguments mattered less than the kinds of arguments being made about how to manage the display. Each group articulated alternative perspectives on the possibility of opening a museum of artefacts and carvings. The elder group expressed the point of view that the museum should be managed by one of the clans of the region. Their work, on behalf of everyone, would be to display material appropriately for visitors to see, and for local residents to view as well. The younger group expressed the point of view in favour of meeting the community's interests in creating a Malanggan display. These junior men sought to recreate the experience of awe at seeing a Malanggan for the first time, as if viewing it in a feast. The museum they sought to build would express their sense of the occasion.

The difference created between them exposed alternative versions of interest in the Malanggan. The older men, voicing the perspective of the clan, created degrees of exclusion from viewing the display. The museum house would be constructed as a series of rooms, each one secluding a more restrictive category of Malanggan carving than the last. In the front room, the most accessible forms of carvings might be shown. Dance masks should be found here, where women might see them. In the next row of rooms, it would be possible to see Malanggans of specific clans, those restricted to viewing by clanspersons with privileges to see specific forms. In a deeper row of rooms the museum would display the objects that only elderly men might view, as befitting their years of apprenticeship in the arts.

In sum, the museum was meant to contain, or hide, Malanggan carvings. It did not display and expose them. Members of some clans were not permitted to enter specific rooms. Women were excluded from viewing most of the exhibit. Younger men were chosen to see some items according to the immediate concerns of the time. Along with the different categories of exclusion from viewing the Malanggan sculptures, there emerged fee schedules to emphasise the points of distinction.[4] Admission for women was higher than for men. Even the first room would cost women a full kina (PNG currency) more than men. In turn, each of the subsequent rooms implied a 'second' fee schedule for those who might not normally view the sculptures therein contained. Setting out fees became a complicated proposal. Over and over again, new fee schedules and new degrees of exclusion were created as the rest of the village entertained the improbability of linking a financial value to the new classifications of the esoteric and sacred. Indeed, the improbability of working out a coherent system of fees became something of a joke, a joke to be told by many people over subsequent months. Even men who one day most seriously committed themselves to the construction of such a maze of chambers found on the following day that the peculiar circumstances amused them, as they smiled at their own predicament.

A cathartic moment arrived to relieve the stress of trying to classify Malanggans and mark the degrees of the sacred with a price of admission. After weeks of recounting various fee schedules, using euphemisms for gender by reference to bodily habits and for age by referring to white hair, a younger man made a new proposal to charge hairless men differently from all the rest![5] Each time the joke was repeated men as well as women would double with laughter. The bald truth exposed, classifications of degrees of sacredness really did not seem very interesting or valuable to the majority of the villagers. The elders' proposal for a museum displaying and categorising sacred objects no longer made sense. Or, did it?

The debate opened a space for a different proposal to be heard, one that was made in the interests of the community rather than the clan. The museum no longer appeared a labyrinthine structure to measure financial and sacred values of specific objects in relation to others. Instead, the younger men planned to display row after row of Malanggan carvings from the rafters of the museum, to create a stunning effect that would cause the visitor to turn away in fear, awe and rapture. This would show the power of the Malanggans' meaning to anyone who visited. Its potency could endure by demonstration.[6]

The admission fee for such a viewing would be 20 kina for each person, regardless of age, gender or hair. It was thought that upon paying the fee the person would enter the house and look up into the rafters. Some people might feel deep terror while others would experience awe. If the visitors felt overwhelmed by the material forms of their own ethnicity, they might leave immediately. Having left once, the person should pay another 20 kina for re-entry. It was agreed that a person might enter as many times as desired, if the full fee was paid upon each entry. The effect of the Malanggan upon the people made the sculpture meaningful. Its classification with other Malanggans had no bearing on its effect and was not a significant part of the museum display.

The calculus of the elders and the passionate attention of the juniors each help define the analytical notion of interest. The interest they define is not a natural capacity of persons limited by their psyche, but it does come into discussion and shared consciousness of people in moments of intense consternation or when overwhelmed by extreme emotional anxiety. Interest does not well up in the person as their individual response, so much as it is the ontological ground which can be rapidly bared for adjudication in relationships between artists, performers, and visitors to the display. However, interests held by diverse persons need not be symmetrical. Notably, the debate exposes radically different grounds *for the determination* of interest. From the perspective of the elders, interest differentiates peoples in a series of formal associations that determine the relational significance of the art object. From the perspective of the youth, interest overwhelms the person, filling their senses and causing awe. In part, that awe includes the fear that the result of the experience should bring a tragic end for some, as it had for the Malanggan carvers of Kavieng Airport Terminal. In part, that awe includes the fascination that marks Malanggan as a distinctive art object that brings about an epiphany, and so is considered worthy to be known as cultural property.

The cross-generational debate shows that different concepts of interest in culture emerge as alternative perspectives in the negotiation. Youth considered the lessons learnt from the older men, whose public display of carvings at the Kavieng Airport Terminal cost them their lives. They tried to incorporate the elders' concerns with the appropriate display of sculpture by building a local museum to manage the viewing of the carvings, rather than display them without restriction in the provincial capital. Youths' advocacy of the community's claims on property expresses a perspective on claims to ownership that highlights meaning in the sensual. Here experience of expressive culture is meaningful; it makes sense because it creates an epiphany, as a moment of revelation, or the 'aha' of culture in shared acumen.

Differently, the elders' advocacy of the clan's claims on property expresses a perspective on claims to ownership that highlights possession in relation to other claims on that form of cultural expression. Here the experience of possessive culture is meaningful because it can be claimed to differ from others' experience of their own forms; for example, the form is valuable to one clan because it evokes meanings that cannot be understood by any other clan. The interest of the clan is distinguished as different from all the rest, and their concerns negotiated on the basis of this essential understanding. The sacred becomes a category, emerging with the elders' perspective that clan interests must select cultural forms to protect.

Negotiating Intergenerational Interests

Contemporary analyses of cultural property debates often assume that disputes arise over the sense of loss experienced by elders through failures of intergenerational transmission over generations. This mistake burdens local groups to prove the transmission of cultural knowledge over the generations, a problem that has moved participants in the dispute to essentialise that knowledge or prove that it is sacred.[7] Debates across the generations on Lelet point to elder and younger men of the same community differentiating themselves on the matter of precisely how to derive meaning from cultural knowledge. Such internal differentiation presents different challenges to the understanding of the making of tradition, but it remains an important part of the explanation as to why people feel their traditions are meaningful. One of the most difficult locations from which to assess the status of interest in claims to cultural knowledge has been from the perspective of contesting intergenerational relations that are internal to group dynamics, such as the Lelet debates suggest. Lelet people merge what they know about their cultural heritage with how they make cultural innovations in their relationships.

Referring to the neighbouring Mandak culture more generally, Clay's analysis of knowledge in *Mandak Realities* (1986) shows that it is the cultural practice that should receive the anthropologist's attention rather than the transmission of knowledge. This will aid the anthropologist in the aim to clarify how culture works innovatively within relations and thereby avoid initiating a study in the terms that a legal analysis (say) might already presume: that culture is a thing in which people have interests. In the main point, this slippage of culture as the way in which people make their lives meaningful into cultural property as the knowledge transmitted from one generation to the next, typifies the larger problem of explaining the substantification of social relations into specific interests apportioned, identified and named as property.

A closer look at intergenerational knowledge practices themselves challenges the familiar rubric that finds indigenous interests in culture legitimated by an account of seamless transmission of knowledge over generations.[8] Intergenerational differentiations present problems for Gell's theorising of tradition as a living thing (Gell 1998). Firstly the conditions in which traditions are formed in Gell's world-wide examples all share the common feature of being the manifestations of efforts made in competition with others, from the struggle to win Kula prestige, through the effort to distinguish an artistic style that marks an oeuvre to the construction of meeting houses of such grandeur that the enemy is overwhelmed by the display. Rejecting attempts to reduce art to interpretations of the form's meanings, Gell explains the artist's intention to engage and overwhelm the viewer or receiver of the expressive cultural forms. For example, a Kula trader expresses his intention to enter into exchange by offering a small beautiful gift suggesting potential fame. Secondly, Gell's examples recover the artist's intention to a discussion of the inventiveness of 'tradition', thereby extending his argument beyond individual artists to include collective works. Thus he examines the Maori debating traditions that build the meeting houses and comprise the work within them, thereby posing the possibility that such enhousement illuminates 'cognitive processes writ large' (Gell 1998: 258).

In reconsidering Gell's assumptions about the habits of intergenerational transmission of knowledge, I would add that he comes close to finding the way in which the nexus of relations fabricates social knowledge ready for a Leviathan, as the constitution of society. Although he does not discuss it directly, Gell seems to be inspired to model society as it is constituted through negotiations in the meeting house. It is a kind of Hobbesian contract made in the belly of Leviathan, a monster that would impress collective will as tradition upon those individuals contained in society and strike guests or enemies of that society with its grandeur and power, and I return to the idea.

Current developments across the generations on Lelet can be better understood if anthropologists displace the common assumption that culture is passed on down the generations as a legacy or a precious heirloom. The habit of thinking about culture as knowledge to be transmitted (that is, a thing or form that can be given through time), depends upon a specific construction of thought that finds itself to be embedded in the Euro-American belief that knowledge is inheritable.

Following Wagner's (1975) assertion that culture is a creative process, it is possible to understand how social change might be analysed as a process internal to the relationships made through the generations. The focus for that learning must challenge common assumptions about inheritability of culture across generations. One instructive location for much of this has been the work of Bateson (1958). His earlier efforts to explain the

Naven ceremony amongst the Iatmul of the Sepik region later generated a theory of schismogenesis: a kind of learning through the juxtaposition of symmetrical or of complementary social forms, such as elder and junior setting out resonant symmetries of difference or male and female foregrounding complementary mirrors of each other's behaviour. As a form of acculturation, schismogenesis can proceed through profound arts of understatement or overstatement. Under the right circumstances, it is the beginning of differentiation that can swing into motion as internally generated social change.

Understanding social change then takes on new dimensions, if it is approached as a problem confronted by people from within the intergenerational relationship of youth and elders. Rather than uncritically assess generational shifts as they occur because the youth have lost or forgotten what the elders once knew, a better model of differentiation understands that dramatic changes across the generations might be a feature of planned and expected acculturation processes, whereby the young learn to become the elders by initially making themselves different from them. Recognising this possibility enables Bateson (1972) to make a later observation that social change begins with the acknowledgement of difference, the process of differentiation, and the recognition of alternative points of view in thoroughly conventional forms. In addition, Bateson's concept of schismogenesis helps us to see that how people come to understand their lives and how social change comes about are deeply entwined processes. Questions about making claims in culture becomes less a matter of how to protect culture against historical contingencies, and more an issue of how people work to make their lives meaningful.

Interests and Property

Such debates over cultural property in Papua New Guinea as the one that occurred on the Lelet Plateau raise significant issues in the anthropology of knowledge that also reflect critically on the legacy of theorising about political and economic life. In the light of this, my focus on 'interest', for orders of relations conceived differently by elders and youth, should not surprise anyone familiar with the history of property debates in Western political economy since Hobbes first theorised the problematic relationship between knowledge, the social contract and property in *Leviathan* (1968 [1651]). If as a matter of epistemological concern Hobbes discussed knowledge and interests adroitly as a crisis of Enlightenment,[9] then Melanesians just as ably debate the ontological terms of intellectual property issues as a crisis over how humans might live meaningfully. The debate on the Lelet in Papua New Guinea requires a researcher to make distinctions as Hobbes did: between form and substance, between categorical knowledge and common sense, between creative inventive expression and conventional routine existence.

Hobbes begins the *Leviathan*, which was to become a major text in political economy, with the question of what he can know as a means of elaborating a picture of 'the nature of man'. After this introspective first section, the famous text lays out the earliest statement of a method of rational inquiry for the social sciences before outlining the groundwork of the modern social contract. This consummation of rational enquiry (enlightenment science) draws comment. Historians of science recognise the inseparability of Hobbes's 'social science' from his political thought (Shapin and Scheffer 1985). In similar light, Sahlins (1995), in urging his reader to compare Hobbes with Sigmund Freud in his book *Civilization and its Discontents* (Freud 1930), points to the later theorists' utilisation of Hobbes's work on interest as if it were the same as desire. His point echoes Shapin and Schaffer's (1985) observation that methods of enquiry are often entwined with the contemporary political theory of its day. But, more than an account of the shifting meanings of interest over time, Sahlins shows his reader that Freud shifts Hobbes's early modern ruminations about the epistemological basis of the distinction between the material and the immaterial forms of social life, to a high modern concern with the repression of the passions as necessary to the creation of civilisation. The anthropologist following Sahlins's suggestion finds out that Hobbes and Freud differ on their understanding of the relationship between human desires and social conventions of association. Hobbes marks them as levels or stages of knowledge in which conventions of rational thought moderate human desires to the end of creating a good life in society, while Freud sees moderation as the repression of creative power with the potential of enchaining personal knowledge to social conventions.

Interest holds different 'sense' in either of these two accounts. Consider the first 200 pages of *Leviathan*, in which Hobbes writes of human nature in his analysis of Man, beginning his meditations on the knowledge that comes by way of the senses. He begins with the nature of human wants and desires, and thereby generates a hierarchy of concepts until the end point, at which he persuasively argues that human reason must triumph over the passions in the negotiation of the social contract. 'Interests' hold a key role in the machinery of the Leviathan, perhaps oiling its action. The expression of an individual's wants and desires as 'interests' moderates those desires into more conventional requests and expectations. This is because desires expressed as interests must take account of another's interests. Negotiation of interests is a central concept of the social contract amongst individuals with different wishes or desires.

Hobbes, writing in the early modern era defines interests as the public expression of the person's wants and desires, which is not transparent in its meaning to me as a reader in a late modern period. Many have elaborated upon this. The social historian Hill (1972) described the ways in which different political and religious groups in the late seventeenth century protested about the abuses of 'self-interest' in the uses of the open ground of the commons. The Levellers and the Diggers each openly and consciously discussed the passions as the motivating force of their respective political movements for property rights in Hobbes's day. Further, Hill acknowledges some of their reciprocal influences with Hobbes's thought. The political theorist Macpherson (1962) elaborated the ideas of a political elite contemporary with Hobbes: in his model the possessive individual is one who is proprietor of the self. A later intellectual historian, Hirschman (1977), showed us that Hobbes's considerations of the link between passions and interests continued to vex the reasoning of the authors of subsequent theorists of capital. Hirschman's book outlines the different attempts to uncover how interest alternatively contained or counted the passions, and by the modern period harnessed and tamed passions to the social good.

One of the oldest critiques of capital focuses on the need to harness the passions against the destruction of society. Locke opened his own discussion of property by reference to human understanding, focusing on interest as it was expressed in rights to the commonwealth, rather than in claims on it. For Locke, the legacy of the concept of interest in political economic theory has been felt as a legal concern, title right or a pecuniary stake. The elaboration of the legal concerns begins what Tully has called *A Discourse on Property* (1980), which positions shared legal interests against individual economic avarice. Tully addressed the absence of any discussion of the concept of 'rights' in Hobbes, illuminating its importance distinct as from interests. Indeed, Tully's revision of Macpherson's thesis argues that the notion of rights emerges distinct from the concept of passions only in Locke's day. In the balance, these theorists of political economy agree that interest belonged to the individual as the capacity to engage with the world, making the social contract the cornerstone of human association.

Other theorists using the (concept) interest after Freud understand differently from their predecessors its work in social relations. It has been variously defined as 'libidinal' or 'invested' by Bourdieu, whose practice theory sought to explain the non-conscious reproduction of belief and structures in society despite the best intentions to alter them into a more heterodox account (Bourdieu 1977a, 1997b). Bourdieu foregoes any attempt to recover Hobbes's pre-Freudian notion for a post-Freudian community of scholars, and thereby sharpens his theory of practice to the difference between desires and interests. Personal desires simply are social interests in such a formulation.

I think that Sahlins approached the scope of the problem of understanding political life somewhat better than Bourdieu when he expanded the definition of interest to include Saussure's (1983) use of the concept of interest in his linguistic theory of meaningful communication. He recognised that a theory of practice also must be a theory of communication, rather than a mute enactment of conventional understandings. Sahlins's marriage of Bourdieu and Saussure makes it possible to consider a theory of meaning beginning from interest as the difference made by expression. Meaning lies in the transformation of values (Sahlins 1981: 241).

By recognising the difference made by the event as significant, the meaning of the transactions can be foretold.

One of the disciplinary points of reference for theories of social change through knowledge transmission has been Saussurean linguistics, upon which Sahlins built his model of change as failed social reproduction. He uses the Pacific (Polynesian) example of Tabu, a cultural practice of prohibition upon specific forms of social relations turned into legal provisions or even codified law, as in the posting of Tabu as a warning against the dangers of trespassing on land kept out of the reach of the common interest. How shifts of meaning that govern specific kinds of relationships (that is, practices of avoidance in some kin relations) become restated as claims about property relations should intrigue any ethnographer, but the theory leaves us gasping for air.

In the last pages of *Historical Metaphors and Mythical Realities* (1981), Sahlins outlines the Saussurean theory of linguistic shift as if it might apply for the analysis of social differentiation. Sahlins's leap of faith is possible because it is rooted in language and sensuality as if they were coterminous practices of meaning making. Saussure's reasoning that language's ability to make meaning by training the human ear to the shifts of different sounds into recognisable patterns is well documented as the relationship between sign, signifier and signified. Attention is given to displacements of conventional forms of that configuration; hence linguistic change can then be marked as the human activity of assimilating historical contingency – the changing world around people – to the configurations by which they make logical sense of experience. Sahlins proposes that it should be applicable to social relations themselves.

The linchpin of his discussion remains the concept of interest, a notion that belongs to the domain of Euro-American common knowledge. Sahlins recalls interest from the Latin for 'it makes a difference', and suggests interest bears a role for human agency in the generation of meaning when event (as historical processes to which people give their interests) alters social structure. The event in Sahlins's reasoning causes a redigitisation of references that conventionally exist between words and meanings. That happens because the symbolic referent always has been free-floating; in Sahlins's theory of social change just as in Saussure's theory there is no inherent link between the sign and the signifier. Following Sahlins's innovation, Graeber (2001) shows his reader how Saussure's examples of the five-franc coin link linguistic theory with the uses of standardised currency in market economy and parallel each other. The power of Saussure's five-franc coin lies in the potential it bears to purchase a wide range of items, not in its reference to a specific purchase. What neither Graeber nor Sahlins points out is that in Saussure's theory, as in Sahlins's own, that potential makes a mystique of interest into something like an economy of meaning. The tension in this concept of interest in the theory of social change advocated by Sahlins might be elaborated to argue that the knowledge practices that express legitimate interest differ from those that express avarice.

The evidence of limits to Sahlins's theory emerges throughout the last decade. It seemed a truism when Sahlins (1999) told anthropologists that just when they thought the culture concept had exhausted its use, people in the postcolonial world invigorated the term with new meaning; but not in ways that Sahlins anticipated. A particular forum for that revitalizsation of 'culture' emerged in the last decade with new discussions of cultural rights in the uses of the environment, and concomitant with that claims to Traditional Knowledge as a new form of property. While Sahlins understood this globally dispersed phenomenon to be indicative of a ground swell of interest in shared cultural heritage, he had less fully theorised the circumstances in which specific hopes came to be expressed.

Wagner's (1975) argument in *The Invention of Culture* makes it possible to say that all debates about cultural property come to look the same because culture itself is a 'cargo cult'. The machinery of Western history remains perpetual because it gives priority to the productive capacity or potential of nature when harnessed to social machinery, as shown in the preceding chapter (see too, Wagner 1986). The caveat drawn from Wagner's most recent proposal for the *Anthropology of the Subject* (2001) recalls the earliest inspirations to a social science as it creates epistemological puzzles, parrying meaning as the knowledge of the sense of experience with the ways in which that experience is shared with other people, and including the recounting of experience in meaningful communication. Wagner's simple and provocative directive, 'A theory of meaning must make sense', remains a helpful compass in the measure of the various uses of the concept of interest as the common point of social negotiations.

I have been concerned to show how 'interest' sits close to a theory of meaning, but is not coterminous with it, thus challenging Sahlins's proposal for a theory of meaning terminally grounded in interest. Sahlins can show how any theory that begins with 'interest' cannibalises meaningful action and speech, yet after this explanation, the larger project of developing a theory of meaningful communication remains. In that larger project I take Wagner's lead and search for a perspective on that process. I argue that subscribing to a theory of interest as meaningful communication makes it necessary to search for a critical perspective on that process; that is, a critical perspective that creates meaning.

Conclusions

Researchers can point to the WTO and WIPO as instruments of the process of globalisation without assessing the nature of the flow through those engines of change, thereby hiding from view the diversity of experience that machinery seeks to cannibalise. In this chapter I have been concerned to show the various ways in which a complex negotiation of 'interest' is mistaken for a claim on culture.[10] A similar point can be made for property. Under the rubric of 'negotiating interests' all exchanges in property appear to be the same, from Adam Smith's discussions of human nature in market transactions to present-day accounts of privatisation as a global economic practice. Here, I critique this long-held rubric that assumes human nature must be enchained productively under legal protections if it is to be protected at all. I argue that anthropological analysis of cultural property debates complicates understandings of interest, creating the need for fuller appreciations of cultural diversity.

Interest has been variously understood as libidinal (Bourdieu), a public expression of personal desires (Hobbesian), a legal concern, title right, or a pecuniary stake (Lockean) or a theory of meaning in the transformation of values that recognises the difference made by the event of the negotiation as significant (Sahlins). An anthropologist choosing to analyse such transactions as the communicative, meaningful domain of interpersonal exchange finds it is possible to assess the effects of global flows and movements in people's life worlds, showing how the loss of meaning is concomitant with the naturalisation of interest in negotiations of the claims to ownership. By de-seating the concept of 'interest' from the individual person to the transactions that make meaning, it is possible to break past an impasse in cultural property debates. It becomes clear that processes of negotiation do not express, rather they make, interests.

A better analysis of the negotiation of interest exposes the processes of naturalisation, creating the grounds by which expression comes to make sense. Wagner argues that confusions in negotiations of interests in culture emerge because people believe meaningful communication must also make sense. He points out that often human nature gains sway over the governance of the meaningful grounds of interaction because 'most of what happens in what we call communication or relating happens too quickly, demands too immediate a response to have any correspondence with any descriptions that might be made of its meaning' (2001: 8).

Another negotiation, internal to the Melanesian village, expressing alternative perspectives across the generations, shows very different ways in which interest can appear as the effect of the negotiation. The elders' perspective approximated a kind of categorical understanding for different degrees of interest, even suggesting the creation of the sacred as a category of understanding amongst a select few people. The elders' knowledge rests on who they are in relationship to the display of the carvings in the local museum, emulating the ritual display of Malanggan. Hence, the arrangements of the sculptures will also enact the presence of the elders as in ritual, including the varying schedules of fees that confirm the elders' control over the categories of their organisation. They do not require the use of the term 'culture' to convey claims to possess such categorical, ritual knowledge.

By contrast, the youth's concern to preserve culture approached something like a sensual interest in culture, suggesting that expressive culture could be almost a 'funhouse' experience for an undifferentiated group of people. The youth pursue the museum project with concern to make an appropriate sculpture display. Although their exhibition would convey emotion, the point is that their efforts would be directed towards a means of communication; that is, to make the audience know through the skill they have put into creating the atmosphere. In the process, they make culture meaningful for themselves and for others because it is precisely about a means of gaining knowledge – and, like the anthropologist, they view culture as capable of 'expression'.

The project flounders because in the elders' eyes cultural preservation remains unnecessary and may even be a dangerously excessive form of Malanggan display, considering the death of the master carvers after the incautious display of their skills for the good of the wider community. Both elders and youth respond emotionally to this, with anxiety and trepidation. For the elders, the ritual enactment of the Malanggan suffices and cultural preservation remains unnecessary. For the youth, the meaning of Malanggan remains bound up, not in selective access to images and skills, but in processes of conveying emotional meaning of culture for undifferentiated groups. At the time, as they acknowledge their mutually constituted identities across intergenerational relations, both youth and elders become aware of their mutual losses: of the potential of authentic expression in the Malanggan arts, and of the possibility of meaningful participation in the Malanggan rituals. It is as if losing the master carvers precipitates actually having interests in Malanggan, as a matter of an essential connection through those elderly men to material cultural forms.

On the Lelet Plateau, in central New Ireland, it is possible to suggest that the emergence of private property also entails the enhousement or enclosure of culture as the new commons. That interest should become a private matter (and not simply personal) comes about as a result of the sense that personal concerns with meaningful existence and expression must be kept as a private affair in either ritual or in sensual experience. Consideration for culture as the new commons emerges out of concern for protecting the well-being of either the elder or junior generations as their 'interests' in it. These correlative and concurrent processes link the emergence of private interests in property to the growing awareness of culture as the new commons.

Notes

1. Chapter 4 sheds doubts upon the habitual recreation of the relations of the social contract in order to protect rights in property, even where individual claims to ownership might not be articulated.
2. For a provocative analysis of Malanggan manufacture as a kind of body outside of the human body and the new questions this would pose for thinking about patents, see Strathern (2001).
3. By tradition, Malanggan makers destroyed the artefacts at the end of feasts. This no longer pertains to all Malanggan carvings, some of which find their way into the tourist trade. The makers of the posts carved for the Kavieng Airport debated their work for a long time, bearing deep concern that they would destroy their traditions by making the display. Finally they chose to display them as artefacts, rather than risk the art form to dying memory.

4. New Irelanders practised the custom of paying to see a Malanggan as part of the funeral ceremony. In mortuary ritual, giving a partial strand of *mis* shells (or money as in contemporary rituals) shows respect to the hosts who risked displaying it to the participants in the feast, and shows the viewer how he might one day plan to host a feast, support a Malanggan carver to come for the preparations, and create the same Malanggan just viewed. As an adaptation of an old practice to new purposes, the payments for the viewing of the Malanggans within the haus touris showed respect for the display, but did not confer any rights.
5. Very few New Irelanders lack hair on their head, and the joke of calling an individual hairless generally evokes good-humoured repartee.
6. And in terms the visitors would understand.
7. See Weiner (1998) for a full discussion of how disputes about cultural property make culture esoteric whereas before the litigation it was not.
8. Cf. Gunn (1987) who tells us of the passing of the lifetime of a generation in the thirty years between first receiving, and then using the Malanggan technologies.
9. Historians generally agree that the intellectual and social revolutions of the Enlightenment did not originate from one nation; rather they began at different times in different places across Europe.
10. And, echoing the concerns of Hayden (n.d.), who points to the way in which all negotiators must presume one another to have interests.

Part III

Creations

Chapter 7

MODES OF CREATIVITY

James Leach

Introduction

Commenting on the current valuation of creativity, Carey Young has written: 'business worth is increasingly evaluated on the proven capacity to innovate. If a business is unable to invent new products and services it will not be seen as competitive. Whatever the economic climate, the endeavour to think and act creatively now runs close to the core of capitalist enterprise' (Young 2002: 7). In its turn, the (UK) Council for Science and Technology tells us that 'successful economies depend increasingly on the creation, communication, understanding and use of ideas and images' (2001: 1). As with business, so with culture.

People across the world express growing interest in protecting or transacting intellectual and cultural productions.[1] It is clear that there is an assumption of creativity written into attempts to protect cultural property, as well as other kinds of intellectual property (IP).[2] Yet amidst these developments, there is little specific anthropological understanding of the modes in which 'creativity' operates.[3] Most discussions of the concept creativity in anthropology are attempts to contest received notions and/or to define it in a way that has cross-cultural relevance (Ingold 1986; Liep et al. 2001). I wish to suggest the possibility that there are different modes in which creativity operates, that creativity is specifically understood and instantiated in different places, and that these differences have consequences in terms of economy and social relations.[4] Creativity is an explicit focus of Euro-American discourse in the realm of art and, increasingly, of business.[5] Intellectual property attribution is apparently vital to both. But art and business do not distinguish modes. We could use either to ask how Euro-Americans think that establishing the conditions for creativity will have an effect.

It might be argued that creativity, as an explicit description of action, is only of interest to Euro-Americans (see Liep 2001). However, with the spread of international intellectual property regimes, this can no longer be the case. Creativity is now a global value and as a Euro-American concept is already apparent in the way international institutions, and indeed anthropologists, approach places such as Papua New Guinea. One of PTC's aims was to capitalise on work already done in Melanesia. Here, I utilise a perspective, understood through a particular case, which crystallises much of what we know from the literature to comment upon the unfamiliar terrain (for anthropologists) of IP and creativity.

I set out to demonstrate that a dominant Euro-American rhetoric points to a modelling of combinations based on appropriation. One could call it an 'appropriative mode' which has creativity as its adjunct. But the thrust of current discussion which implies that this is the only mode of creativity is simply not true. Counter-examples of creativity abound. Some hit Euro-Americans from elsewhere, some from practices with which many are familiar. What prevents Euro-Americans from seeing other forms is their division between persons and things. The procreation of persons is generally excluded from creating and appropriating things. This then gives us at least two modes from the outset.

It is my argument that one can find a mode of what we can rightly call creativity in Melanesia that at one and the same time contains familiar elements, and yet relies upon different premises. By uncovering these specificities, I look to highlight how the concept of intellectual property is embedded in a matrix of Euro-American thinking, in suppositions about being and doing, subjects and objects, agency and personhood.[6] These are thrown into relief by comparison with Melanesia. Given that there has been little written in anthropology directly on creativity,[7] the themes that I select to focus upon have to be of interest both in Melanesia and in Euro-America. The way I set out to delineate intellectual property is given by what I will say about the Melanesian material.

Comparing modes of creativity as modes of action demands a working definition of creativity. The aim at this point is to find a conceptualisation wide enough to move between contexts, comparing processes and the conceptual worlds they engender. My definition is a distillation of the main ways creativity has been recognised, specifically in anthropological writings,[8] but also more generally (see Arieti 1976; Ingold 1986). For the purposes of this chapter, let us take creativity as consisting of three major elements. The first is combination – creativity can be recognised where combinations of things or ideas are apparent. The second is that this process of combination is directed by a will or intent. The third is novelty of form or outcome.[9]

If we take this definition we can 'see' creativity on the part of Papua New Guineans. It sets up a comparative frame. But that leads the investigator into considering a set of ground rules and conditions which could never have produced the ideas of property in creations, let alone intellectual property, found in Euro-American imaginings.[10] I start with the third of my elements: innovation.

Contemporary Creativity 1

There has recently been a public reiteration in Britain that creativity lies in the ability to combine elements drawn from many sources. The UK government currently seeks secondary and higher education policies which encourage a diverse knowledge base explicitly to encourage innovation. Narrow specialisation is not the way forward, rather a wide range of subjects should be taught to each child right up to university level (UK Government/DfES 2002). Creativity can be contrived in the population by forcing combination upon it. Indeed, the development of science and technology is imagined to lie in combining the 'imagination and understanding' of the arts and humanities with the specific information bases of science.[11] There is a more or less explicit motivation in all this: economic regeneration, growth in the national economy and 'self-fulfilment' for society's members. Fostering the capacity for creativity in education will create the conditions under which business will flourish. In other words, creativity has an objectified instantiation that generates wealth. 'In our ever changing world, one quality will be valued above all others: *creativity*. Our children, as no generation before, will need to think outside the norm, to be able to use their *imagination* and to *innovate*' (Coxon 2001: 34).

British society itself may be judged on its success in fostering and recognising innovation. As the British minister for Culture, Media and Sport recently wrote: 'The most successful economies and societies in the twenty-first century will be creative ones. Creativity will make the difference – to businesses seeking a competitive edge, to societies looking for new ways to tackle issues and improve the quality of life. This offers the UK enormous opportunities. We have a well-deserved reputation for creativity' (Smith 2001).

There must also be mechanisms in place with which this innovation may be harnessed.[12] The promise of intellectual property rights can be seen as both the motivation for acting creatively (a mechanism to encourage creative thinking by rewarding its application), and the instrument through which certain kinds of persons (those in competition with one another and needing a way of publicising their work, while protecting it) are mobilised (Barry 2000; Strathern 2002).[13]

Education and business models alike (and they flow into one another) emphasise adaptability and flexibility as necessary attributes for working effectively in the modern world. In extolling the virtues of developing people's capacities and rewarding their manifestation in innovative objects (property), a recursive logic is established. The process of complexification which 'adaptation' must be tailored to is generated within a culture itself technologically driven. The effect is a perception of the world speeded up.

The admonishment in the focus on creativity is that people need to speed up themselves. But the logic is almost narcissistic. The more creative people become, the more creative they have to become to keep pace with the apparent 'runaway' (Leach 1967; Beck 2001) character of the world outside them. Change and speed is projected outward as a (structural) condition (technical advance), and working to establish flexible and adaptable people (Martin 1997) as a response to this acceleration is in fact the engine of perceived change and acceleration. The fact that creativity is cited as the necessary tool amounts to a self-sustaining loop in the projection and reflection of conceptual categories. One might even call it an autopoietic mode of generating meaning, social relations and appropriate objects (Luhmann 2000: 2). The effect of people feeling they are 'left behind' by the world reconstitutes it as separate from individual efforts (and thereby available for appropriation).

In these constructions, human creativity is primarily intellectual creativity. It exists as abstract thought. How is the intellect produced as such? This is an interesting question when considering IP. An economy that constantly sees the need to innovate (or in earlier times improve) also has an investment in making people add their labour to create goods (add value), which, as Marx pointed out, was valued as *abstract* labour. Abstract labour is not the work of particular individuals (social labour) but effort which could be commuted into an impersonal general measure (labour time). The work of the mind is similarly constituted as abstract by the very conceptualisation of creativity as something into which anyone can tap. It is the work of instantiation which makes distinctions (property). The fact that creativity is thus contingent (neither logically necessary nor logically impossible) for any particular person can be managed by facilitating conditions, that is establishing the right situations in which creativity (a particular kind of intellectual work) can be first expressed, and then exploited. The reverse side is that without such effort on the parts of educationalists, business managers, state laws, and so forth, creativity would not appear. In this mode, creativity is contingent to the world. It is a capacity some people demonstrate at certain times. The rhetoric is directed to generalising the capacity. In this way, it has been turned into something like the labour potential of a workforce that needs to be tapped through human organisation. Labour of the mind is embodied in material outcomes. These can be owned.[14]

Contemporary Creativity 2

On precisely these themes of innovation and economy, I was struck recently by a contrast in the (lack of) claims people made to innovations in business practices, and the (constant, highly articulated) claims they made to innovations in religious and musical practice on the Rai Coast of Papua New Guinea.[15] As someone there explained,

> whatever you find through your own endeavour in the arena of the spirit cult belongs to all of us as a family. It is for us all to generate a name for

ourselves and consume pigs on the basis of this name. But whatever innovations you accomplish on the side of business, you cannot claim [the idea behind].

In those villages, people often try new ways of making money. One will construct an oven from an old oil drum and cook cakes for sale in the market; another develop a system of gambling for plates of cooked rice and meat. Yet such new ideas are not equivalent to a new spirit. People complain that whenever anyone comes up with a new idea for a business venture, everyone else follows suit, and soon the market is flooded with cakes, or with gambling for rice plates. They describe this as 'an idiotic custom of ours', to copy and repeat others' ideas (*tawa'narnung*). The word is the *same* as is used for the defamation (inappropriate use, copying) of a spirit voice. Yet it does not bring the same penalties. When questioned about someone copying their business idea, people reply that everyone wants to make money, and it is open for anyone to try any way to do so. What is not 'public' (*pablik*) on the Rai Coast is the particular creativity which is understood to be part of a family and its interactions with its ancestors, spirits and lands. New *ideas* just do not figure centrally in this. It is a form of creativity based on combinations of people. Spirits/songs are seen as a resource – a powerful one, as they elicit the currency of kinship, the currency through which affinal (reproductive) relations are managed. Because of the kind of resource that this is, a resource commensurate with other means of reproduction – understood as the regeneration of people and places through the work of family groups – it is inappropriate for any one person to claim (as an individual idea), even though the new song originated in their mind. People achieve prominence and authority through these creations. They do not achieve exclusive control over them, however.

As the resources generated by this mode of action are multiply owned, those that appeal to the form of familial creativity in their business enterprises run the risk of invoking multiple claims to ownership. This point is clearly illustrated in the case of cocoa fermentary businesses that have been undertaken in the area. Opening a fermentary on the Rai Coast is a large undertaking in terms of labour. The two fermentaries that have been opened there to date have both relied on variations of residence group (kin) formations for the recruitment of that labour. And there is a rhetoric employed by the organisers of these businesses which deploys the notion of communal enterprise by an extended family group to recruit labour. Promises are made about access to the facilities in terms of the customary needs of the residence group. The form of words is usually: 'we all face difficulties in finding enough wealth to fulfil our affinal obligations – for marriage, child and death payments. The fermentary is for everyone and will help with the kinds of difficulties we all face'.

Both fermentaries are the site of conflict and dispute, and thus experience difficulty in retaining labour. The history of one is illustrative. A succession of 'managers' (younger kin to the 'owner') have given up buying, drying and organising the transportation of cocoa because the original owner of the fermentary, who is also one of the elders of the residential group in whose name it was established, has not distributed the profits. He has not paid much in the way of wages either. In addition, he has often complained that those resident in the village and managing the facility misuse (his) money. The complaint is based on his perception that as the investor of capital, and the elder of the people who work there, both custom (kastom) and business sense dictate that he should receive all the profit of the enterprise and then redistribute it as he sees fit. As there are constant tensions and multiple claims, he does not see fit to make such distributions, and instead channels the money to his own children's school fees. One rationalisation I have heard of this use of the money is that they are the children of the residential group, and thus an investment in the future of the village as a whole. For nine or ten months of the year the fermentary remains unused – a kind of sad memorial to the complaints it has generated – standing in the village plaza.

This set of circumstances fairly describes not only fermentary businesses in the area, but also small stores, coffee-buying schemes, and also 'Youth Group' and 'Mother's Group' activities. Always, it seems, there is someone who claims the enterprise is the result of their own strength and endeavour, ignores those who have provided labour and support, and consumes the capital of the business. I suggest here that expectations of multiple ownership, based on customary principles of shared interest in the products of people's labour, conflict with a convenient reading of capitalism where having an innovative idea and making it a reality is enough to claim exclusive control. This reading places power and resources in the hands of the capitalist at the expense of others' interests. 'Convenient', because at the same time, the entrepreneur appeals to customary authority and multiple interests, rather than wage-labour payments, to recruit their major resource (labour).

Rai Coast people are clearly able to understand different modes of action (innovation in business is not the same as innovation in reproductive endeavour), even if these modes get mixed up in practice. This means we must look to the conditions under which different kinds of imaginative action appear and have effect (become modes of action). While Reite people do not themselves talk about IP, it seems one can find a mode of creativity here which is at once of the kind appealed to in IP concepts (innovative and useful development), and different from it.

Modes of Creativity

The rhetoric of creativity in contemporary Euro-America is driven by commerce, and relies upon property. Intellectual property law demonstrates this forcefully with the explicit suggestion that there would be no innovation or creative endeavour without the promise of private reward to motivate individuals. But there is no surprise to find an indigenous critique, as the construction I have outlined above is all about people's capacities. There are a number of places we could look for such critiques, and I do not see it as the task here to catalogue and discuss each of them. Here instead are some suggestive moments where Euro-Americans have made different models to that outlined in IP. For example, a close study of the poetry and artistic work of William Blake, or the political economy of Marx, reveals certain critiques. Recent feminist scholarship has been explicit in focusing on creativity as an ideological device (Delaney 1986). When Marx pointed out the appropriative nature of capitalist relations of production, he focused upon exactly that which is hidden within the dominant mode of production, yet upon which it necessarily relies: the reproduction of labour power. The 'mind forged manacles' and 'dark satanic mills' of Blake's poems were a critique of constraint, objectification, and the hoarding of creative authority that detracted from people's capacity to know creative power.[16]

In the epic poems which he wrote towards the end of his life, Blake returns to central moments from many angles. He seems to suggest that any one perception contains a miniature of the whole. These poems are hard to comprehend because chronology is fragmented, but this structure points to Blake's concern (Fox 1976). Blake's model of a 'distributed' creativity in persons and imagination (explicitly fashioned against an appropriative mode) is perhaps most clearly expressed in the poem *Milton* (Blake 1886). At the end of that poem, the reader and the poet are drawn into a single moment, a single image of Blake himself in his garden at Felpham, which contains within it the whole vast panorama of creation and eternity. The poem, fifty pages or so in length, is focused upon a single event, which happens in an instant. This is the 'moment in each day' when 'the poet's work gets done'. That moment, like the moment of 'an artery's pulse', is at once minute and vast, 'as brief as inspiration and as long as all lifetime' (Fox 1976: 153).

> Seest thou the little winged fly, smaller than a grain of sand
> It has a heart like thee; a brain open to heaven and hell,
>
> *(Milton*: 20: 27–28)

The brain of the smallest of Nature's creations is open to both heaven and hell, which for Blake meant to the creative oppositions of eternity, just as the poet's brain, in the instant of inspiration, becomes open to this reality:

> There is a moment in each day that Satan cannot find,
> Nor can his Watch Fiends find it, but the industrious find
> This moment and it multiply.
>
> *(Milton*: 35: 42–45)

In one moment then, the whole exists, and thus we are to understand that creativity is immanent in all moments, and distributed through creation. It is not the preserve or property of a particular institution or deity ('all that lives is holy'). In Blake, it is the forces of constraint, of authority, and of property, which blind Blake's contemporaries, in his view, to a mode of action which is consistent with the mode of creativity that I call appropriative here:

> For Blake, the essence of human life is not thought but experience, the imaginative apprehension of the unseen worlds which we believe will always exist for the joy of man's discovery. These may as well be the worlds of thought, but for Blake the experience of discovering them rather than the *intellectual possession* of them is paradise, Eden… (McGann 1973: 18 emphasis added).

Alternate modes then exist for Euro-Americans and, as I will outline further, on the Rai Coast of Papua New Guinea. The rhetoric of commerce precipitates a modelling of combination in one mode. This rhetoric, however, relies upon the contingency of creativity in the world, locating it within the minds of individuals and constituting the material as the register of creative intervention. What are the other aspects of this mode of action?

Anthropological Creativity

In his famous discussion of the engineer and the bricoleur, Lévi-Strauss (1966) introduces a metaphor for two different types of creativity.[17] Whereas for the engineer, problems can be solved through creating an abstract model or formula to solve the problem at hand, for the bricoleur, projects always involve the reuse of existing elements which were not specifically designed for any purpose but – in novel combinations – can be put to other purposes. The former begins with the abstract, the latter with the concrete. Both create structures but from (apparently) different starting points. The difference between the engineer and the bricoleur, Lévi-Strauss argues, can be applied more widely to the difference between scientific and mythic thought. While all human beings have a capacity for abstract thought, 'primitive' thought locates abstractions in existing symbols which relate to (but are not the same as) concrete units in the world (1966: 17–21).

Relying upon the distinction between signifier and signified to discuss the operation of the mind, Lévi-Strauss locates the creative process, be it bounded by past concrete reality in the case of 'savage thought'/the bricoleur or open in the case of the scientist/engineer, at the level of the signifier. These images of different types of combination have gained great currency. However, I locate his fundamental premise of the separation of signifier from signified as an aspect of a *particular mode* of creativity. For Lévi-Strauss, what is significant about combination could not be properties of things themselves. All must be returned to the level of symbolisation. '[T]he prohibitions [in food taboos] result not from intrinsic properties of the species to which they apply but from the place they are given in one or more systems of significance …' (1966: 99).

How is it that 'the science of the concrete' ended up outlining the play of signification (where the 'signified' is not the world of objects but what is created by the sign) as the prior and essential element in his two kinds of creative process? There is an 'ethnographic' observation here, which is to note the abstraction of the will, of agency and of purpose from physical matter. The mentalist approach makes these elements not only human attributes *in relation* to the natural, nonhuman *and* extant cultural world, but thus locates them outside that world (including the already created world of human society and culture), which the bricoleur utilises in his combinations, *and* which the engineer draws upon in thinking up new structures to realise in concrete form. The principle of stability and structure is prior to any particular (human) intervention.

> The meaning of the adjective *physical* underwent a significant change in connotation with the new seventeenth-century conception of nature as matter. In terms of that conception the word *physical* i.e. 'natural' came to mean 'material', and since matter is 'bodily', *physical* also came to mean 'bodily' – but 'body' in a sense quite excluding 'soul'. This meaning of *physical* stands in contrast to the antecedent scholastic Aristotelianism, in which *physical* was certainly 'bodily', but not to the exclusion of 'soul' (Leclerc 1990: 5).

The abstraction of the mental from material left nature, or even society, apparently without human purpose:

> [T]he biological theory of evolution explains the origin of new species by invoking spontaneous mutations and with reference to selection in the struggle for survival. Novelty or creativity appear nowhere as independent concepts. This same reductive strategy is applied in order to explain the development from a fertilised seed to a fully grown living being. The procedure applied is analogous to the one employed to deduce the production of the physical properties of the macroscopic body... from the constitution of their respective elements (Rapp 1990: 77).

What is it that, *by its absence*, makes biological evolution and human culture, mechanical, functional and self-sustaining (Franklin n.d.)? The short answer is agency. People have projects (are authors). The bricoleur and the engineer are both creative in the limited sense of generating combinations to fulfil purposes. For Lévi-Strauss agency is on the level of epistemology, not ontology (Viveiros de Castro 1998). The position he establishes, with human beings sifting and combining already existent symbolic elements (Lévi-Strauss 1961: 160), making sense at the level of signifier, has to assume human cultures as already created objects. That is, even when it is the abstracted mind which gives form to perception and thus experience, the human will acts at the level of reorganisation, not ex-nihilo creation. Human cultures are obviously created objects, they arise in social relations between persons. But they are not directed.[18] The human mind in this view is the vehicle for the replication of cultures (Ingold 1986: 200). There is a similarity to views of biological evolution here, wherein individual organisms are the vehicles for the transmission of genes. Both nature and culture in this Euro-American construction are created objects, but not the product of human creativity because creativity requires intention or will in the authoring of combination (Lévi Strauss 1966: 64).[19]

Natural Creativity

In his discussion of the place of creativity in Darwinian models of evolution, Ingold notes that '[t]here are two facets to the meaning of creativity, as it is commonly understood. The first is the implication of subjective *agency*. To create is to cause to exist, to make or produce. The second ... is that what is brought into being is *novel*. There is no creativity in the mechanical evolution and replication of a preformed project' (Ingold 1986: 177). There is, then, a difference between what is produced as novel by an agent, and what is produced by random chance, by mutation under the constraints of natural selection. Ingold goes on: 'it would seem that, so long as we insist that the implication of agency is essential to our conception of creativity, we would have to deny the operation of a creative principle in Darwinian evolution' (1986: 178). In other words, discovery is not creativity (Hastrup 2001: 31, 32), and revelation of form is not the generation of form.[20]

There is a consistent distinction made in the literature Ingold reports upon. This lies in the difference between what people *do* and what they *undergo* (1986: 209). This relates to IP. While one might attribute a kind of creativity to the ongoing development of species in evolution, or indeed to the constant negotiation of novel situations by human subjects, neither are recognisable in IP law because of the distinction enshrined there between intentional creativity and plan-less generation. As intention resides in the human mind alone, creativity is given a particular meaning. The outcomes of creative action are explicitly objects or practices which bear the imprint of planning (novelty, inventive step, utility). These in turn become properties of the object, while creativity remains with the person.

The compact Oxford English Dictionary gives a definition of creativity that highlights another two, related types in which Euro-Americans imagine it. These are 'the action or process of creating; the action of bringing into existence by a divine power or its equivalent', and 'an original production of human intelligence or power especially of imagination or imaginative art'. They are qualitatively different. Yet the overlap between them is also significant. And both distinction and overlap have analogies within the current rhetoric of human creativity. The intellect is seen as separate, in much the same way as the deity (see Mimica 1991: 50–51). Novelty and agency combine in a validating concept – creativity – which in its own conceptual combination invokes the first instance of creativity, the exercise of divine power. The promise is an ability to change the conditions of being. The fact that so much weight is put upon the abstracted and transcendent *intellect* in Euro-American formulations, both in the recognition of original expression (copyright), and invented objects (patents), and in the ontological issue of ex nihilo origination, alerts us to the fundamental disjuncture between differentiated intelligence and material realisation. The control that humans exercise over nature comes about through their intellect, and it is the projection of that intellect into objects, which then in turn reflect back the workings of intelligence and thus foster identification. A Lockean understanding of labour is extended to the intellect, and thus the objects that demonstrate the imprint of the intellect can be regarded as property. Something has been appropriated from the common heritage of humanity.

At the same time as being valorised as the solution to everything from the decline in manufacturing industry to personal *anomie*, creativity also carries dangers for Euro-Americans. While there is a 'natural' right to appropriate, there is a moral imperative not to appropriate too much. When considering creativity, that 'too much' starts to look like power itself. This is another aspect of understanding appropriative creativity. A leading economist (Rifkin), writing recently on the subject of human cloning in a national newspaper, outlined a critique of human creativity with a long history. He is explicit about the correct, transcendent, position of a being who can change the destiny of the human race (as cloning could do): we 'play God with our evolutionary destiny' and thus 'endanger the future of civilisation' (Rifkin 2001) by interfering with evolution. Human control over the natural world, through the abstract activities of the intellect, carries real dangers. There is an admonition in the language used, familiar to us all, that creativity is also potentially destructive. Usurping the deity and allowing 'each person [to] become their own private god' (ibid.) shows the extent, and the limits, of current Euro-American belief in the creative power of the mind and its works. Human knowledge is limited and flawed, but powerful.[21] In fact, the psychological approach to creativity would confirm these observations. 'Creativity, a prerogative of man, can be seen as the humble human counterpart to God's creation … human creativity uses what is already existing and available and changes it in unpredictable ways' (Arieti 1976: 4). My point here is that this idea of creativity as a transcendent force accords with a notion of the intellect as separate and organising. With the removal of God, the notion of transcendence is replaced by notions of contingency.

Directed novelty and creativity are perceived as extra to physical processes. As creativity is separated from the process of becoming, it is valued and validated as an contingent extra to the mechanistic (that is undirected) recombination of elements, in novel forms, through the dual interplay of chance and necessity (Ingold 1986). Not all combination then demonstrates creativity.[22] The difference that will or agency makes is that there is a conscious organisation of elements in the mind which is then realised in the world.[23] Thus the correct conditions for recognising personhood among Euro-Americans – control over the object world by the thinking subject – are fulfilled. The operation of will connects abstract mental elements to the world in particular projects, which are then thought of as creative. The world goes on itself, independent of the will which created such interventions. The natural world, scientifically understood, is full of structures (chemical, physical) already given, quite aside from the question of materiality. In the social world, the Euro-American understanding of creativity as remaining with the person puts an inflection on creativity as a continuing active or reproductive force. What is being reproduced is the Euro-American self, and it is the materiality of the object (its lack of creativity) that effectively enables the reproduction of the self in relation to the material, at every turn. This holds as much for intellectual property (realised in objects) as any other form of property.

Strathern (1992) has pointed out that our notions of culture, and of change, rely on the perception of new and unique combinations coming deliberately into being. Thus culture change and creative moments are often seen as synonymous. The notions of creolisation (Hannerz 1987) and of the disruptive yet creative potential of cultures meeting have been well rehearsed in anthropology (and see Löfgren 2001). If new cultural forms are made up of unique combinations, so too are people. That internal qualities of the mind allow control over the external environment defines personhood as exactly the ability to contain both abstract thought and the will to harness objects to its intentions. This combination is a condition for making new combinations. The psychologist with an interest in creativity and the educationalist who promotes the development of the child both encourage us to understand, and therefore have in place, the conditions under which one may think creatively (Arieti 1976; Coxon 2001).

To distil, I am pointing to six interlinked elements that contribute to an appropriative mode of creativity. Firstly, that Euro-Americans are interested in the intellect itself as a site of powerful combination. Secondly, that the outputs of the intellect must appear in physical form if they are to be realised. Thirdly, that such interventions have potential for novelty against a background of perceived stability. There is no agency or will embedded in the physical, including the structures of human society. There may be evidence of past creative input, but, fourthly, once realised in an object, creativity can no longer be in that object because will or agency are seen to lie in the subject. The imprint of form from the intellect is a stamp, it does not transfer will or organisational capacity to objects. And fifthly, that this makes creativity an occasional, human intervention. It is contingent to 'the world' which is already structured; as a mode of action, it can be encouraged or suppressed. Finally, the transcendence of the abstracted intellect/will combination finds resonances with a Euro-American tendency to locate reason or knowledge in the individual mind, and thus reproduces the self through its operation.

Rai Coast Combinations

I now move on to outline a modelling of combination in Melanesia which is differently structured. Whether attempting business projects, or attending to kin, Reite people are interested in the ways in which persons combine, or differentiate themselves.[24] This produces a mode of action which is not founded upon appropriation. Individual will is an element, novelty appears, but the logic of the mode of creativity puts emphasis elsewhere.

Nekgini speakers live in small hamlets that are based around a meeting house and a cult house. People become related to one another there by co-residence in these hamlets. The residential group is named the *palem*, and this word refers to a platform on which ceremonial payments to affines are piled. The cult house contains the paraphernalia of different spirits (*kaapu*) which are called upon exclusively by men. *Kaapu* are musical, known by their 'voices', which are the melodies of sacred songs. They reside in specific places in the landscape, and are called to the hamlet for specific purposes: life cycle changes, exchanges and ceremonial performances. Each spirit is owned by particular *palem* members. They are transmitted through inheritance of a *palem* identity, and also transacted between *palem*. In transaction, they become wealth items.

Palem are the focus of a *generative* system. Persons *become* related to one another through living together in a *palem*. All second-generation residents of a *palem* are siblings. *Palem* are combinations of people which, through the work involved in growing the next generation, become a single entity. *Palem* are recognised as whole units (*palem konaki*) at the point where they collectively produce a payment to another residential group. These payments are made for women who arrive in marriage, and for their children. The payments take the form of an effigy, made up of garden produce, wealth items and a live pig. These items are explicitly named as body parts. The *kaapu* animate this body, giving it voice and calling for the recipients.[25] *Palem* are named after the site of their cult and meeting house, and the effigy is 'at their door', born from their collective work. Places as combinations of people and spirits come to have identity through the recognition they gain in dramatising their existence through exchange. Each payment made as a *palem* constitutes the work of the *palem* as the work of producing its children, and acknowledging the unique combination which has gone to make it up as a viable social entity (i.e. with connections beyond itself).

Palem children then are also combinations: of the labour, nurture, knowledge and spirits of a particular place. Such children are siblings because they embody elements from the same place. They are differentiated from one another, just as *palem* themselves are, through the relationships they have *external* to the *palem*. It is in these relationships that the particularity of the person/*palem* emerges because of its unique position (name) and unique set of constitutive relations to other places, affines or maternal kinsmen. As a system that generates new *palem*, new named social groups, new spirits and designs to accompany them, and new persons as the conscious effort of others, I think we might call these combinations 'creative'. The combinations are not mental, but bodily and substantive.

Relationships within and beyond the *palem* are not contingent to the person, their identity or their bodily substance. They *are* that body, identity and person. The distinctions noted in the prevalent Euro-American mode of creativity, between mind and matter, reproduction and mental creation, are not present in the mode of Reite people making new *palem*. They are 'creations' because they bring into being a microcosm of the social cosmos, a single entity which embodies in its own constitution, the power of its relational make-up. Thus generativity is willed by persons and that will is embodied by the novel outcomes of their combinatorial acts. It remains with the products. Thus people as creations of other persons, not nature or biology, are able to create other bodies.

Palem first came into being through the actions of beings Nekgini speakers know as *patuki*. *Pomo patuki* is a particular narrative of the actions of certain *patuki*, which tells of the transition from a primordial state without gender, marriage or exchange, to existence as it is currently experienced. The characters (*patuki*) presided over the first *palem* formation in a place called Pomo, and the first exchange relations. Their actions caused the emergence of reproductive species in the environment, and differences between the character, material culture, and geography of people and places. All this followed from an initial act of differentiation. A 'mother' or 'sister' had a vagina/design tattooed between her legs. This act precipitated anger and fighting between the other characters of the myth (a pair of siblings), and in the subsequent movements of their fight, chase, and eventual reconciliation through exchange (from different positions in the emergent landscape), human existence came into being (Leach 2003).

On the evidence I have presented this is a large claim to make. However, it is not my claim, but that of Nekgini speakers. All they now know and experience followed from the initial gendering, fight and separation. *Pomo Patuki* is *pablik* (public), a *patuki* belonging to everyone.

Pomo patuki is the condition of human existence. The term *patuki* covers not only the narrative *and* characters in what anthropologists call 'myth'. It also designates knowledge itself, and the power of knowledge to have effect as the magical names of these powerful beings. The appearance of *patuki* is in the physical forms of the landscape, of different exchange items produced in various places, and most fundamentally in the gendering of bodies. All this is to say that 'myth' (knowledge) itself is not thought of by these people as intellectual *as opposed* to physical. Differences are between kinds of people with different control over knowledge, not between intellectual and other forms of activity. Narrative, character and power are in the form of persons, and are distributed, *pablik*, through and in the persons who embody this power. *Pomo patuki* is not abstract knowledge but *is* the existential condition which persons exhibit in their distinct gendered forms, belonging to and constructing *palem*.

Now if Nekgini speakers see *Pomo patuki* as the practice which is generative of their particular social form then they assume that this is how people must *be* as humans. Each marriage is an instantiation of that *patuki*. Reproduction, then, as the initial condition of human emergence, is always present in the form and generation of persons as *palem* members. Social life does not have a structure independent of the creative power of *patuki* (people's action).

Creativity, in terms of combination and in terms of generating other persons (novelty) is thus intrinsic, necessary to this personhood. It is also why one can sensibly think of creativity as distributed, and why the myth of *Pomo*, distributed ('public') knowledge of the condition of human life, is cited *as* the human condition. Such narratives do not outline possibilities, they outline a necessity – that is, the necessity of keeping the *human* world in existence (Mimica 1991), a necessity in no dependable (mechanical) sense. The emphasis on establishing creativity in Euro-America is not the same as this necessity. The Euro-American myth is one of competitive creativity. It is based on the notion of appropriation (property). The Nekgini necessity requires further action to be taken to keep the world in human form. This is not a constant search for novel acts of appropriation.

Rai Coast Agency

In what form does will or agency, another aspect of our working definition of creativity, appear? An ethnographic example illustrates how the distribution of creativity is also the distribution of will or agency. Early in 1999, a young woman from the hamlet of Sarangama made a payment to some of her kinsmen within the hamlet.[26] There was some controversy and ill feeling about the payment as it was *requested* by those kinsmen. Requesting payment for anything in this region is seen as shameful. In both the general principle, and in the particular instance I outline, knowing one's obligations (Crook 2001a) is seen as a mark of an adult person. Obligations are intrinsic to the definition of personhood, not just morality. Asking for something implies the other does not know how to behave.

In essence, the case refers to a girl (Yatat) who was connected to two groups of people (Sarangama and Kumundung). She had kin in each group, and had been nurtured on both their lands when her father became too ill to bring her up. Prior to her marriage, it was seen as necessary to define the interests each group had in her. Senior Sarangama men made plain their wish that Yatat should make them a presentation of wealth, payment for their nurture, before she left them in marriage.[27]

The example illustrates two points. Firstly, that persons are explicitly viewed as combinations of the work and input of other people. There was no question that Sarangama were entitled to a share of Yatat's bride-payments whatever their previous connection. They had worked to grow her. Secondly, that moral personhood is the knowledge of these connections *appearing as* the transaction of wealth items.

This notion of 'work' is foreign to the Euro-American mode of creativity I have outlined. As we have seen, physical conception is not a 'a work' (Ingold 1986: 180). Rather, creativity is recognised when it involves input from outside physical matter, the imprint of reason or purpose.[28] The Euro-American idea that evolution or nature can go on without will and effort confirms these things as elements of human existence, and therefore contingent 'in the world'. Only what persons themselves produce, the change or development that they partake in, are seen as 'works'.

Nekgini speakers class actions that have effects in the bodies and minds of other people as 'work'. For example, horticulture involves the manipulation and coercion of spirit bodies and cooperation from wives; a gardener also needs knowledge derived from his maternal kin to be successful. Garden produce is the outcome of one agent acting upon others, and thus involves 'work' in this sense. A man organising a payment solicits advice, guidance and magical assistance from his elders. Those who receive the payment are described as the *origin* or reason for the work. Without the cooperation of widely distributed kin, the event will never take place. Spirits are essential to the process, constructing the *palem* structure and drawing the receivers to the exchange.[29] Though the work of organising may be attributed to one person, or husband/wife pair, it is explicit that many work and receive recognition for it.

Obligations are substituted in exchanges, as we see with Yatat, where obligations incurred through receiving nurture are substituted for obligations incurred through the receipt of 'help'. The named recipient or donor does not undertake such work as an option. That one person is seen as a combination themselves, of the input, the will, knowledge and agency of others, both receivers and supporters. The obligation that Yatat feels, that her brothers feel, in making a payment to her mother's brothers (MBs) is a moral duty already in place within her bodily constitution. Others' work in producing that placed and connected body is thus made visible. As the work of others, Yatat and her brothers are already constituted in the will and agency of others. It was those others' intention to grow her body through their actions. Nekgini speakers do not imagine the body growing automatically without specific kinds of action on the part of kinsmen. Thus Yatat and her siblings are themselves the creations of those particular relationships.

Now if this payment is an acknowledgement of the common moral duty of all persons to recognise the 'work' inputs of others, this implies that persons are *made up of* the will of others. The will/intention of others is manifest in them, not as a contingent addition (I am this person, now I am being forced to do something by someone else), but as a necessary constitutive factor of their being (being this person, I am obligated to others).

What then is the person on the Rai Coast? They are the 'works' of other people, and thus they are what we might call the 'instruments' for those others' will and personhood to expand through relationships. Or rather, they are both instrument and relationship because these things come together in any person. The mode in which will, agency and work appear as persons does not allow their abstraction as the person *is* the combination of these aspects of other persons.

Now speaking broadly for Euro-Americans, a person's body originated in their father and mother's bodies, but not in *their* creativity. Intent and will are encompassed by instinct, and control over the outcome does not exist as control over an object, but an entity with developing subjectivity in its own right. In this construction, a child 'belongs' to its parents, but not as an object. Appropriative creativity is a mode in which objects are realised and controlled. This is not strictly true when children come into being. A different mode of creativity is in evidence, which is problematic for property. Thus as Strathern (n.d.) has recently written, 'the arena of family and kin relations is exactly where the Euro-American arithmetic that creates objects in the world falters'.

Mental and Material

How then do items that are created and held in the mind, recombined and presented as novel, figure in the characterisation of Nekgini speakers that I am drawing? Surely the fact that these people have a spirit cult, that they design and carve decorations to accompany the appearance of the spirits, that such things are owned and transacted, disproves my assertion that the same distinction between the mental and the material is not made here?

During the 1970s, a particularly prominent elder man revealed two new spirit voices. New spirits are described as appearing in the heads and thoughts of a particular person. Ancestors or *patuki* gave the person the thought, and it was 'because they wanted to give a child to' another spirit. Authorship lies beyond the person, yet not in a realm of transcendence, but in the *work* of others.[30] New spirits are born, the children of other spirits. Emphasis is placed not on the intellectual aspect of the creation (a single mind labouring), but on the reproductive potential of the thing itself. The 'work' involved in revealing the spirit voice turns out to be the same work that is required for having effects in the minds and actions of others. The dreamer feeds both spirits and people with cooked pork. It is this that establishes the spirit voice as his, and it is *this work* that is cited as the reason that others may not appropriate the spirit.

There are other aspects to a performance of spirit voices (Leach 1999). Long wooden poles are carved in secret by men of the cult. These poles (*torr*) are carried by a single man during the dancing. They stand vertically in a frame upon the man's shoulders, and thus reach high into the air. They carry shapes of snakes and lizards, and have designs associated with the spirits of the *palem* group (who are dancing) carved upon them. *Torr* are kept hidden until the night of the performance, and are revealed only briefly by the light of flaming fire-brands, which are readied for the purpose.[31]

A recent innovation in the carved designs displayed to accompany spirit voice renditions was shown in 1999. It came into being when an elder saw a snake twined around a tree in the sacred grove of a particular spirit. When he cooked pigs for a life cycle payment, he unveiled this new design. Yet such an originator has no right to dispose of this design. In the same way as a new tambaran song has a single creator, yet is owned multiply by the residential group that its creator belongs to, so a design is multiply owned by a residential group.

The forms of *torr* posts must not be copied exactly. Reproducing the same combination of images and figures would be seen as shameful by the owners, and as inappropriate copying, by others. Each element that goes to make up a *torr* (particular snakes or lizards, particular designs) are owned by *palem* groups. These elements are held in the memories of men from these groups, and combined in new forms for each occasion.[32]

Interestingly, appropriation of spirit voices, designs, or even *patuki* are offences which incur fines among Nekgini speakers. In essence, making payments in the currency of kin transactions (the charge for the theft of a spirit voice is to cook pigs and distribute them to the owners) establishes the inclusion of the wrong-doer in the kin group of those he has wronged. If spirits and persons are substitutable, if they constitute one another's existence and identity, then 'theft' is not really the right gloss for appropriation. Claims of inclusion might be a better explanation for what has happened when a spirit is used without authority (Leach 2000). The consequence is a call by those who do have authority for the person to establish his connection to them. This can be done in retrospect through 'work', though making presentations which do include him within the relationships which have as one of their nodes, particular spirits, songs or designs. These items are not primarily mental abstractions, but elements in the relational constitution of particular persons. '[T]he Melanesian "right" to reproduce [an image/design/song] is sustained not by a legal apparatus but by the person being in the appropriate and necessary ontological state to exercise the right ... the very exercise of the right is an instantiation of the substance of the right itself. Making "duplicates" *is* (to reproduce) the capacity for creation' (Strathern n.d.: 22).

The authors of new spirit voices are party to, or facilitators of, the reproductive potential embodied in the image / song / artefact itself. Thus the significant point about such things is not their status as things in the mind, but their analogy with and positioning within, the reproductive capacity of relationships between persons. A spirit can reproduce itself. It is not a mental addition or creation in the thought processes of the person who dreams the thing.

Memories of *torr* posts allow carvers to make new ones. There is a novel combination of elements, which to Euro-Americans looks remarkably like the operation of intellectual creativity. And the restrictions on others copying the images seems to confirm this (in the model of copyright). But, as I pointed out, it is not the novel combination (as a mental appropriation from a common pool) but the elements themselves which are 'protected'.

Indeed the authors may not copy the combination of images from any previous post of their own creation. This then is nothing like copyright, where the original idea is instantiated in material composition, and then the rights to copy that composition are attached to the originator of the idea. Here *no one* can copy the specific forms (i.e., combinations) of *torr* posts. The images that are combined are kept separately available for new creative projects. It is not then a particular instantiation and material realisation of *ideas* that is valued, but the elements, which are valued as *instruments* for future action. People do own images, ideas, but these are not owned *in* objects. In other words, they do not rely on the separation of mental/ideational creativity from its instantiation in an object which can then be owned as property. The same goes for people themselves. They too have reproductive potential because of their constitution in the work of others. They can be owned and transacted, but not as property, rather as instruments of others' past and future projects.

Conclusion

My argument has been that a Euro-American mode of creativity in the realm of knowledge making, as it is apparent in policy statements to encourage the phenomenon, and in legislation designed to protect intellectual property, assumes it is contingent to social life. This is 'contingent' in the sense it is used in logic: neither logically necessary, nor logically impossible. I argued that this contingency is related to a particular construction of the person found in such statements, and more generally. For contemporary Euro-Americans, it seems, human creativity is first and foremost constituted as an intellectual phenomenon. When instantiated, it may have the effect of altering an already-structured environment, or producing new objects. But creativity itself is already absent from structures and objects. It exists within the mind/person. The creative process, exemplified in occasional and significant interventions, is abstracted from the everyday and from 'the world'. This conceptual sequence makes for the high *valuation* placed upon creativity as a description of a kind of action.

Among Nekgini speakers emphasis is placed on achieving the correct form of relationships to other people. This form contains creative force. If Euro-Americans separate that which gives purpose (the mind/will) from the physicality of the body then their physical bodies are entities devoid of creativity, even though they change and develop. In contrast, Nekgini speakers see subjectivity distributed in objects. This allows for a conception of a distributed creativity, an animated landscape composed of different kinds of bodies in which change and effect are events with meaning on the same level as human actions. Will and control of the object world are not defining factors of personhood against the physical. Rather, particular positioning within a network of subjective positions on which the person can have an effect (through work) is both the substance and the realisation of personhood. Nekgini weather magicians see their own actions manifest in the change of weather patterns. Like illness, all weather is caused by *someone*. That is, in an intersubjectively constituted landscape, all effects are caused by the actions of other subjects.

One way to express this would be to say that intersubjectivity is not contingent but necessary to the particular being, substance, body and effect of each person. Subjects are different from one another because the 'necessity' of their being *is* their specific position in relation to other agents/persons. This all has consequences for how and what people own. The Euro-American conceptualisations of the intellect we have been considering position it outside the ongoing processes of physical regeneration. In the domain of knowledge making, creativity is contingent. It can be encouraged or discouraged, stifled or suppressed. The ability to 'think creatively' is not necessary to human being itself. Rather the correct control over objects in the material world through the use of the intellect is. Symbolic or mental work of innovative combination is viewed as input into an artefact. The object comes to have abstract attributes of its own (covered in patent legislation by recognition of the object's 'novelty', or as an embodiment of an 'inventive step'), which thus are abstracted from the person who produced it. Creative work is solidified and abstracted. It is no longer available for use, but must be recaptured in manipulating the conditions under which thinking can manage directed and intentional combinations again. This conceptualisation re-embeds creativity in the person just as its effects are made apparent in external physical objects.

Rai Coast people have it a different way around. They do appropriate from nature, produce objects, and own them, but they understand this as the creation of persons. Thus the models of ownership which Rai Coast dwellers operate most of the time are not models based on an appropriative creativity, but on a distributed creativity.

Why make this contrast? Is it just another version of a projected absolute difference between Melanesia and Euro-America? Absolutely not, as the two modes here identified exist already within Euro-American thinking.[33]

For Reite people creativity is a necessary process. Human life does not continue without it. Humanity is not defined by the contingency of creative action (in thought/mental operation) but by the necessity of embodying and acting creatively. Relations established with others create those others and oneself in the work of differentiation. We come to this insight through the contrast with intellectual property rights, which make creativity into a specific resource, its presence contingent upon certain conditions of emergence. The notion of resource implies scarcity, and scarcity is a measure of value. But creativity is not scarce in Reite. Resources for these people lie elsewhere. People themselves are valuable, not what they produce as objects. As Wagner points out, 'Westerners' value the objects, the outcomes of creativity: 'we keep the ideas, the quotations, the memoirs, the creations and let the people go. Our attics ... [and] museums are full of this kind of culture' (Wagner 1975: 26). In contrast, *palem*s do not last. *Torr* posts rot away in the bush. Their effect is to maintain separations between people, to distribute 'creativity' throughout existence. IPR has the effect, to the contrary, of concentrating creativity in particular individuals, and then in individual kinds of mental operation which amount to forms of appropriation by the subject.

To close, I note as a finding of this exploration that the way that production and consumption is handled by Chris Gregory, utilising Marx (1982: 30–32 and *passim*), has parallels with the two modes of creativity that I have outlined. Appropriative creativity is what I describe for Europe or America, and includes an anthropological approach. The critique or alternative mode that I have outlined comes from Melanesia, but it could equally easily come from Euro-America itself. This is because each mode contains the seed of its alternative. Locke, in his reliance on labour as appropriative, does not consider what reconstitutes labour. But the reconstitution of labour (the production of persons) is exactly what Reite people are interested in. The production of objects is incidental, yet it does occur. As there is a domain outside appropriative creativity within our own understanding, we need not identify a culture or a region with one mode alone. Thus we could perhaps follow Gregory, and label the appropriative mode 'consumptive production'. Consumptive production as a mode uses up resources, and therefore 'contains' questions about how these resources will be replaced and renewed. (In Marx, this becomes the question of how to maintain labour power.)

Creativity for Nekgini speakers is not a mode of individual appropriation. People do not think of asserting rights over 'inventions' (business developments) because it is the people they seek to control, not the objects. *Palem* leaders 'appropriate' persons, they incorporate them into their endeavours, but since these endeavours are the production of persons or person-like objects, these creations are already connected to their producers. There is no need for a further appropriation sanctioned in law. But in business, which does not seem to produce persons, the mode of creative endeavour breaks down, people cannot control people (through reciprocal obligation), and the system seems to run out of control. Applying a distributed mode of creativity to business (a Euro-American form of transaction and personhood) results in innovations which are not claimed, while claims over people (from either the entrepreneur or his workers), escalate out of hand.

Acknowledgements

Special thanks to Fleur Rodgers, who was wonderful in her support while this was being written. The editors have spent much time and energy trying to bring order to my unruly thoughts, while the other members of PTC have provided much inspiration. Simon Biggs, Alan Blackwell, Lissant Bolton, James Carrier, Cori Hayden, Martin Holbraad, Andrew Moutu and Nigel Rapport have made comments and discussed aspects of this paper. Of course, they cannot be held responsible for it in the Euro-American mode of creativity.

Notes

1. The World Intellectual Property Organisation (WIPO), for example, reconstituted by the UN in the 1970s, is pursuing its mission to 'promote the protection of Intellectual Property throughout the world' as an adjunct to the General Agreement on Tariffs and Trade (GATT) negotiations. Inclusion in the World Trade Organisation (WTO) for nations such as Papua New Guinea has been made conditional upon their adoption of the WIPO-formulated treaty on 'Trade-Related Intellectual Property Protection' (TRIPs). Interest comes both from developed nations looking to protect their publishing and music industries, and from developing nations looking to protect local inventions and innovations, and indigenous knowledge.
2. For example, a recent UNESCO document reporting on the 'UNESCO-WIPO World Forum on the Protection of Folklore' states: 'in contrast with the individual, personal nature of the creativity represented by literary and artistic works proper – it [cultural heritage] is the result of impersonal creativity of unknown members of the nation or communities thereof'.
3. Although see Wagner (1975).
4. While I explore different modes of creativity, it is important to understand that I do not promise to replace a universal definition with multiple, alternative definitions. Rather I look to suggest how different modes of creativity may be examined. I relate the results of this examination in two instances to different forms of transaction and personhood.
5. Although see Barron (1998), who argues against the assumption of a romantic sensibility in the development of authorial copyright. If she is right, the question remains as to why that assumption should have been read into IPR in Euro-America.
6. I pursue this through the comparison of an understanding of creativity which is dispersed through media, government and business literature, as well as UNESCO and WIPO policies, and the specificity of creative endeavour in a particular location, the Rai Coast of Papua New Guinea. In the latter case, calling a constellation of elements 'creativity' is my gloss on how a mode of action operates, and how it is understood and valued. Thus creativity can 'appear' for me in Reite. Armed with the notion of different modes, however, I do not assume that the understandings or operations are similar in their social conditions or consequences. The first question that must be addressed is the basis on which we may compare Euro-America and Melanesia in examining conceptions of creativity. The Rai Coast language with which I am familiar (Nekgini) does not seem to have a word with the same associations as the English 'creativity'. However, as a concept which is already used in representations of Melanesia, both anthropological and institutional, it seems justifiable to try and work out where creativity fits in IP, and what the comparable processes might look like elsewhere.
7. A notable recent exception being John Liep's volume *Locating Cultural Creativity* (2001).

8. See Liep (2001). Contributors to Liep's volume in the main examine the kinds of combinations and innovations in which anthropologists can see the creation of novel forms in culture. Different cultures are an explicit focus, but different modes of creativity are not.
9. The focus on combination is important for my argument as it allows different constellations of elements to be compared as combinations. Some might object in that we would be hard pressed to find something new that was not made up of familiar constituents. In fact human culture itself has been seen as remaking meaning in ever changing situations. This is an aspect of the Euro-American view of culture as a human project. Our being is constituted by our biology, which then transcends itself. We create our own conditions of existence, as Marx says, not from conditions of our choosing. Combination then is an expression of our understanding of creativity. How it operates, however, in different social settings, is what I wish to focus upon here.
10. It may be that we cannot even begin to talk of a specialised domain of knowledge production, thus *intellectual* property is not appropriate in such places for exactly this reason (Kalinoe n.d.).
11. 'An education which introduces students to different ways of thinking and different approaches to knowledge is likely to encourage the qualities which will be of lasting importance over a lifetime of employment' (Council for Science and Technology 2001).
12. These lie in intellectual property regimes. 'Recent management theory has prompted businesses to redefine their strategic assets including intangibles such as brand and organisational knowledge; to innovate new processes, products and services; and to start finding ways to engage more creatively with customers, employees and partners' (Kimbell 2002: 6).
13. 'If competition emanates from the agent's own sense of agency, a firm's fear of or readiness for battle, then this internal motivation (competitiveness) is being *externalized*. To be precise, it is externalized in so far as competition is anticipated, even imagined. The blocking patent can even create competitors in the abstract' (Strathern 2002: 254, original emphasis).
14. '[D]uring the 1980's it [creativity] had become increasingly popular in the media and public discourse. The virtues of creative solutions, creative people and creative attitudes were extolled in judgements of artistic and occupational success or failure, they were celebrated in career profiles and in high demand in recruitment advertisements' (Löfgren 2001: 71).
15. I do not mean to imply that this difference is the same as that between art and business endeavour for Euro-Americans. These innovations/creations are not 'art' in the Euro-American sense (see Gell 1998).
16. It is worth the detour via Blake here as he was undeniably 'creative' and his creativity relied upon combinations of previous images and ideas (Raine 1962).
17. Although he does not use the word.
18. There is also much more that could be said in ethnographic mode here. Sociobiology as a theory, for example, gives a certain kind of 'will' to nature, and thus places creative agency at the level of genes. Without intellect or purpose, however, this is a mechanical expansion rather than creative in the way IP would recognise. There is no identifiable labourer and instigator, thus no owner/property.
19. Something that is also discernible in IP law.
20. The premise that discovery is not creativity is a central tenet of patents. In the difference between what is produced as novel by an agent, and what is

produced by random chance, we see something of the logic which maintains a difference between discovery and invention. In the first, an agent seeks things which exist. This is not enough to warrant a patent. Novelty is not the work of an agent. In the second, an agent utilises what has been discovered or revealed in a directed way, and thus *makes* a novel outcome which has the imprint of the mind as integral to its form. As such, a form of abstract labour is apparent in that form, and can be claimed under IP law.

21. '[T]he notion of the *ex nihilo* is a clear fascination in our world. It harbours the heroic so dear to the intellectual heart or, perhaps, ego. Creativity in the arts has often been represented in such terms' (Friedman 2001: 46).
22. Darwin, it is reported, acknowledged that he was in a 'hopeless muddle' about what started the process of evolution going (Ingold 1986: 175). Where mechanistic connections are distinguished from willed, intellectual leaps of imagination (creativity), one is left with this kind of 'ontological' question.
23. Marx's comment that what distinguishes the worst of architects from the best of bees is that the architect raises the building in his mind 'before he builds it in wax' (1930: 170).
24. Reite is the name of the hamlets on the Rai Coast in which I conducted fieldwork. People there speak a language called Nekgini.
25. The payment itself in this form is called a *'palem'*, and the co-resident group who generated it are known thereafter as 'one *palem'*.
26. This example is a typical one in that it shows how separations are generated and combinations achieved as a matter of course here.
27. Yatat was clearly positioned by this exchange. She had fulfilled obligations to a set of people who were thus separated from her. Those that helped her in this action became 'closer' in that they were now the significant 'siblings' to whom she would distribute her marriage payments. What was unclear because of Yatat's unusual position is only made clearer by degree in the case of children who grow up with the support of their father's siblings (i.e., in his *palem*). The work, nurture and wealth they are able to give to their MB's makes a comparable, if more conventional, separation between places and kin groups prior to marriage. Sarangama were obviously concerned that the legacy of their work might be overlooked because of the unconventional position (living with cross-cousins) of Yatat prior to marriage.
28. A Lockean conception of the identification of a person and what they own through the series: purpose, work and object.
29. This example takes male action in gardening and exchange as its focus. It would be equally true to say that women's work in nurturing children, for example, requires recognition. That is, its effect on the bodies and minds of children and fathers is made apparent in exchanges with 'mothers' as the recipients (see *kalawung* payments in Leach 2003: 129).
30. 'Work' in the Nekgini context is always described as things people do in aid of growing other people, and the corollary, making ceremonial payments to affines. In the sense that both have an effect on others, and register in their future actions, work is the way that relationships are made (cf. Marx for whom production [work] was co-operative).
31. *Torr* are only ever used once, and are taken back to the spirit abodes in which they were carved, to rot after their single use.
32. Strathern has written 'the ornaments and songs and habits of comportment which these PNG people produce are not "representations". They are more like demonstrations or certifications' (Strathern n.d.: 12). Images such as the

elements that are combined in *torr* posts are not particularly 'intellectual', she argues. The fact that they appear in the heads or thoughts of carvers or dreamers does not make them different from the physical instances of those images.

33. The very processes that Euro-Americans focus upon most neatly exclude the focus of action we see on the Rai Coast because these are explicitly about the reproduction of persons. Rai Coast people see other *people* as what they 'create', and the *way* they do this, how they conceptualise what they see of themselves *in* other people, is thus comparable on an analytic level to more familiar notions of authorship. In fact, such a juxtaposition highlights many assumptions about the person-as-author. The framing interest in creativity makes the connections people see between themselves and the things or objects that they help produce, commensurable. It suggests that we need not become embroiled in positioning objects, persons and things within 'regimes of value' (Appadurai 1986) which themselves become abstract objects of attention and description. Rather we examine how different regimes of value may be generated by the very interest people have in their creations. Comparison may occur on the grounds of a common focus which transcends distinctions in *what* is produced (persons, things, rituals and so forth) and distinctions between *kinds* of producers (indigenous, technological, capitalist, subsistence, artistic) as a priori definitions.

Chapter 8

Boundaries of Creation: the Work of Credibility in Science and Ceremony

Eric Hirsch

Introduction: an Attention to Form

It could be argued that one of the central endeavours of anthropology has been to describe the forms taken by subjects and by objects, in diverse areas of the world. Through their use of the notion of form, anthropologists highlight issues of limits and finiteness. It is evident that there is an almost infinite number of ways in which subjects and objects can appear in the imagination – the contents of myth are a case in point. However, anthropology has routinely shown that when it comes to social action concrete limitations are enjoined on these infinite possibilities. What is socially possible among Melanesian peoples is not the same amongst South Asians, or again is different among Euro-Americans. Each perceives different kinds of relevance and recognises distinct limits to the way forms of subjects and objects can appear.

Law is similarly attentive to the forms taken by these entities. But this is for different purposes from that undertaken by anthropology. (Where law designates the limits of what it authorises, anthropology describes the grounds of diverse social perceptions of limits.) In the area of intellectual property, for example, this becomes apparent with respect to claims to originality: that is, specifying the author of a musical composition or the inventor of a technical artefact. '[I]n law, originality is … the description of a causal relationship between a person and a thing: to say that a work is original in law is to say nothing more than that it originates from [can be attributed to] its creator' (Barron 1998: 56). In Barron's reading of claims to intellectual property, which I follow in this chapter, the central issue is the attribution of a creation (object/thing) to a creator (subject/person); law acts as a technical device for these purposes of identification. This 'technical' paradigm of intellectual property contests the popular view that evaluates intellectual property as an outgrowth of concerns with creativity, bound up with Romantic conceptions of the artist and author.[1] While not concerned with creativity per se, an alternative model of intellectual property has suggested that the modern legal process is itself creative: that it creates its own subject matter – that of intangible or intellectual property – through its technical procedures (Sherman and Bentley 1999: 57). Both paradigms can be viewed as complementary: techniques of attribution are *creative* of a creator/creation relation which can be socially enacted by intellectual property law.

The stress on law as a technique of attribution and identification is significant. This is in effect a technique of boundary perpetuation. Only particular arrangements of subjects and objects are perceived as amenable to the dictates of law. The integrity of law depends on the ability to maintain its boundaries; to resist the influence of other ways of conceiving, for instance, the creator and creation relation (Barron 1998: 86).[2] The law can only appear credible by limiting what it authorises in this regard. The work of sustaining credibility, then, is simultaneously the work of sustaining boundaries.

This chapter will scrutinise examples of creations – scientific and artistic – in order to probe the work of credibility and of boundaries that attend these creations. Such an examination implicates what is regarded and claimed as intellectual property (IP) and what does not necessarily fall within its scope. The range of Melanesian and Euro-American examples considered draws attention to the limits of the mutual relations between IP and ordinary understandings of creations and creators.

Boundaries and Creations

Gieryn (1999) extensively documents the processes of boundary work entailed in modern science. He draws on the metaphor of a map to argue that scientific credibility is established through creating 'bounded territories of knowledge'. Scientific credibility can only be established when knowledge has assumed an appropriate bounded form, a process which often involves lengthy public contests of persuasion regarding the new boundaries created. One instance is that of the science of 'cold fusion': 'a "sustained nuclear fusion reaction at room temperature" by passing an electric current between a palladium electrode and a platinum anode submerged in an insulated tube filled with heavy water' (Gieryn 1999: 183).[3] This is an example where the credibility contests – played out before the media and the US Congress – did not convince the scientific establishment that nuclear power could be produced in this 'cold' fashion without waste (Gieryn 1999: 183–232; Sismondo 2004: 99–100).

The boundaries of science and its credibility is thus the outcome of complex interpretative work, occurring in numerous settings – downstream, so to speak, from the laboratories and other conventional sites of science. Intellectuals and public commentators are crucial to the way such boundaries are established and whether a particular scientific endeavour gains credibility. But this is not only the case for science. As we shall see below, this is as true for evaluations of ceremony and what are perceived as local 'traditions'. In contemporary Papua New Guinea (PNG), for instance, such boundary work and credibility contests are also informed by analogous interpretative work, involving intellectuals and commentators of various kinds.

Boundaries thus draw attention themselves and render visible specific conceptual effects which were not necessarily apparent. Gell (1998) highlights a not dissimilar procedure at work in the establishment of artworks, including ceremonial forms. What he designates as the 'art nexus' is the outcome of shifting connections between relatively bounded aspects of the 'agent' and the 'patient'. Distinctive artistic forms exhibit different boundaries between the constituent elements of specific agents and patients. The credibility of the artwork is connected with its capacity to captivate through intentionality, in a manner analogous to persons' own intentionality. For example, instances where the boundaries of the *artist's* agency are most evident frequently occur in post-Renaissance Western art: 'The brushwork in works by Van Gogh emanates an almost palpable sense of the artist's presence, smearing and dabbing the still viscous oil paint. Jackson Pollock's "drip" paintings provide even more striking examples. They have no subject at all except the agency of Jackson Pollock himself' (Gell 1998: 33). Much public controversy surrounded the artworks of Pollock at the time of their first display: were they still within the boundaries of what, during the period, was considered art?

In orthodox Euro-American conceptions a creation needs to be identified with a creator – a specific 'subject' such as an author or inventor; or a creation can be recognised as 'unauthored', deriving from multiple origins where no single origin can be identified.[4] Even in the case of a 'single' identifiable author, for instance, issues of multiple influences and origins often emerge to contest claims to originality. The invention of the light bulb is credited to Edison, although the narrative of this creation is more complex than the efforts of a single individual (see Hughes 1983: 25–28). Similarly rock 'n' roll was a new form of music during the 1950s; a creation with no specific author, although Elvis Presley is often spoken of as its 'king'. It derived from jazz, country-and-western and blues music – a new form was created by redefining the boundaries between established musical genres. In either case, creations conceived in this manner redefine the boundaries of conventional forms. At the same time, to endure, creations must be credible. The creation must be able to persuade, to give evidence of its value. This is as true with 'scientific' creations (where cold fusion was not successful) as it is with 'artistic' creations (where Jackson Pollock succeeded), but always in ways appropriate to 'science' and to 'art'.

Creation is a notion that abides both within Euro-American everyday discourse and within IP law. The boundary between these is equivocal. In everyday conceptions creation is the action of making, forming, producing or bringing into existence. This set of ideas about creations is allied with a more mental conception: an original production of human intelligence or power; especially of imagination or imaginative art. IP law and mundane Euro-American conceptions of creations provide for one another. But this occurs with respect to the boundary work entailed in keeping each affiliated. The credibility of IP contends with how its conception of creations are perceived outside the legal domain. But these everyday evaluations – in everyday action as much as media portrayal – simultaneously lead to reframing of ordinary conceptions. This is because the forms assumed in any local setting must persuade – must appear tenable to those involved – both legally and ordinarily. Without this mutual work, IP law lacks the capacity to identify the creator/creation relation in a plausible fashion. Each form of credibility informs the other. For instance, the kinds of subject-object relationships that can count within the realm of IP law are *not necessarily* those ordinarily conceived (cf. Barron 1998: 55).

Witness the recent public dissent against attempts to 'patent DNA'. This was an ordinary view, promoted by critics of biotechnology companies that failed to give patent law its technical interpretation (that is, the rights to prevent others from exploiting the assay kits that derived from DNA analysis, or the programmes with which DNA was identified). Instead, the critics promoted the idea that what was happening was claims over the substance, that is, DNA itself. A significant operative boundary here was between patent legislation narrowly defined and the evident and huge advantage that commercial companies could reap if they owned the patent. The rhetoric of an encroachment on commons – a sense that property was being taken away – raised the issue of who created the patented entities. The ordinary view came to assume that 'persons' were being 'patented' like commodities.[5] There were also questions about the relation between the creation and creator: were the biotechnology companies the creator (subject) or general humanity? As a result of these contests about boundaries and their credibility the 'Human Genome' is now widely conceived of as a common human creation and resource, where before the legal claims were made, it would not have entered ordinary perceptions in this way. Thus the bounds between IP and ordinary understandings of creations recurrently alter. This is especially the case at the current conjuncture where the boundaries of what is regarded and claimed as IP rapidly change. In fact, one of the rationales made for the recent dissemination of intellectual property regimes worldwide, through agencies such as the WTO and WIPO, is that they enable creations to be fashioned more rapidly and marketed more effectively than before. In short, they help overcome vested 'traditions', thereby engendering a 'liberalised' level playing field in a globalized economy. Places such as Melanesia are typically regarded as requiring such 'reform'. This chapter seeks to highlight the limitations of such a view.

As noted, the credibility of intellectual property – its capacity to identify the link between creator and creation – coexists with the credibility of what it technically attributes and identifies in mundane understandings. This is as true for Melanesian circumstances as it is for Euro-American, or elsewhere. If IP law is a technical device then its credibility rests not only on what is integral to law – authorising the creation/creator relation – but on the credibility of its potential for creating new (ordinary) ways of envisioning this relation. However, the recent expansion of IP, beyond the confines of publishing and industrial development has led to a crisis in its legitimacy (see Chapter 4; cf. Coombe 1998): is IP law capable of legally authorising an expanded array of creations and creators? This is an international predicament as IP law is now on the agenda in a majority of national contexts; legal authenticity cannot be divorced from everyday considerations. The Euro-American and Melanesian instances considered here echo the recommendation of Sherman and Bentley (1999: 220):

> [I]f [intellectual property] law is to achieve what we demand of it, it is not only necessary to recognise the influence the various narratives in operation have upon the law [by which IP law is explained and justified], it is also important that we set about inventing new narratives. As intellectual property grapples with the issues that flow from its attempt to regulate [among other things] indigenous artistic and cultural expression, these needs are as urgent and pressing as they ever were.

Proliferating Ownership Claims

Scholarly attention to matters of IP has increased substantially throughout the last decade. This is no less true of anthropology and its concern with non-Euro-American as much as Euro-American circumstances. At the same time this scholarly attention has been matched by a journalistic interest, attesting to more widespread concerns.[6]

Why has there been this proliferation of ownership claims and affiliated concerns? Mirowski and Sent have proposed an interpretation for science – especially American science – which, it would seem, has wider applicability. They suggest that scientific research – large-scale, publicly funded – based in industry and university alike, was the outcome of the Cold War arrangements following the Second World War (cf. Edgerton 1996). Unlike the prewar arrangement ('proto industrial regime', in their terms), which had a strong structure of intellectual property protection, the Cold War regime was characterised by a weak IP legal structure, associated as it was with the looming presence of the military in science funding (Mirowski and Sent 2002: 20). With the demise of the Cold War during the late 1980s the regime of science funding from state and federal agencies could no longer be legitimated, either economically or politically. This led to new arrangements for funding scientific research, where an emphasis was placed on transforming research outcomes into profitable

IP. Whereas the postwar ideology of the 'freedom' of the scientist was positively reinforced by the Cold War arrangements of research funding, the current regime appears to undermine this legacy.[7]

This change played itself out among universities as much as corporations. In this reworked regime of scientific research the key idiom was 'privatisation' of those functions and entities that were previously funded by government. In this new environment corporate R&D could be isolated as a modular profit centre and targeted for restructuring as part of its subordination within the competitive strategic position of the multinational company. 'The mutual interaction of the induced vulnerability of the universities with the novel corporate drive to reinvent contract research, itself the outcome of a change in federal government policy, has resulted in new science policy for a global privatized economy of information' (Mirowski and Sent 2002: 31).

In this new 'globalised privatisation regime', concerns with IP have assumed a prominence they lacked in previous decades. This is not just true of science but of 'art' (among other creations), where the capacity to copy artistic creations through the use of digital technologies has expanded exponentially (compare the concluding discussion in Chapter 3).[8] As Mirowski and Sent's examination indicates, this is now a 'global' regime. We only need to consider the remarks of the former Chief Ombudsman of Papua New Guinea (PNG) concerning these widespread effects. He has recently argued 'that the [PNG] government should take immediate steps to protect traditional material including music and dance by way of legislation "to ensure the traditional music and dance belonging to certain ethnic groups are protected [for their own] their purposes"' (quoted in Kalinoe and Simet 1999: 12).[9] The Chief Ombudsman's perspective has been formed by the conjunction of international shifts and local practices: i.e. 'the ease and frequency at which local contemporary artists take either by way of adaptation or rearranging traditional songs, dance and music, and churn them out in the local entertainment industry' (Kalinoe and Simet 1999: 13). In light of the Chief Ombudsman's remarks, a PNG lawyer (see Chapter 2) and an anthropologist (Simet) have argued together apropos PNG's customary law:

> [I]f a clan or tribe wishes to protect and/or enforce its proprietary interest or copyright over its traditional songs, dance or music, it will have to adduce evidence of where ownership rights to these materials are claimed. If the courts decide to accept the evidence it will then proceed to accept it as law and apply and enforce it (Kalinoe and Simet 1999: 13).

Both sets of commentators are concerned about proper legal authorisation and recompense. The law is creative here in formulating a context for these issues to be addressed. However, what is specified in Euro-American understandings in terms of the relevant creators and creations does not necessarily have the same resonance in situations found in PNG (see Leach's argument in Chapter 7, and below). Legal and ordinary ideas of credibility by definition do not align. Boundaries may appear plausible from one Euro-American perspective (science/law) and not from another (everyday). Such contests of credibility are far from novel.

The Work of Credibility and its Transformation

Consider the classic scientific case of Galileo documented by Biagioli (1993). As the subtitle of his volume indicates, this was 'the practice of science in the culture of absolutism'. To operate effectively Galileo needed to engage in the complex patronage regime of the period. This was not an 'option': 'Unless one was engaged in a complex network of patronage relationships, a career and social mobility were impossible, especially if one belonged or wanted to belong to the upper classes' (Biagioli 1993: 16). This was especially true of scientists and their lives at court: a 'close connection between social status and epistemological credibility characterised early modern Europe' (Biagioli 1993: 16–17). The patron both enabled and authored the work produced by the client. Science as it was practised during this period was unimaginable outside these constraints.

Biagioli's study of Galileo's court-based strategies concludes with reflections on the subsequent emergence of explicit scientific institutions during the later part of the seventeenth century, documented for the English context by Shapin and Schaffer (1985). With this study in mind, Biagioli notes: 'Credibility began to be no longer exclusively linked to one's *personal* status or *personal* relationships with a patron. Rather, it became associated to one's membership in scientific *corporations* like the early academies [e.g. the Royal Society]' (1993: 354–55, original emphasis). In particular, there is a transformation of the person of the patron into the that of the *personification* of the corporation.

This change precipitated the onset of experimental science, where the legitimation of scientific discourse authorised by the patron was now settled by 'matters of fact'. Under the regime of absolutist patronage the patron was credited with what had been discovered by the client.[10] In more recent times these came to be known as 'scientific advisors', persons of social standing and scholarly credentials, who became central to the work of credibility. Hong (1996) documents an early twentieth-century example regarding Marconi and his efforts to secure the scientific credibility of his experiments with wireless telegraphy. Hong's account highlights the subversion perpetrated on Marconi's scientific advisor by a competitor. This potentially jeopardised Marconi's public demonstrations of syntony (tuning).

Most recently, as highlighted earlier, the academy has been reconfigured in a way that many see as inimical to the very practice of science and its credibility. One of the central issues is 'the extent to which universities have ceased to serve as repositories for wisdom and have become profit centres for the generation of intellectual property' (Mirowski and Sent 2002: 10).[11] The transformation of the academy to this purpose also overlaps with new sites for the production of science in commercial settings prominently influenced by company patent lawyers and market analysts (see Ziman 2002: 334–36).[12] These are sites where the boundaries between academy and business are purposely obscured. The emergence of the biotechnology industry during the 1980s exemplified this trend most potently. It was this novel convergence of scientific creations and intellectual property that came to hold the attention of anthropologists, such as Rabinow.

It is noticeable that Rabinow chose a synonym for creation – making – as the title of his study of PCR (the polymerase chain reaction). His account highlights the inherent instability of creations (things) in connection with their multiple origins. As he notes, this is 'arguably the exemplary biotechnological invention to date' due to the way it has transformed molecular biology. Now, with PCR, genetic material can be quickly identified and manipulated for experimentation (Rabinow 1996b: 1). His study, though, interrogates the question of who 'invented' PCR; when did this new form emerge (see Rabinow 2000)? The answer depends on where one focuses: the concept, the technique, or the experimentation? 'Was the inventor the inspired scientist who first glimpsed the possibility or the technician who made PCR work when this scientist could not? Or was it the group that made PCR a refined, commercially viable technology two years later' (Gusterson 1998: 793)?

The creation emerged not only through the work (conceptual and manual) of different persons in their distinctive domains, but also through the negotiations between domains (Rabinow 1996b: 111–33). Whereas the boundaries between the conceptual, technical and experimental are significant in the organisational matrix of a scientific establishment (such as Cetus Corporation, where Rabinow conducted his study), they become obscure when one attempts to assign an advent point for a new form such as PCR. In other words the new form appears to *comprise* the multiple relations and negotiations which brought it about.

Rabinow's account draws attention to, but does not analyse explicitly, the negotiations that facilitate the processes of emergence, and *simultaneously* obscure the boundaries of these multiple origins. In the case of PCR, for instance, the relations and negotiations brought about between persons with different capacities a series of disparate situations: where a 'concept' exists as a hybrid 'concept-technique' or as a 'technique-experiment', neither of which is credible until it unreservedly exists certain within its bounded domain of operation. There are a set of concerns about getting PCR 'to work' and a set of issues about the claims made about PCR once it works, once it appears credible. Although one person was credited with 'inventing' PCR and subsequently received a Nobel Prize in recognition, Rabinow's investigation reveals a more complex account. In short, PCR was an operation whereby the enterprises of different persons culminated in a single, identifiable and therefore credible creation.

The case of PCR is comparable to the 'trading zones' investigated by Galison (1996: 13); the boundary areas 'between the disunified bits of science'. In particular, Galison studied the historical emergence of the

Monte Carlo method: a statistical procedure where mathematical operations are performed on random numbers. This form emerged in the distinctive research environments created during and following the Second World War.

> What happens when an H-bomb designer, a logician, an aerodynamical engineer, and a statistician sit down together? Whatever else they do ... they do not found a League of Nations with simultaneous translators (or their scientific equivalents) perched over the assemblage in metaphorical glass booths. No: they work out an intermediate language, a pidgin, that serves a local, mediating capacity (Galison 1996: 14).

The pidgin emerged in these contexts of negotiation and transaction; the boundaries between the domains involved were both eclipsed and then reasserted, as we have seen with PCR.

In Euro-American contexts, the interpretation disclosed by the study of Rabinow addresses a different set of issues to those focused upon by IP law. When Rabinow (1996b: 8) asked Norman Arnheim, a former Cetus scientist: 'Who invented PCR?', he replied: 'Conception, development and application are all scientific issues – invention is a question for patent lawyers.' Rabinow later notes in his account how those factors which facilitated the rise of the biotechnology industry included a reformed regulatory environment, one 'that encouraged the rapid application of research to applied problems, as well as changes in the patent laws directed at actively encouraging (almost forcing) the commercialization of inventions in both industrial and academic settings' (Rabinow 1996: 19). Both the market and the law were reconfigured to speed matters up.

Speeding Things Up

PCR provided a different and, importantly, *quicker* answer to the problem that cloning genes was to solve. Scientific convention prior to the advent of PCR was devoted to the 'mimicry of nature' and this is what the cloning of genes was to achieve.[13] Mullis's concept, though, was not enough to make PCR a reality. It required sustained dealings and effort on the part of numerous other persons within different divisions of Cetus to make the concept workable and credible. Once PCR does emerge, however, the object becomes different again – a legal entity, patentable, where issues of scientific processes, authority and responsibility are potentially altered. Biagioli (2000: 104), suggests that scientific processes, authority and responsibility are a 'set of relations among colleagues', which is ill-suited to the characterisation as a 'legal entity'. '[I]n scientific credit there is no monetary reward, only citations and prestige'. Strathern (this volume) follows his lead in looking for comparisons to this situation. She suggests as a candidate the notion of 'cultural property' – which now covers both tangible and intangible 'indigenous knowledge'. Its recent expansion from the confines of the museum world of national monuments and heritage conservation signals a shift in its operation: 'it rendered "indigenous knowledge" transactable'. Viewed in this way, then, we might begin to envision the actual scientific practices that transpire in the laboratories of Cetus or other similar biotechnological setups as exemplifying a kind of 'indigenous knowledge' – both internally and externally directed zones of trade (cf. Cambrosio and Keating 1988; Cambrosio et al. 1990; Pottage 1998b: 752 n. 54, 758 n. 73).

But this raises the issue of what counts as 'indigenous' knowledge – what and where is the location, the boundaries, of the indigenous? Consider for a moment a very different example from the one just considered: disco. Who created disco? This is clearly a Euro-American creation – like rock 'n' roll noted above. It emerged during the period of the mid-1960s to late 1970s: as first, a distinctive music rhythm and later a new movement in pop music itself, exemplified by the ultra-chic Studio54 in New York City. This form of disco also came to Papua New Guinea (PNG) and was (and still is) evident in the hotels and nightclubs found in the capital Port Moresby, as well as other cities and towns.

But there is another form of disco evident in places away from the cities, where the conventions of 'villages' hold sway. I became attentive to this form of disco first in the mid-1980s and again during 1999. Disco in this case refers to string-band music accompanied by a 'stereotypical Polynesian dance, with swaying hips and undulating hand movements' (Niles 1998: 78). Among the Fuyuge people with whom I encountered this kind of disco, men and women dance in the same area but in single gender groupings, and never explicitly touching. The specific form and dynamics of Fuyuge disco are not of central concern here. Rather, I am interested in one of the rationales offered for its adoption. Unlike the conventional forms of Fuyuge dance, and in particular the processes of preparation they entail, disco could be accomplished much quicker; it could speed up matters.

I heard this expressed during the mid-1980s when disco was performed outside the central events of Fuyuge collective performance known locally as *gab*. Younger men said that like more conventional dances performed in *gab*, disco could be performed in the daytime and nighttime, but the time devoted to preparing adornments and musical instruments (drums) would be far less. These young men perceived a way of achieving a similar effect – appearing strong and efficacious – but one that was less 'wasteful' of time. These men were interested in incorporating disco into *gab* so that they could achieve the relations between persons performed in the ritual in a quicker and more contemporary way. It was not that disco was 'modern' and *gab* 'traditional', although these distinctions could be perceived (see Hirsch 2001: 302–4). Rather, *gab* had to become more disco-like as this was seen as the appropriate way of the moment to attain the effects achieved in *gab*. For this to occur required a complex set of dealings whereby 'disco *gab*' could be revealed as a credible alternative to more conventional dance arrangements. How could disco *gab* be persuasive? For it to be so, many aspects of the headdresses and bodily adornments had to be maintained. Most significantly, collective bodily appearance in performance had to attain a unity, a 'oneness'. The appearance or 'skin' of the disco performers had to be perceived as appropriately displayed and unified. By 1999 disco had begun to achieve this status, although it was contested. It had locally come to be spoken of as 'law' – 'disco is law' – as a convention of the moment that required observance (see Hirsch 2001).

However, my Fuyuge associate Alphonse was not so enamoured with disco's status in *gab* and intellectualised his reasons. For him, at least, disco was not 'indigenous' – was not Fuyuge and not of the place. Alphonse's educated derived views are more 'modernist' – his is a world of increasingly visible and apparently bounded 'cultures'. He was concerned that local people would come to view disco as 'their own' and forget what is 'really' theirs. He expressed similar concerns with regard to the way Fuyuge migrants returning home changed the names of local places, giving them names deriving from elsewhere (cf. Hirsch 1995). In short, Alphonse was concerned about the boundaries of Fuyuge 'culture' as a modernist conception and about what were and were not credible alterations with these boundaries (compare the intergenerational negotiations described in Sykes's chapter). For Alphonse the boundaries were a limit, while for other Fuyuge speakers the boundaries did not exist in this manner. If anything, the boundary of what was disco and what was *gab* was a potential for incorporation; of presenting a new way to appear effective and credible in the social alignments that make up *gab*.

In many respects Alphonse's view, informed by the perspective of the 'village', is akin to that of the former Chief Ombudsman referred to earlier. Indeed it is likely that Alphonse's views are informed by those expressed by the former Chief Ombudsman as much as by Lawrence Kalinoe. Alphonse avidly reads the national press when he has the opportunity (and has appeared in it himself in connection with the promotion of coffee growing in the area).[14] The concern of Alphonse echoes that of the former Chief Ombudsman and both illustrate the dilemma highlighted by Kalinoe in his chapter: the 'nonidentical twins' of IP and cultural protection. Whereas the former Chief Ombudsman is speaking of IP *and* cultural protection, Alphonse is only concerned with the latter. Neither Alphonse or other Fuyuge-speakers perceive the 'creator' of disco *gab* as an issue. What is of concern is the capacity to make the form itself appear – through magical power and other 'secret/sacred' knowledge addressed by Kalinoe. This capacity has no specific creator as it derives from ancestral sources. Before the dancers perform, this secret knowledge is applied to their bodies as much as to the dancing ground. It is this which affects the success of the performance. That is taken as given. Fuyuge speakers have a long history of transforming *gab* performance through the introduction and alteration of outside influences. However, Alphonse's concern about cultural protection raises the modernist question of what is 'traditional'.

In a similar way Euro-Americans have no problem seeing songs, dance and music as exemplary expressions of 'culture' – as potential 'cultural property'. But as widely recognised in PNG, 'traditional' songs are known to have originated from other places in the near or distant past (see Rumsey and Weiner 2001a). Thus what belongs to one people may have originated elsewhere. The negotiations which brought this about *are* the boundary making that keeps the value of the foreign items, as in the case of disco. The debate signalled by Kalinoe and Simet, echoed by Alphonse, draws attention to a new perspective on boundaries in PNG and an explicitly 'authored' view of 'creations'.

Old Boundaries and New Boundaries

During the Cold War era of science funding, several decades before the emergence of disco *gab* a very different form appeared in connections sustained between PNG and Euro-America. This was known locally as *kuru* (lit. extreme shivering), a condition attributed to sorcery.[15] It was a fatal disease occurring among the Fore people of the eastern New Guinea highlands, most notably during the 1950s and 1960s. In an era before IP expanded beyond the confines of industrial development and publishing, the 'possession' of *kuru* by the medical anthropologist Gajdusek was conducted in an environment dictated by local and translocal transactions and colonial relations. In effect a 'trading zone' was created that was as much discursive as material (Anderson 2000: 716).

Anderson (2000) has extensively documented how Gajdusek negotiated a complex set of transactions with the Fore and with senior medical colleagues in Australia and the USA in order to 'possess' *kuru*: both to possess the body parts necessary to make his investigations, and to make *kuru* his own (compare Crook's chapter where an exchange network with different implications is analysed). It would be Gajdusek's because he was the discoverer of what was causing this disease that afflicted a substantial number of the local population.

After Gajdusek established himself in Fore, a flow of autopsied organs and tissues, along with containers of blood and urine, were air-freighted out to metropolitan laboratories. To obtain body parts from the Fore, Gajdusek had to create a complex set of exchange relations and obligations. 'Some things had a price, but the ones that Gajdusek most wanted – blood, body fluids, corpses – either were out of circulation altogether or could only be given as gifts' (Anderson 2000: 728). He needed to transgress local boundaries of exchange – especially where autopsied bodies were concerned – in order to obtain the 'things' he required. From the Fore perspective these were not things but persons and the axes and salt provided were of little interest (Anderson 2000: 728). At the same time, he needed to secure his scientific credentials and status among senior colleagues on different continents. To do this Fore body parts had to appear as if they were his possession, which he could bestow upon his seniors in the gift regime that has long characterised scientific knowledge and authority, the public sharing of data and results as noted by Biagioli (1998).[16] As gifts from these persons, the objects – blood and brains – 'would remain to some extent inalienable from their original owner' – that is, of course, the Fore (Anderson 2000: 730). For Gajdusek alone to gain the credit and visibility in these exchanges he needed to construct a clear boundary between local and translocal transactions (Anderson 2000: 730). Conferring these gifts whilst obscuring their origins enabled him to win recognition, a secure institutional and research base and eventually a Nobel Prize.[17]

Anderson speaks of Gajdusek becoming a 'big man' of science in the 1980s. During the 1990s he was a director in the US National Institute of Neurological Disorders and Stroke. Under his directorship a patent was applied for on a cell line from a Hagahai man of New Guinea.[18] (By this period Anderson's account is current with that related by Rabinow in his narrative of PCR.) Whereas in the 1950s and 1960s such materials circulated widely in the gift-like reward system of science, by the 1990s the medical scientist was instead creating a potential market commodity of Hagahai cells through a patent (Anderson 2000: 735). (See Chapter 1 for a discussion of this case.)

The Hagahai case is an outgrowth of the same sort of medical scientific research conducted on *kuru*. In this instance, however, IP was implicated and a creation[19] formed by a creator.[20] This is a consequence of the reformed regulatory environment which virtually forced the commercialisation of 'inventions' in academic as well as industrial settings (see Rabinow 1996b: 19). Voices both within and outside PNG were raised to force the withdrawal of this patent. Now, much as in the 1950s, the global enterprise of science arises out of political and economic accomplishments realised in local settings. The difference, however, is that now 'governments and corporations ... can designate brains, cells, and DNA as intellectual property, and ... can trade them as commodities in a global market' (Anderson 2000: 735). But in this instance national (PNG) and international views (promulgated by the NGO RAFI [Rural Advancement Foundation International]) of the legal claim argued that the patent lacked credibility. The patent appeared to transgress conventions of ownership concerning subjects and objects that was summoned up by ordinary views of the creator/creation relation. Although there was technically no ownership of 'a person' by the US government – as some media reports trumpeted (see Strathern 2001: 148–58) – the accusation of 'biopiracy' meant the patent had to be dropped in order to maintain scientific credibility (Anderson 2000: 743, n. 114).

Conclusion: Big Men of Science and of Ceremony – Symmetrical Anthropology and Its Limits

It is a shrewd observation by Anderson (2000: 731) to draw an analogy between Melanesian big men and the big men of science such as Gajdusek. 'Among the Fore, Gajdusek had observed big men manipulating competitive ceremonial exchange systems in order to enhance their social status. In science, too, one could manage networks of exchange partnerships in a drive for credit.' It would be mistaken to see Melanesian big men[21] as a relic of the past, as they are implicated in current social and political institutions – as much locally as nationally (see Gregory 1997: 70, n. 2).

We can also discern a parallel between the analysis of PCR and that of disco *gab*. Not only did each speed up previous conduct but, as Rabinow's narrative emphasises, there was no single 'creator' of this 'creation' (although Mullis and Cetus were legally identified and attributed as the originators). In the story of multiple origins that Rabinow documents the ultimate objective is to get the thing to work: the enterprises of numerous individuals were perceived to have been added together.

In the contemporary Melanesian material I have considered this additive procedure is *not* the focus of people's interest. This is where anthropology delineates different forms. It is also where the 'symmetrical anthropology' (Latour 1993) I have pursued in this chapter reveals its limits. The conventions of social actions lead to different forms of subjects and objects (see Pottage 2001: 133). Rather, as in case of disco *gab*, Fuyuge men and women are interested in being able to *divide* themselves from one another in order to attach themselves in different ways: to engender images of unity, oneness – a unified 'skin', as this is locally assessed (cf. Strathern n.d.). Disco *gab* is the most recent way of achieving this effect. This is what people value, not disco *gab* the 'thing', but as a way of enabling persons to detach and attach themselves to and from one another. If we begin to apply IP to this form of subject and object a real impasse arises. The identification and attribution of creator and creation does not appear relevant. There is no identifiable creator (whether singular or collective) of the creation – the thing. What is of concern in ordinary conceptions is what Kalinoe refers to as 'secret/sacred knowledge'. It is this which authorises forms to materialise. But this is not 'intellectual property' because it does not derive from the intellect or imagination of any single person. It is 'property' of ancestors and of ancestral knowledge. To assume to be the originator is to assume to be an ancestor, which is a contradiction in terms. One can 'look after' such knowledge and thus become ancestor-like, but this is very different from assuming the role of creator.

PNG law derives from the common law of Britain as well as having its own provision of customary law. IP is part of the legal arrangements of contemporary PNG and the country is a signatory of the international WTO/TRIPS agreement. IP law has been creative here in providing the context for the discussions involving the former Chief Ombudsman, the lawyer Kalinoe, the anthropologist Simet, and including the other authors of this volume. But the technical aspect of IP – the identification and attribution of the creator/creation – is often not matched by everyday conceptions in either Euro-America or Melanesia. Yet without this mutual implication of the legal and ordinary, IP lacks credibility. It is an impasse this chapter has sought to describe, an impasse that has resonances in the

Euro-American context, as we have seen. These are some of the current boundaries of creation that arise from the work of credibility in science as much as in ceremony.

Acknowledgements

I warmly thank all those of Visi in the Udabe Valley, PNG, who facilitated my initial research; to Alphonse Hega and those of Yuvenise village, with whom I stayed during my most recent visit (1999), I offer much gratitude. As were a number of others in this volume, earlier versions of this chapter were presented at the 7th biennial EASA conference, August 2002, Copenhagen, and at the AAA annual meeting, November 2002, New Orleans. Many thanks to participants on each occasion for their stimulating questions and discussion. Drafts of the chapter were also kindly read and very helpful comments received from Gisli Pálsson and Alison Shaw.

Notes

1. However, a convergence has been noted between a discourse of creativity and intellectual property law in 'pre-modern times' (Sherman and Bentley 1999: 44–47).
2. This is highlighted by the case of Terry Yumbulbul, analysed by Barron (1998) and similarly by Kalinoe in this volume. What came to be seen as Terry Yumbulbul's creation was not seen as credible by his local people when it appeared on the Australian $10 banknote. Its very public appearance in this form occurred because he had been assigned copyright for his artistic work, his creation. The credibility of IP law was tested hand in hand with the credibility of the creation's appearance. The courts found Terry Yumbulbul did possess copyright. 'Predictably, French J. felt unable to acknowledge that such a claim was capable of recognition under Australia's copyright law. ... French J ... expressed himself to be personally sympathetic to Yumbulbul's predicament – but [what the plaintiff encountered] was an incommensurability between two ways of thinking about objects and the possible forms of relationship subjects may have with them, and the intractability of positive law as the instituted structure of authority in the modern nations of the West' (Barron 1998: 51).
3. The portion in double quotes is from a statement issued by Pons and Fleischmann, the 'creators' of cold fusion.
4. During the early modern period in Europe concepts such as 'create' and 'creativity' begin to take on their present-day character, as deriving from individual authorship. This was part of a transition whereby forms – such as poetic texts – came to be envisioned as 'things', where before they were perceived as 'actions'. As late as 1711, Alexander Pope 'could still evoke the idea of the poet as the reproducer of traditional truths' (Rose 1993: 13); poetic texts were dispatchers of divine gifts. During this period it became a question of where to place boundaries so as to stop or facilitate the commercialisation of cultural forms – especially texts (see Hirsch 1998).
5. Marilyn Strathern, personal communication.

6. For example, the US legal scholar Lessig argues against the extension of copyright beyond the current seventy posthumous years. He claims this is not in the public interest, while maintaining that the rights of copyright holders to be paid should, if anything, be strengthened. His tome is not an argument against IP, but an analysis of its current limitations. Significantly Lessig's (2002) text has not been of concern to the legal academy alone. It has provoked widespread interest, especially its implications for internet use and the copying of creations from the internet. IP – patent and copyright – are, it is declared in more journalistic circles, 'going to be one of the most contested issues of our ... century' (Lanchester 2002: 37; cf. Pálsson and Harðardóttir 2002).
7. '[B]ecause the R&D budget of the federal and state governments was so widely dispersed among numerous agencies and programs, and so devoid of co-ordination and effective interest-group mobilisation ... they made an inviting target if and when budgetary stringencies would prompt belt-tightening measures' (Mirowski and Sent 2002: 23).
8. Lessig's text addresses this trend from the perspective of US copyright law.
9. The portion in double quotation marks are the words of the Chief Ombudsman.
10. 'As shown by later scientific academies, for individual authorship to emerge, it was not enough for the prince to stay incognito; he had to leave the stage altogether' (Biagioli 1993: 362). If he had to leave the stage, other persons came to occupy it.
11. Mirowski and Sent (2002: 10) present a graph which vividly highlights the number of patents granted to US academic institutions between 1974 and 1995. There is a steady upward trend from approximately 250 in 1974 to around 1,850 in 1995; more than a sevenfold increase in just over twenty years.
12. A consequence of the commercialisations of scientific research is that publishing is often discouraged, so as to avoid disclosing industrial secrets. This ensures a form of 'territoriality': one might draw an analogy with societies based around hunting and fishing, where there is the refusal to disclose good sites (Gisli Pálsson, personal communication).
13. The former line of scientific thinking and research had been followed since the work of Khorana and the concepts and systems he developed in molecular biology and biochemistry during the late 1960s. PCR as it emerged registered a change from this research agenda. Rabinow states that 'Mullis's decontextualisation and exponential amplification was the *opposite* of Khorana's efforts at mimicry of nature. Mullis conceived a way to turn a biological process (polymerization) into a machine; nature served (bio)mechanics' (Rabinow 1996b: 9, original emphasis). Originally Mullis had been employed by Cetus to make oligonucleotides which was a very time-consuming and repetitive undertaking. His 'concept' was a way of speeding the whole process up.
14. In a recent personal correspondence Alphonse drew my attention to an article written by Sir Paulius Matane in *The National* (PNG) newspaper. The article is titled 'Destruction of PNG Culture' and was presented at a symposium on decolonisation of PNG held at the University of Sydney during July 2002. Alphonse said in his letter that he shared the view of culture expressed by Matane. The latter speaks of the 'rape and destruction' of PNG social life over 120 years ago when Christian missionaries 'came to our shores and stopped our people practising their traditional dances, and removed some carvings which represented the invisible spirits'. Matane goes on to note how the

government 'set up some schools, and how people were forced to learn English and not to speak our own languages'. He mentions how we learnt foreign verse, such as 'Baa Baa Black Sheep', and became more and more separated from traditional ways of living. 'Today, some do not or even know their cultures and traditions. They have become strangers in their own homes'. This last sentiment, in particular, is one that Alphonse aligned his own views with, especially those concerning disco.

15. What was *kuru*? 'The Fore believed that a sorcery poison [was its cause]; [the first anthropologists to work among the Fore] suggested that the stresses of culture contact might produce emotional insecurity and psychosomatic disorders, perhaps even something as lethal as *kuru*' (Anderson 2000: 721). The local medical officer, who would later brief Gajdusek (see below) and was himself based at the nearby government station of Kainantu, suspected it was an inflammation of the brain, a manifestation of encephalitis.
16. Knorr (1999) has argued that modern experimental sciences include different exchange conventions. Her two case studies are high-energy physics (where the exchange ethos is 'communitarian') and molecular biology (described as having a highly 'individualistic' view of exchange) (see Pálsson n.d.: 3).
17. The Nobel Prize was for recognition of his discovery of a 'slow virus' – a new etiology of human disease – that seemed to explain *kuru*: '[h]is model of causation also appeared to explain Creutzfeldt-Jakob disease and, later BSE' (Anderson 2000: 734).
18. A form of leukaemia had been found in the blood of these people, but it rarely resulted in the disease.
19. Patent Number 5,397, 696 – for the DNA sequence 'PNG human T-lymphtrophic virus (PNG-1)' (Anderson 2000: 743, n. 114).
20. Carol Jenkins, the medical anthropologist involved, among others.
21. Strathern (1991) elucidates the comparisons between big men, great men (and chiefs), each as distinctive personifications of power.

Notes on Contributors

Tony Crook is a Lecturer in Social Anthropology at the University of St Andrews. He began research in the Min area of Papua New Guinea in 1990; this short study in Telefomin was followed in 1994–96 by doctoral research on knowledge practices in Bolivip. Further fieldwork in 1997, and in 1999 and 2000–1 as a British Academy postdoctoral fellow, has increasingly focused on relations produced by the Ok Tedi mine. *Kim kurukuru: An Anthropological Exchange with Bolivip, Papua New Guinea* is forthcoming as a British Academy monograph.

Melissa Demian obtained her PhD from the University of Cambridge, and has since taught at Bard College, Rutgers University and the New School, New York. She has published on dispute settlement, legal pluralism, gender and adoption in Papua New Guinea. Her work has been published in *Oceania*, the *Journal of the Royal Anthropological Institute* and in several edited volumes. She is currently at work on her first ethnographic monograph.

Eric Hirsch is Senior Lecturer of Social Anthropology at Brunel University. His current research includes work on the historical anthropology of landscape, power and property relations (first elaborated in the co-edited *Anthropology of Landscape* 1995); and research on historical and ethnographic issues in connections between new technologies and new forms of social relations (see the co-edited *Consuming Technologies*, 1992, *Inside Organisations*, 2001, and the co-authored *Technologies of Procreation*, 1993, 2nd edn. 1999).

Lawrence Kalinoe is Executive Dean of the School of Law, University of Papua New Guinea. He was a member of the National Intellectual Property Rights Committee (NIPRC) of Papua New Guinea from 1999 to 2001. As a member of the NIPRC, he has been involved in the discussion leading up to the eventual enactment of the copyrights, patents and industrial design legislation in 2000. He also practises law with the firm of Harricknen Lawyers in Port Moresby

Stuart Kirsch is Assistant Professor of Anthropology at the University of Michigan. He completed his PhD at the University of Pennsylvania. His research interests include ritual and myth, political ecology, indigenous political movements, and cultural property debates. His essays have been published in *Current Anthropology, Social Anthropology, Critique of Anthropology* and *The Contemporary Pacific*. He has consulted widely on mining and land rights issues in the Pacific.

James Leach completed his PhD at the University of Manchester in 1997, and is now a Research Fellow at King's College, Cambridge. He conducted fieldwork in Madang Province, Papua New Guinea during 1994–95, 1999 and 2000–1. His research interests include: kinship, place and personhood; art, aesthetics and material culture; creativity, intellectual property and ownership; ethnographic description and theories of modernity. Recent publications include *Creative Land: Place and Procreation on the Rai Coast of Papua New Guinea* (2003) and 'Drum and Voice' (2002; J.B. Donne Prize in the Anthropology of Art, 1999).

Marilyn Strathern is Professor of Social Anthropology at the University of Cambridge. A long-standing interest in gender relations (*Women in between* 1972) and kinship (*Kinship at the Core*, 1981) led to a critical appraisal of transactions in Melanesian societies (*The Gender of the Gift* 1988), and of consumer society in Britain (*After Nature* 1992). Interest in reproductive technologies (*Reproducing the Future* 1992; co-authored *Technologies of Procreation* 1993) sharpened a concern with new property forms. Drawing some of these strands together, *Property, Substance and Effect: Anthropological Essays on Persons and Things*, appeared in 1999.

Karen Sykes is Senior Lecturer in Social Anthropology at the University of Manchester. She gained her PhD from Princeton in 1995. Her research in Papua New Guinea began in 1990 and since then she has returned several times to New Ireland, especially to the villages of the Lelet Plateau where she has lived for three years in all. With a particular interest in schooling and education, she has published in *American Ethnologist, Critque of Anthropology,* and *Journal of Pacific Studies*.

Bibliography

Abada S. 1999. 'Sui Generis Protection of the Artistic Expression of Folklore: UNESCO/WIPO Model Provisions for National Laws, 1982'. SPC/ UNESCO Symposium on the Protection of Traditional Knowledge and Expressions of Indigenous Culture in the Pacific Islands, Technical Paper No. 215. Noumea: SPC/UNESCO.

Abramson, A. 1999. 'Sacred Cows of "Development": the Ritual Incorporation of a Dairy Project in the Eastern Interior of Fiji (c. 1980–1997)', *Oceania*, 69: 260–81.

Abramson, A. 2000. 'Mythical Land, Legal Boundaries: Wondering about Landscape and Other Tracts'. In A. Abramson and D. Theodossopoulos (eds.), *Land, Law and Environment: Mythical Land, Legal Boundaries*. London: Pluto Press.

Akin, D. and J. Robbins (eds.). 1999. *Money and Modernity: State and Local Currencies in Melanesia*. Pittsburgh: University of Pittsburgh Press.

Alexander, C. (n.d.) 'Value, Relations and Changing Bodies: Privatisation And Property Rights in Kazakhstan'. Presented at Wenner-Gren symposium on 'Changing Property Relations at the Turn of the Millennium', Ronda (Spain), 2001.

Alpers, M.P. 1996. 'Perspectives from Papua New Guinea'. In Robert Friedlaender (ed.), 'Genes, People, and Property: Furor Erupts over Genetic Research on Indigenous Groups', *Cultural Survival Quarterly*, 20(2): 32.

Altman, D. 2002. 'Just How Far Can Trading of Emissions be Extended?' *The New York Times* (31 May 2002), Business Day. C1, 13.

Anderson, W. 2000. 'The Possession of Kuru: Medical Science and Biocolonial Exchange'. *Comparative Studies of Society and History*, 42: 713–44.

Appadurai, A. (ed.). 1986. *The Social Life of Things: Commodities in Cultural Perspective*. Cambridge: Cambridge University Press.

Araho, N. 2000. Presentation of Discussion group 2. In K. Whimp and M. Busse (eds.), *Protection of Intellectual, Biological and Cultural Property in Papua New Guinea*. Canberra and Port Moresby: Asia Pacific Press and Conservation Melanesia Inc.

Arieti, S. 1976. *Creativity. The Magic Synthesis*. New York: Basic Books.

Arizpe, L. (ed.) 1996. *The Cultural Dimension of Global Change: an Anthropological Approach*. Paris: UNESCO (Culture and Development Series).

Asad, T. 1972. 'Market Model, Class Structure and Consent: A Reconsideration of Swat Political Organisation', *Man* (n.s.), 7: 74–94.

Bainbridge, D. 1999. *Intellectual Property*. 4th edition. London: Financial Times Management and Pitman Publishing.

Banks G. and C. Ballard (eds.). 1997. *The Ok Tedi Settlement: Issues, Outcomes and Implications*. National Centre for Development Studies, Pacific Policy Paper 27, Research School of Pacific and Asian Studies, Canberra: The Australian National University, and Resource Management in Asia-Pacific, Research School of Pacific and Asian Studies, Canberra: The Australian National University.

Barron, A. 1998. 'No Other Law? Author-ity, Property and Aboriginal Art'. In L. Bentley and S. Mariatis (eds.), *Intellectual Property and Ethics*. London: Sweet and Maxwell.

Barry, A. 2000. 'Invention and Inertia'. *Cambridge Anthropology*, 21: 62–70.

Barth, F. 1959. *Political Leadership among the Swat Pathans*. London: Athlone Press.

—— 1966. *Models of Social Organization*. Occasional Paper 23. London: Royal Anthropological Institute.

—— 1975. *Ritual and Knowledge among the Baktaman of New Guinea*. Oslo: Universitetsforlaget, and New Haven, CT: Yale University Press.

—— 1987. *Cosmologies in the Making: A Generative Approach to Cultural Variation in Inner New Guinea*. Cambridge Studies in Social Anthropology 64. Cambridge: Cambridge University Press.

—— and U. Wikan. 1982. *Cultural Impact of the Ok Tedi Project: Final Report*. Boroko: Institute of Papua New Guinea Studies.

Bateson, G. (1958 [1936]). *Naven*. Palo Alto, CA: Stanford University Press.

—— 1972. 'Schismogenesis and Culture Contact'. In G. Bateson, *Steps to an Ecology of Mind*. Northvale, New Jersey: Dell.

Battaglia, D. 1994. 'Retaining Reality: Some Practical Problems with Objects as Property'. *Man* (n.s) 29: 631–44.

Beck, U. 1992. *Risk Society: Towards a New Modernity*. London: Sage.

—— 2001. 'Living Your Own Life in a Runaway World'. In W. Hutton and A. Giddens (eds.), *On the Edge: Living with Global Capitalism*. London: Vintage.

Belejack, B. 2001. 'The Professor and the Plants: Prospecting for Problems in Chiapas'. *Texas Observer* (Austin), 22 June 2001, 8–13, 29. Available at: http//www.texasobserver.org

Bentham, J. 1791. *Panopticon* [etc.]. Dublin printed; London reprinted; and sold by T. Payne.

Bhat, A. 1996. 'The National Institutes of Health and the Papua New Guinea Cell Line'. In R. Friedlaender (ed.). 'Genes, People, and Property, *Cultural Survival Quarterly*, 20(2): 29–31.

Biagioli, M. 1993. *Galileo, Courtier: the Practice of Science in the Culture of Absolutism*. Chicago: University of Chicago Press.

—— 1998.'The Instability of Authorship: Credit and Responsibility in Contemporary Biomedicine', *FASEB*, 12: 3–16.

—— 2000. 'Rights or Rewards? Changing Contexts and Definitions of Scientific Authorship', *Journal of College and University Law*, 2: 83–108.

—— 2003. 'Rights or Rewards?: Changing Frameworks of Scientific Authorship'. In M. Biagiolo and P. Galison (eds.). *Scientific Authorship: Credit and Intellectual Property in Science*. New York: Routledge.

Biersack, A. 1982. 'Ginger Gardens for the Ginger Woman: Rites and Passages in a Melanesian Society', *Man* (n.s.), 17: 239–58.

Blake, C. 1993. 'An Atmosphere of Effrontery: Richard Serra, *Tilted Arc*, and the Crisis of Public Art'. In R.W. Fox and T.J. Lears (eds.), *The Power of Culture: Critical Essays in American History*. Chicago, IL: University of Chicago Press.

Blake, J. 2001. *Developing a New Standard-setting Instrument for the Safeguarding of Intangible Cultural Heritage*. Paris: UNESCO.

Blake, W. 1886. *Milton*. Edmonton: W. Muir et al.

Blakeney, M. 1995. 'Protecting Expressions of Australian Aboriginal Folklore under Copyright Law', *European Intellectual Property Review*, 9: 442–45.

—— (ed.). 1999a. *Intellectual Property Aspects of Ethnobiology*. London: Sweet and Maxwell.

—— 1999b. 'Intellectual Property Rights in Dreamtime – Protecting the Cultural Creativity of Indigenous Peoples', *Oxford Electronic Journal of Intellectual Property Rights* (www.oiprc.ox.ac.uk/EJWP1199.html).

—— 1999c. 'The International Framework of Access to Plant Genetic Resources'. In M. Blakeney (ed.), *Intellectual Property Aspects of Ethnobiology*. London: Sweet and Maxwell.

—— 1999d. 'What is Traditional Knowledge? Why Should it be Protected? Who Should Protect it? For Whom?: Understanding the Value Chain'. WIPO Roundtable on Intellectual Property and Traditional Knowledge, Geneva, 1999.

—— 2000. 'The Protection of Traditional Knowledge under Intellectual Property Law', *European Intellectual Property Review*, 6: 251–61.

BMA, 2001. *Gene Patenting: a Discussion Paper*. London: Medical Ethics Department, British Medical Association.

Bolton, L. (n.d.) 'What Women Know, What Women Transact: Perspectives from North Vanuatu'. Paper given to 2nd PTC Colloquium, *Inter-gender and Inter-generational Transactions*, Girton College Cambridge, June 2002.

—— 2003. *Unfolding the Moon: Enacting Women's Kastom in Vanuatu*. Honolulu: University of Hawaii Press.

Born, G. 1996. '(Im)materiality and Sociality: the Dynamics of Intellectual Property in Computer Software Research Cultures'. *Social Anthropology* 4(2): 101–16.

Bourdieu, P. 1977a. *Outline of a Theory of Practice*. Cambridge: Cambridge University Press.

—— 1997b. *Practical Reason: On the Theory of Action*. Chicago and Oxford: Polity.

Boyd, D.J. 1996. 'A Tale of "First Contact": The Hagahai of Papua New Guinea', *Research in Melanesia*, 20: 103–40.

Brandt, F. 1927. *Thomas Hobbes' Mechanical Conception of Nature*. Copenhagen: Levin & Munksgaard.

Brennan, T. 2000. *Exhausting Modernity: Grounds for a New Economy*. New York: Routledge.

Breton, S. 2000. 'Social Body and Icon of The Person: a Symbolic Analysis of Shell Money among The Wodani, Western Highlands of Irian Jaya', *American Ethnologist*, 26: 558–82.

Brown, M. 1998. 'Can Culture be Copyrighted?' *Current Anthropology*, 39(2): 193–222.

—— 2003. *Who Owns Native Culture?* Cambridge: Cambridge University Press.

Browne, N., T. Cooke et al. 1983. *Ok Tedi 24:00*. Brisbane: Thomas Cooke and Associates for Ok Tedi Mining Limited.

Brush, S.B. 1993. 'Indigenous Knowledge of Biological Resources and Intellectual Property Rights: the Role of Anthropology', *American Anthropologist*, 95(3): 653–86.

—— 1994. 'A Non-Market Approach to Protecting Biological Resources'. In T. Greaves (ed.), *Intellectual Property Rights for Indigenous Peoples: a Source Book*. Oklahoma City: Society for Applied Anthropology.

—— 1996. 'Indigenous Knowledge of Biological Resources and Intellectual Property Rights: The Role of Anthropology', *American Anthropologist*, 95(2): 653–86.

—— 1999. 'Bioprospecting the Public Domain', *Cultural Anthropology*, 14(4): 535–55.

—— and B. Orlove. 1996. 'Anthropology and the Conservation of Biodiversity', *Annual Review of Anthropology* 25: 329–52.

—— and D. Stabinsky (eds.). 1996. *Valuing Local Knowlege: Indigenous Peoples and Intellectual Property Rights*. Washington DC: Island Press.

Burton, J. 1997. '*Terra nugax* and the Discovery Paradigm: How Ok Tedi was Shaped by the Way it was Found and How the Rise of Political Process in the North Fly took the Company by Surprise'. In G. Banks and C. Ballard (eds.), *The Ok Tedi Settlement: Issues, Outcomes and Implications*. National Centre for Development Studies, Pacific Policy Paper 27, Research School of Pacific and Asian Studies, Canberra: The Australian National University, and Resource Management in Asia-Pacific, Research School of Pacific and Asian Studies, Canberra: The Australian National University.

Busse, M. 2000. 'The National Cultural Property (Conservation) Act'. In K. Whimp and M. Busse (eds.), *Protection of Intellectual, Biological and Cultural Property in Papua New Guinea*. Canberra and Port Moresby: Asia Pacific Press and Conservation Melanesia Inc.

—— and K. Whimp. 2000. 'Introduction'. In K. Whimp and M. Busse (eds.), *Protection of Intellectual, Biological and Cultural Property in Papua New Guinea*. Canberra and Port Moresby: Asia Pacific Press and Conservation Melanesia Inc.

Byrne, J. 1995. '*Rex Dagi et al. v. The Broken Hill Proprietary Company Limited*'. No. 5782 of 1994 and others, Victorian Supreme Court of Melbourne, 10 November 1995.

Callon, M. 1998. *The Laws of the Markets*. Oxford: Blackwell.

Cambrosio, A. and P. Keating. 1988. 'Going Monoclonal: Art, Science, and Magic In the Day-To-Day Use of Hybridoma Technology'. *Social Problems*, 35: 244–60.

——, P. Keating and M. MacKenzie. 1990. 'Scientific Practice in The Courtroom: the Construction of Sociotechnical Identities in a Biotechnological Patent Dispute', *Social Problems*, 37: 275–93.

Carrier, J.G. 1995. *Gifts and Commodities: Exchange and Western Capitalism since 1700*. London and New York: Routledge.

Chapman, P., M. Burchett, P. Campbell, W. Dietrich and B. Hart. 2000. 'Ok Tedi Mining, Ltd. (OTML) Environment Peer Review Group (PRG): Comments on Key Issues and Review Comments on the Final Human and Ecological Risk Assessment Documents'. April 2000. Available at: http://www.oktedi.com

Cheal, D. 1988. *The Gift Economy*. London: Routledge.

CIPR. 2002. *Integrating Intellectual Property Rights and Development Policy*. London: Department for International Development, Commission on Intellectual Property Rights.

Clark, J. 1991. 'Pearlshell Symbolism in Highlands Papua New Guinea, with Particular Reference to the Wiru Peoples of the Southern Highlands Province', *Oceania*, 61: 309–39.

Bibliography

Clay, B. 1986. *Mandak Realities: Person and Power in Central New Ireland*. New Brunswick, NJ: Rutgers University Press.

Clifford, J. 1997. *Routes*. Berkeley, CA: University of California Press.

Cohen, A. and J. Comaroff. 1976. 'The management of Meaning: on the Phenomenology of Political Transactions'. In B. Kapferer (ed.), *Transaction and Meaning: Directions in the Anthropology of Exchange and Symbolic Behaviour*. Philadelphia: Institute for the Study of Human Issues.

Coombe, R. 1993. 'The Properties of Culture and the Politics of Possessing Identity: Native Claims in the Cultural Appropriation Controversy', *Canadian Journal of Law and Jurisprudence*, 6(2): 249–85.

—— 1994. 'Challenging Paternity: Histories of Copyright' (Review article), *Yale Journal of Law and the Humanities*, 6: 397–422.

—— 1996. 'Left Out on the Information Highway', *Oregon Law Review*, 75(1): 237–47.

—— 1998. *The Cultural Life of Intellectual Properties: Authorship, Appropriation, and the Law*. Durham, NC: Duke University Press.

de Coppet, D. 1985. ' ... Land Owns People'. In R.H. Barnes, D. de Coppet and R.J. Parkin (eds.), *Contexts and Levels: Anthropological Essays on Hierarchy*. Oxford: *Journal of the Anthropological Society of Oxford*.

Council for Science and Technology (CST). 2001. 'Imagination and Understanding. A Report on the Arts and Humanities in relation to Science and Technology'. UK Government/DTI.

Cowan, J., M-B. Dembour and R. Wilson (eds.). 2001. *Culture and Rights: Anthropological Perspectives*. Cambridge: Cambridge University Press.

Coxon, K. 2001. 'How to Have a Creative Child', *Junior*, 24(June): 34–39.

Cronon, W. 1995. 'Introduction: In Search of Nature'. In W. Cronon (ed.), *Uncommon Ground: Toward Reinventing Nature*. New York: W.W. Norton and Company.

Crook, T. 1999. 'Growing Knowledge in Bolivip, Papua New Guinea', *Oceania*, 69: 225–42.

—— 2000a. 'Briefing Paper on West Ningerum Pressure Association Petition: Issues for the Consultation Process', 26 December 2000.

—— 2000b. 'Disputing Resolution: Differing Responses to Two Plane Crashes'. In C. Banks (ed.), *Developing Cultural Criminology: Theory and Practice in Papua New Guinea*. Sydney Institute of Criminology Monograph Series No. 13. Sydney: The Institute of Criminology.

—— 2001a. 'Combining Rationales from Bolivip'. In L. Kalinoe and J. Leach (eds.), *Rationales of Ownership*. New Delhi: UBSPD.

—— 2001b. 'Observer's Notes on the Lower Ok Tedi Consultation Meeting, Kiunga, 20th February 2001'.

—— forthcoming. 'Machine-Thinking: Changing Social and Bodily Divisions Around the Ok Tedi mine'. In S. Bamford (ed.), *Embodying Modernity and Postmodernity in Melanesia*. Ann Arbor: University of Michigan Press.

Cunningham, H. 1998. 'Colonial Encounters in Postcolonial Contexts: Patenting Indigenous DNA and the Human Genome Diversity Project', *Critique of Anthropology*, 18(2): 205–33.

Daes, E.I. 1993. *Study of The Protection of the Cultural and Intellectual Property of Indigenous People*. New York: UN Economic and Social Council Commission on Human Rights.

—— 1997. *Protection of the Heritage of Indigenous People*. Human Rights Study Series. New York and Geneva: United Nations.

Defoe, D. 1719. *The Life and Strange Surprizing Adventures of Robinson Crusoe*, [etc.]. London: printed for W. Taylor.

Derlon, B. 1997. *De Memoire et d'ouble: Anthropologie et objects Malanggan de Nouvelle-Irlande*. Paris: CNRS.

Delaney, C. 1986. 'The Meaning of Paternity and the Virgin Birth Debate', *Man* (n.s.), 2: 494–513.

Dijksterhuis, E.J. 1961. *The Mechanization of the World Picture*, trans. C. Dikshoorn. Oxford: Oxford University Press.

Divecha, S. 2001. 'Private Power'. Originally published on ZNET (http://www.zmag.org). Available at: http://www.mpi.org.au/oktedi/private_power.html

Dombrowski, K. 2001. *Against Culture: Development, Politics, and Religion in Indian Alaska*. Lincoln, NE: University of Nebraska Press.

Dominguez, V. 1992. 'Invoking Culture: The Messy Side of Cultural Politics', *South Atlantic Quarterly*, 91(1): 19–42.

—— 2001. 'Reply to Stuart Kirsch, "Lost Worlds: Environmental Disaster, 'Culture Loss', and the Law"' *Current Anthropology*, 42(2): 182–83.

Dove, M.R. 1994. 'Marketing the Rain Forest: "Green" Panacea or Red Herring?' *Asia Pacific Issues*, 13: 1–8. Honolulu: East-West Center.

—— 1996. 'Center, Periphery, and Biodiversity: A Paradox of Governance and a Developmental Challenge'. In S.B. Brush and D. Stabinsky (eds.), *Valuing Local Knowledge: Indigenous People and Intellectual Property Rights*. Washington, DC: Island Press.

Drabkin, I.E. 1960 [1613]. 'On Motion.' In *On Motion and On Mechanics*, trans. G. Galili. Madison, WI: The University of Wisconsin Press.

Drahos, P. 1999. "Biotechnology Patents, Markets and Morality", *European Intellectual Property Review*, 21(9): 441–49.

—— 2000. 'Indigenous Knowledge, Intellectual Property and Biopiracy: Is a Global Collecting Society the Answer', *European Intellectual Property Review*, 22(6): 245–50.

Dutfield, G. 1999a. 'Protecting and Revitalising Traditional Ecological Knowledge: Intellectual Property Rights and Community Knowledge Databases in India'. In M. Blakeney (ed.), *Intellectual Property Aspects of Ethnobiology*. London: Sweet and Maxwell.

—— 1999b. 'The Public and Private Domains: Intellectual Property Rights in Traditional Ecological Knowledge', *Oxford Electronic Journal of Intellectual Property Rights* (www.oiprc.ox.ac.uk/EJWP0399.html).

Dwyer, P.D. 2000. '*Mamihlapinatapai*: Games People (Might) Play', *Oceania*, 70: 231–51.

Edgerton, D. 1996. *Science, Technology and the British Industrial 'Decline' 1870–1970*, Cambridge: Cambridge University Press.

Eisenberg, R. 1996. 'Public Research and Private Development: Patents and Technology Transfer in Government Sponsored Research', *Virginia Law Review*, 82: 1663–1727.

Ellinson, D. 1994. Unauthorised Reproduction of Traditional Aboriginal Art', *Univ. New South Wales Law Journal*, 17: 327–44.

Environmental Defense. 2002. 'Farmers and Electric Company Strike a Unique Deal to Slow Global Warming'. Available at: http://www.environmentaldefense.org/article.cfm?contentid=1669

Eriksen, T.H. 2001. 'Between Universalism and Relativism: a Critique of the UNESCO Concept of Culture'. In J. Cowan, M-B. Dembour and R. Wilson (eds.), *Culture and Rights: Anthropological Perspectives*. Cambridge: Cambridge University Press.

Ernst, T.M. 1999. 'Land, Stories, and Resources: Discourse and Entification in Onabasulu Modernity', *American Anthropologist*, 101: 88–97.

Errington, F. and D. Gewertz. 1995. *Articulating Change in the 'Last Unknown'*. Boulder, CO: Westview Press.

Escobar, A. 2001. 'Culture Sits in Places: Reflections on Globalism and Subaltern Strategies of Localization', *Political Geography*, 20(2): 139–74.

Evans, G. 2002. 'Dealing with the Hardest Issues', *Mining Monitor*, 7(1): 11.

Feeny, D., F. Birkes, B.J. McCay and J.M. Acheson. 1990. 'The Tragedy of the Commons: Twenty-two Years Later', *Human Ecology*, 18(1): 1–19.

Fernandez, J.W. 2001. 'Creative Arguments of Images in Culture, and the Charnel House of Conventionality', In J. Liep (ed.), *Locating Cultural Creativity*. London: Pluto Press.

Filer, C. 1997a. 'Compensation, Rent and Power in Papua New Guinea'. In S. Toft (ed.), *Compensation for Resource Development in Papua New Guinea*. Port Moresby and Canberra: Law Reform Commission of Papua New Guinea, Monograph no. 6, and National Centre for Development Studies, Pacific Policy Paper 24.

——— 1997b. 'West Side Story: The State's and Other Stakes in the Ok Tedi Mine'. In G. Banks and C. Ballard (eds.), *The Ok Tedi Settlement: Issues, Outcomes and Implications*. National Centre for Development Studies, Pacific Policy Paper 27, Research School of Pacific and Asian Studies, Canberra: The Australian National University, and Resource Management in Asia-Pacific, Research School of Pacific and Asian Studies, Canberra: The Australian National University.

——— 2003. 'The Role of Landowning Communities in PNG's Mineral Policy Framework'. In E. Bastida, T. Wälde and J. Warden (eds.), *International and Comparative Mineral Law and Policy: Trends and Prospects*. The Hague: Kluwer Law International.

——— n.d. 'How can Western Conservationists Talk to Melanesian Landowners about Indigenous Knowledge?' Paper given to 1st PTC Colloquium, *Intellectual and Cultural Resources*, Girton College, Cambridge, March 2000.

Fishlock, T. 1993. 'Brawling over Souls in God's Last Battlefield: Lost-Tribe Missionaries Damned as UnChristian', *The Sunday Telegraph*, 22 August, NEXIS Library, News.

Forty, A. and S. Küchler. 1999. *The Art of Forgetting*. Oxford: Berg.

Foster, A.L. 2001. '2 Scholars Face Off in Copyright Clash', *Chronicle of Higher Education*, 10 August.

Foster, R. 1995. *Social Reproduction and History in Melanesia: Mortuary Ritual, Gift Exchange, and Custom in the Tanga Islands*. Cambridge: Cambridge University Press.

——— (ed.) 1995. *Nation Making: Emergent Identities in Postcolonial Melanesia*. Ann Arbor, MI: Michigan University Press.

Foucault, M. 1977. *Discipline and Punish: the Birth of the Prison*. London: Penguin.

Fox, S. 1976. *Poetic Form in Blake's Milton*. Princeton, NJ: Princeton University Press.

Franklin, S. n.d.. 'Biological Propriety'. Paper presented in panel 'Forms of Intellectual Creativity' at conference. *Innovation, Creation and New Economic Forms*, Cambridge, December 2001.

Freud, S. 1930. *Civilization and its Discontents*. London: Hogarth Press and The Institute of Psycho-analysis.

Freudenthal, G. 1986. *Atom and Individual in the Age of Newton: On the Genesis of the Mechanistic World View*. Dordrect and Lancaster: Reidel.

Friedlaender, J. 1996. 'Introduction'. In J. Friedlaender (ed.), 'Genes, Peoples, and Property', *Cultural Survival Quarterly*, 20(2): 22–25.

Friedman, J. 2001. 'The Iron Cage of Creativity: An Exploration'. In J. Liep (ed.), *Locating Cultural Creativity*. London: Pluto Press.

Galison, P. 1996. 'Computer Simulation and the Trading Zone'. In P. Galison and D. Stump (eds.), *The Disunity of Science: Boundaries, Contexts, and Power*. Stanford, CA: Stanford University Press.

Garrity, B. 1999. 'Conflict Between Maori and Western Concepts of Intellectual Property', *Auckland University Law Review*, 8: 1193–1210.

Gell, A. 1998. *Art and Agency. An Anthropological Theory*. Oxford: Clarendon Press.

——— 1999. 'The Language of the Forest: Landscape and Phonological Iconism in Umeda'. In A. Gell, *The Art of Anthropology: Essays and Diagrams*. London: Athlone Press.

Gieryn, T. 1999. *Cultural Boundaries of Science: Credibility on the Line*. Chicago, IL: University of Chicago Press.

Goddard, M. 2000. 'Of Cabbages and Kin: the Value of an Analytic Distinction between Gifts and Commodities, *Critique of Anthropology*, 20: 137–51.

Goldman, M. (ed.). 1998. *Privatising Nature: Political Struggles for the Global Commons*. New Brunswick, New Jersey: Rutgers University Press.

Gordon, J. 1997. 'The Ok Tedi Lawsuit in Retrospect'. In G. Banks and C. Ballard (eds.), *The Ok Tedi Settlement: Issues, Outcomes and Implications*. Canberra: National Centre for Development Studies and Resource Management in the Asia-Pacific.

Görlich, J. 1998. 'The Construction of Social Meaning and Material Value: A Note on Trade in Melanesia', *Oceania*, 68: 294–301.

Graeber, D. 2001. *Toward an Anthropological Theory of Value: The False Coin of Our Own Dreams*. New York: Palgrave.

Gray, K. 1991. 'Property in Thin Air', *Cambridge Law Journal*, 50(2): 252–307.

Greaves, T.C. 1995. 'Cultural Rights and Ethnography', *Bulletin of the General Anthropology Division (American Anthropological Association)* 1: 1–6.

——— (ed.). 1994. *Intellectual Property Rights for Indigenous Peoples: a Sourcebook*. Oklahoma City: Society for Applied Anthropology.

Greely, H.T. 1998. 'Legal, Ethical, and Social Issues in Human Genome Research', *Annual Review of Anthropology*, 27: 473–502.

Gregory, C. 1982. *Gifts and Commodities*. London: Academic Press.

——— 1997. *Savage Money. the Anthropology and Politics of Commodity Exchange*. Amsterdam: Harwood Press.

Grossman, H. 1987 [1935]. 'The Social Foundations of Mechanistic Philosophy and Manufacture', *Science in Context*, 1(1): 129–80.

Gudeman, S. 1996. 'Sketches, Qualms, and Other Thoughts on Intellectual Property Rights'. In S.B. Brush and D. Stabinsky (eds.), *Valuing Local Knowledge: Indigenous People and Intellectual Property Rights*. Washington, DC: Island Press.

Gunn, M. 1987. 'The Transfer of Malagan Ownership on Tabar'. In L. Lincoln (ed.), *Assemblage of Spirits: Image and Idea in New Ireland*. New York: George Braziller and The Minneapolis Institute of Arts.

Gusterson, H. 1998. 'Review of "Making PCR", by P. Rabinow', *Technology and Culture*, 39: 792–94.

Hadden, R. 1994. *On the Shoulders of Merchants: Exchange and the Mathematical Conception of Nature in Early Modern Europe*. Albany, NY: State University of New York Press.

Hagström, W. 1965. *The Scientific Community*. New York: Basic Books.

——— 1982. 'Gift Giving as an Organising Principle in Science'. In B. Barnes and D. Edge (eds.), *Science in Context: Readings in the Sociology of Science*. Milton Keynes: Open University Press.

Hann, C.M. (ed.). 1998a. *Property Relations: Renewing the Anthropological Tradition*. Cambridge: Cambridge University Press.

——— 1998b. 'Introduction: The Embeddedness of Property'. In C.M. Hann (ed.), *Property Relations: Renewing the Anthropological Tradition*. Cambridge: Cambridge University Press.

Hannerz, U. 1987. 'The World in Creolization', *Africa*, 57(4): 546–59.

Hardin, G. 1968. 'The Tragedy of the Commons', *Science*, 162(3859): 1243–48.

Harrison, S. 1992. 'Ritual as Intellectual Property', *Man* (n.s.), 27: 225–44.

——— 1993. 'The Commerce of Cultures in Melanesia', *Man* (n.s.), 28: 139–58.

——— 1999. 'Identity as a Scarce Resource', *Social Anthropology*, 7: 239–51.

——— 2000. 'From Prestige Goods to Legacies: Property and the Objectification of Culture in Melanesia', *Comparative Studies in Society and History*, 42: 662–79.

Harvey, P. et al. 1998. 'Exploitable Knowledge Belongs to the Creators of it: a Debate', *Social Anthropology*, 6(1): 109–26.

Hastrup, K. 2001. 'Othello's Dance: Cultural Creativity and Human Agency'. In J. Liep (ed.), *Locating Cultural Creativity*. London: Pluto Press,

Hayden, C. 1998. 'A Biodiversity Sampler for the Millennium'. In S. Franklin and H. Ragoné (eds.), *Reproducing Reproduction: Kinship, Power, and Technological Innovation*. Philadelphia, PA: University of Pennsylvania.

——— 2003. *When Nature Goes Public: The Making and Unmaking of Bioprospecting in Mexico*. Princeton, NJ: Princeton University Press.

——— forthcoming. 'Presumptions of Interest: Bioprospecting and Postcolonial Science Studies'. In C. Castañeda (ed.), *Science as Culture*. Special issue on Science Studies and Postcolonial Studies.

——— n.d. 'Presuming Interests'. Paper presented at the University of Cambridge (Dept. of Social Anthropology), 2002.

Heath, A.F. 1976. 'Decision Making and Transactional Theory'. In B. Kapferer (ed.), *Transaction and Meaning: Directions in the Anthropology of Exchange and Symbolic Behaviour*. Philadelphia, PA: Institute for the Study of Human Issues.

Helgason, A. and G. Pálsson. 1997. 'Contested Commodities: the Moral Landscape of Modernist Regimes', *Journal of the Royal Anthropological Institute* (n.s.), 3: 451–71.

Higgins, R.J. 2002. 'Ok Tedi: Creating Community Partnerships for Sustainable Development'. Available at: http://www.oktedi.com

Hilgartner, S. 1997. 'Access to Data and Intellectual Property: Scientific Exchange in Genome Research'. In National Research Council, Intellectual Property Rights and Research Tools in Molecular Biology, Washington, DC: National Academy Press.

——— and S.I. Brandt-Rauf. 1994. 'Data Access, Ownership, and Control: Towards Empirical Studies of Access Practices', *Knowledge: Creation, Diffusion, Utilization*, 15: 355–72.

Hill, C. 1972. *The World Turned Upside Down: Radical Ideas During the English Revolution*. Harmondsworth: Penguin.

Hirsch, E. 1995. 'Local Persons, Metropolitan Names: Contending Forms of Simultaneity among the Fuyuge'. In R. Foster (ed.), *Nation Making: Emergent Identities in Postcolonial Melanesia*. Ann Arbor, MI: University of Michigan Press.
—— 1998. 'Ownership of Cultural Practices in Melanesia and Euro-America: Back to the Future?', *Cambridge Anthropology*, 20: 52–58.
—— 2001. 'New Boundaries of Influence in Highland Papua: "Culture", Mining and Ritual Conversions', *Oceania*, 71: 298–312.
—— 2002. 'Malinowski's Intellectual Property', *Anthropology Today*, 18(2): 1–2.
Hirschman, A. 1977. *Passions and Interest*. Princeton, NJ: Princeton University Press.
Hobbes, T. 1946 [1651]. *Leviathan or the Matter, Forme and Power of a Commonwealth Ecclesiastical and Civil*, with an Introduction by M. Oakeshott. Oxford: Basil Blackwell.
—— 1968 [1651]. *Leviathan*, with Introduction by C.B. Macpherson. Harmondsworth, Middlesex: Penguin.
Holding, A. n.d. 'Background Report on Fieldwork in Tanga'. Paper given to 3rd PTC Colloquium, *The Commodity and its Alternatives*, Girton College, Cambridge, September 2001.
Hong, S. 1996. 'Syntony and Credibility: John Ambrose Fleming, Guglielmo Marconi, and the Maskelyne affair'. In J. Buchwald (ed.), *Scientific Credibility and Technical Standards in 19th and Early 20th Century Germany and Britain*. Dordrecht: Kluwer.
Horowitz, G.M. 1996. 'Public Art/Private Space: The Spectacle of the *Tilted Arc* Controversy', *Journal of Aesthetics and Art Criticism*, 54: 8–14.
Hughes, T. 1983. *Networks of Power: Electrification in Western Society, 1880–1930*. Baltimore, MD: Johns Hopkins University Press.
HUGO. 2000. *Statement on Benefit-sharing*. Vancouver: Hugo Ethics Committee, Human Genome Organisation.
Humphrey, C. 1999. 'Rituals of Death in Mongolia: Their Implications for Understanding the Mutual Constitution of Persons and Objects and Certain Concepts of Property', *Inner Asia*, 1: 59–86.
—— 2000a. 'An Anthropological View of Barter in Russia'. In P. Seabright (ed.), *The Vanishing Rouble: Barter Networks and Non-Monetary Transactions in Post-Soviet Societies*. Cambridge: Cambridge University Press.
—— 2000b. 'How is Barter Done? The Social Relations of Barter in Provincial Russia'. In P. Seabright (ed.), *The Vanishing Rouble: Barter Networks and Non-Monetary Transactions in Post-Soviet Societies*. Cambridge: Cambridge University Press.
Humphreys, D. 2000. 'Mining as a Sustainable Economic Activity'. Paper presented to OECD, Paris, 9 February 2000.
Hyndman, D. 1988. 'Ok Tedi: New Guinea's Disaster Mine', *The Ecologist*, 18(1): 24–9.
—— 1994. *Ancestral Rainforests and the Mountain of Gold: Indigenous Peoples and Mining in New Guinea*. Boulder, CO: Westview Press.
Ibeji, Y. and K. Gane 1996. 'The Hagahai Patent Controversy: In Their Own Words'. In J. Friedlaender (ed.), 'Genes, People, and Property', *Cultural Survival Quarterly*, 20(2): 33.
IGH. 2001. *Intellectual Property Rights and Global Health: Challenges for Access and R & D*. Consensus statement from Global Health Forum II, University of California, Berkeley and San Francisco: Institute for Global Health.

Ingold, T. 1986. *Evolution and Social Life*. Cambridge: Cambridge University Press.
——— 1993. 'Globes and Spheres: The Topology of Environmentalism'. In K. Milton (ed.), *Environmentalism: The View from Anthropology*. ASA Monographs 32. London: Routledge.
Jackson, J.E. 1995. 'Culture, Genuine and Spurious: The Politics of Indianness in the Vaupés, Colombia', *American Ethnologist*, 22(1): 3–27.
Janke, T. 1997. 'UNESCO-WIPO World Forum on the Protection of Folklore: Lessons for Protecting Indigenous Australian Cultural & Intellectual Property', *Copyright Reporter*, 15(3): 104.
Jean-Klein, I. 2002. 'Alternative Modernities or Accountable Modernities? The Progressive Movement and Political (Audit) Tourism during the Palestinian Intifada'. *Journal of Mediterranean Studies*, 12(1): 43–81.
Jenkins, C.L. 1987. 'Medical Anthropology in the Western Schrader Range, Papua New Guinea', *National Geographic Research*, 3: 412–30.
Jolly, M. 2000. 'Woman ikat raet long human raet o no? Women's Rights, Human Rights and Domestic Violence in Vanuatu'. In A-M. Hilsdon, M. Macintyre, V. Mackie and M. Stivens (eds.). *Human Rights and Gender Politics: Asia-Pacific Perspectives*. London and New York: Routledge.
Jorgensen, D. 1990. 'Secrecy's Turns', *Canberra Anthropology*, 13: 40–7.
Josephides, L. (n.d.). 'Explicit Meanings: Transacting Change across Gender Aand Generation'. Paper given to 2nd PTC Colloquium, *Inter-gender and Inter-generational transactions*, Girton College, Cambridge, June 2002.
Kalinoe, L. 1999. *Water Law and Customary Water Rights in Papua New Guinea*. New Delhi: UBS Publishers Ltd.
——— 2001. 'Expressions of Culture: A Cultural Perspective from Papua New Guinea'. WIPO Sub-Regional Workshop On Intellectual Property, Genetic Resources and Traditional Knowledge, Brisbane, Australia, 2001.
——— (n.d.). 'Ascertaining the Nature of Indigenous Intellectual and Cultural Property and Traditional Knowledge and the Search for Legal Options in Regulating Access in Papua New Guinea'. Paper given to 3rd PTC Colloquium, *Inter-gender and inter-generational transactions*, Girton College, Cambridge, June 2000.
——— and J. Leach (eds.). 2001. *Rationales of Ownership: Ethnographic Studies of Transactions and Claims to Ownership in Contemporary Papua New Guinea*. New Delhi: UBS Publishers' Distributors Ltd. 2nd edn. Wantage: Sean Kingston Publishing, 2004.
——— and J. Simet. 1999. 'Cultural Policy to Oversee Management of Cultures, Cultural Material', *The Independent* [PNG], 23 September1999, 13.
Kambuou, R. 2000. 'Plant Genetic Resources of Papua New Guinea: Some Thoughts on Intellectual Property Rights'. In K. Whimp and M. Busse (eds.), *Protection of Intellectual, Biological and Cultural Property in Papua New Guinea*. Canberra and Port Moresby: Asia Pacific Press and Conservation Melanesia Inc.
Kant, I. 1915 [1795]. *Perpetual Peace: A Philosophical Essay*. London: Allen & Unwin.
——— 1998 [1785]. 'On the Wrongfulness of Unauthorized Publication of Books'. In M.J. Gregor (ed.), *Kant's Practical Philosophy*. Cambridge: Cambridge University Press.
Kapferer, B. (ed.). 1976. *Transaction and Meaning: Directions in the Anthropology of Exchange and Symbolic Behaviour*. Philadelphia, PA: Institute for the Study of Human Issues.

—— 1976. 'Introduction: Transactional Models Reconsidered'. In B. Kapferer (ed.), *Transaction and Meaning: Directions in the Anthropology of Exchange and Symbolic Behaviour*. Philadelphia, PA: Institute for the Study of Human Issues.

Keesing, R. 1989. 'Creating the Past: Custom and Identity in the Contemporary Pacific', *The Contemporary Pacific*, 1-2: 19-42.

Kennedy, D.M. 2001. 'A Primer on Open Source Licensing Legal Issues: Copyright, Copyleft and Copyfuture', *Saint Louis University Public Law Review*, 20: 345-78.

Kimbell, L. 2002. 'Some Ways of Working'. In *Ways of Working. Placing Artists in Business Contexts* (CD-ROM). London: Arts Council of England.

Kimbrell, A. 1996. 'Biocolonization: The Patenting of Life and the Global Market in Body Parts'. In J. Mander and E. Goldsmith (eds.), *The Case Against the Global Economy: And for a Turn toward the Local*. San Francisco, CA: Sierra Club.

King, S., T. Carlson and K. Moran. 1996. 'Biological Diversity, Indigenous Knowledge, Drug Discovery and Intellectual Property Rights'. In S. Brush and D. Stabinsky (eds.), *Valuing Local Knowledge: Indigenous Peoples and Intellectual Property Rights*. Washington DC: Island Press.

Kirsch, S. 1997a. 'Indigenous Response to Environmental Impact along the Ok Tedi River'. In S. Toft (ed.), *Compensation for Resource Development*. Papua New Guinea Law Reform Commission Monograph 6, Pacific Policy Paper 24. Law Reform Commission and National Centre for Development Studies, The Australian National University: Port Moresby and Canberra.

—— 1997b. 'Lost Tribes: Indigenous People and the Social Imaginary', *Anthropological Quarterly*, 70(2): 58-67.

—— 2001a. 'Property Effects: Social Networks and Compensation Claims in Melanesia', *Social Anthropology*, 9(2): 147-63.

—— 2001b. 'Lost Worlds: Environmental Disaster, "Culture Loss" and the Law'. *Current Anthropology*, 42(2): 67-98.

—— 2002. 'Anthropology and Advocacy: A Case Study of the Campaign against the Ok Tedi Mine', *Critique of Anthropology*, 22(2): 175-200.

Knorr, C. 1999. *Epistemic Cultures: How the Sciences Make Knowledge*. Cambridge, MA: Harvard University Press.

Konrad, M. 1998. 'Ova Donation and Symbols of Substance: Some Variations on the Theme Sex, Gender and the Partible Person', *Journal of the Royal Anthropological Institute*, (n.s.) 4: 643-67.

Kopytoff, I. 1996. 'The Cultural Biography of Things: Commoditization as Process'. In A. Appadurai (ed.), *The Social Life of Things: Commodities in Cultural Perspective*. Cambridge: University of Cambridge.

Kramer A. 1925. *Die Malanggan Von Tombara*. Munich: Georg Mueller.

Küchler, S. 1987. 'Malangan, Art and Memory in a Melanesian Society', *Man* (n.s.), 22: 238-55.

—— 1992. 'Making Skins: Malangan and the Idiom of Kinship in Northern New Ireland'. In J. Coote and A. Shelton (eds.), *Anthropology, Art, and Aesthetics*. Oxford: Clarendon Press.

—— 1997. 'Sacrificial Economy and its Objects: Rethinking Colonial Collecting in Oceania', *Journal of Material Culture*, 2: 39-60.

—— 1999. 'The Place of Memory'. In A. Forty and S. Küchler (eds.), *The Art of Forgetting*. Oxford: Berg.

—— 2002. *Malanggan: Art, Memory and Sacrifice*. Oxford: Berg.

Kuper, A. 1999. *Culture: The Anthropologist's Account*. Cambridge, MA: Harvard University Press.

Lambert, P. 2001. 'Copyleft, Copyright and Software IPRs: Is Contract Still King?', *European Intellectual Property Review,* 23: 165–71.

Lanchester, J. 2002. 'Diary'. *London Review of Books*, 25 April 2002, pp. 36–37.

Latour, B. [1991] 1993. *We Have Never Been Modern*, trans. C. Porter. Hemel Hempstead: Harvester Wheatsheaf.

—— 1999. 'On Recalling ANT'. In J. Law and J. Hassard (eds.), *Actor Network Theory and After*. Oxford: Blackwell Publishers/The Sociological Review.

Laurie, G. 2002. *Genetic Piracy: a Challenge to Medico-Legal Norms.* Cambridge: Cambridge University Press.

Leach, E. 1967. *A Runaway World? The 1967 Reith Lectures*. London: British Broadcasting Corporation.

Leach, J. 1999. 'Singing the Forest. Spirit, Place and Evocation among Reite Villagers of Papua New Guinea', *Resonance: Journal of the London Musicians Collective*, 7(2): 24–27.

—— 2000. 'Situated Connections: Rights and Intellectual Resources in a Rai Coast Society', *Social Anthropology*, 8(2): 163–79.

—— n.d. 'Creativity, Ritual Process, and the Valuation of Knowledge'. Paper given to 1st PTC Colloquium, *Intellectual and Cultural Resources*, Girton College, Cambridge, March 2002.

—— 2003. *Creative Land. Place and Procreation on the Rai Coast of Papua New Guinea*. Oxford: Berghahn Books.

Leclerc, I. 1990. 'Whitehead and the Dichotomy of Rationalism and Empiricism'. In F. Rapp and R. Weihl (eds.), *Whitehead's Metaphysics of Creativity*. Albany, NY: State of New York Press.

Lessig, L. 2002. *The Future of Ideas: The Fate of the Commons in a Connected World.* New York: Vintage.

Lévi-Strauss, C. 1961. *A World on the Wane*, trans. J. Russel. New York: Criterion Books.

—— 1966. *The Savage Mind*. London: George Weidenfeld and Nicolson Ltd.

Lewis, P. 1969. 'The Social Context of Art in Northern New Ireland', *Fieldiana: Anthropology*, 58. Chicago: Field Museum of Natural History.

Libling, D.F. 1978. 'The Concept of Property: Property in Intangibles', *Law Quarterly Review,* 94: 103–19.

Liep, J. (ed.). 2001. *Locating Cultural Creativity*. London: Pluto Press.

Liloqula, R. 1996. 'Value of Life: Saving Genes Versus Saving Indigenous Peoples'. In J. Friedlaender (ed.). 'Genes, People, and Property', *Cultural Survival Quarterly*, 20(2): 42–45.

Lincoln, L. 1987. *Assemblage of Spirits: Idea and Image in New Ireland*. New York: George Braziller in Association with the Minneapolis Institute of Arts.

Lock, M. 1994. 'Interrogating the Human Diversity Genome Project', *Social Science and Medicine*, 39(5): 603–6.

Locke, J. 1960 [1698]. *Two Treatises of Government*. Cambridge: Cambridge University Press.

Löfgren, O. 2001. 'Celebrating Creativity: On the Slanting of a Concept'. In J. Liep (ed.), *Locating Cultural Creativity*. London: Pluto Press.

Luhmann, N. 2000. *Art as a Social System*. Stanford, CA: Stanford University Press.

Macfarlane, A. 1998. 'The Mystery of Property', In C. Hann (ed.), *Property Relations: Renewing the Anthropological Tradition*. Cambridge: Cambridge University Press.

Macintyre, M. 1984. 'The Problem of the Semi-Alienable Pig', *Canberra Anthropology*, 7: 109–21.
—— n.d. '"Mani bilong mi o mani bilong mipela? (My money or our money?)" Wage-earners, Decision-Makers and Ways that Cash and Commodity Ownership Redefine Social Relations in Contemporary Melanesia'. Paper given to PTC conference, *Innovation, Creation and New Economic Forms*, Cambridge, December 2001.
Macpherson, C.B.1962. *The Political Theory of Possessive Individualism: Hobbes to Locke*. Oxford: Oxford University Press.
Maine, H. 2000 [1861]. *Ancient Law*. Washington, DC: Beard Books.
Mangi, J. 1988. 'On the Question of the "Lost Tribes": A Report on a Field Trip of 24–20 April 1985'. University of Papua New Guinea Schrader Mountains Report No. 4. *Research in Melanesia*, 9: 37–65.
Martin, E. 1997. 'Designing Flexibility: Science and Work in an Age of Flexible Accumulation', *Science as Culture*, 6(3): 327–62.
Marx, K. 1896 [1867]. *Capital: A Critical Analysis of Capitalist Production*. London: Sonnenschein & Co.
—— 1930 [1867]. 'Capital', vol. 1, trans. E. and C. Paul, from 4th edn. *Das Kapital* (1890). London: Dent.
Matainaho, L. 2000. 'Genetic, Biochemical and Medicinal Resources: How Much can we Own, Protect and Receive Credit for?' In K. Whimp and M. Busse (eds.), *Protection of Intellectual, Biological and Cultural Property in Papua New Guinea*. Canberra and Port Moresby: Asia Pacific Press and Conservation Melanesia Inc.
Maurer, B. 1999. 'Forget Locke? From Proprietor to Risk-Bearer in New Logics of Finance', *Public Culture*, 11(2): 365–85.
Mayr, O. 1986. Authority, Liberty and Automatic Machinery in Early Modern Europe. Baltimore: The Johns Hopkins University Press.
McGann, J.J. 1973. 'The Aim of Blake's Prophecies and the Uses of Blake criticism'. In S. Curran and J. A. Wittreich (eds.), *Blake's Sublime Allegory*. Madison, WT: University of Wisconsin Press.
McNeilly, R. 1999. 'Mining's Modern Paradigm: A Sustainable Future'. The Essington Lewis Memorial Lecture, 1999.
McSherry, C. 2001. *Who Owns Academic Work? Battling for Control of Intellectual Property*. Cambridge, MA: Harvard University Press.
—— 2003. 'Uncommon Controversies: Legal Mediations of Gift and Market Models of Authorship'. In M. Biagioli and P. Galison (eds.), *Scientific Aurhorship: Credit and Intellectual Property in Science*. New York: Routledge.
van Meijl, T. and F.L. von Benda-Beckmann (eds.). 1999. *Property Rights and Economic Development. Land and Natural Resources in Southeast Asia and Oceania*. London: Kegan Paul International.
Merton, R.K. 1942. 'The Normative Structure of Science', in R.K. Merton (ed.), *The Sociology of Science: Theoretical and Empirical Investigations*, Chicago,IL: University of Chicago Press.
Merry, S.E. 2001. 'Changing Rights, Changing Culture'. In J. Cowan, M-B. Dembour and R. Wilson (eds.), *Culture and Rights: Anthropological Perspectives*. Cambridge: Cambridge University Press.
Milne, T. (ed.). 1981. *Collected Works of Jeremy Bentham: Volume 4, Correspondence*. London: Athlone Press, 1981.
Milton, K. 1996. *Environmentalism and Cultural Theory: Exploring the Role of Anthropology in Environmental Discourse*. New York: Routledge.

Mimica, J. 1991. 'The Incest Passions. An Outline of the Logic of Iqwaye Social Organisation', *Oceania*, 62(1): 34–58 and 62(2): 80–113.

Mirowski, P. and E-M. Sent. (eds.). 2002. *Science Bought and Sold: Essays in the Economics of Science*. Chicago, IL: University of Chicago Press.

Mondragon, C. 2002. 'Extending Agency and Incorporating Value in the Torres Islands, Vanuatu'. (University of Cambridge, ms, written in response to 3rd PTC Colloquium.)

Moore, A. 2000. 'Owning Genetic Information and Gene Enhancement Techniques: Why Privacy and Property Rights may Undermine Social Control of the Human Genome', *Bioethic,s* 14: 97–119.

Mosko, M. 1999. 'Magical Money: Commoditisation and the Linkage of *maketsi* ("market") and *kangakanga* ("custom") in Contemporary North Mekeo'. In D. Akin and J. Robbins (eds.), *Money and Modernity: State and Local Currencies in Melanesia*. Pittsburgh, PA: University of Pittsburgh Press.

—— 2001. 'Syncretic Persons: Sociality, Agency and Personhood in Recent Charismatic Ritual Practices among North Mekeo (PNG)'. In J. Gordon and F. Magowan (eds.), *Beyond Syncretism: Indigenous Expressions of World Relations*. *Australian Journal of Anthropology*, Special Issue, 12: 259–74.

—— 2002. 'Totem and Transaction: the Objectification of "Tradition" Among North Mekeo', *Oceania,* 73(2): 89–110.

Muehlebach, A. 2001. 'Making Place at the United Nations: Indigenous Cultural Politics at the UN Working Group on Indigenous Populations', *Cultural Anthropology,* 16(3): 415–448.

Munn, N. 1986. *The Fame of Gawa*. Cambridge: Cambridge University Press.

Negativland, 1995. *Fair Use: The Story of the Letter U & the Numeral 2.* Concord, CA: Seeland.

Nelson, R.D. and R. Mazzoleni. 1997. 'Economic Theories about the Costs and Benefits of Patents'. *Intellectual Property Rights and the Dissemination of Research Tools in Molecular Biology: Summary of a Workshop Help at the National Academy*. National Academy Press. Available at: http://www.nap.edu/openbook/0309057485/html/17.html

Nihill, M. 1996. 'Beyond Bodies: Aspects of The Politicisation of Exchange in the South-West Highlands of Papua New Guinea', *Oceania,* 67: 107–26.

Niles, D. 1998. 'Papua New Guinea: an Overview'. In S. Cohen (ed.), *International Encyclopedia of Dance*. New York: Oxford University Press.

Nonggorr, J. 1995. 'The Development of an "Indigenous Jurisprudence" in Papua New Guinea: the Past Record and Future Prospects'. In J. Aleck and J. Rannells (eds.), *Custom at the Crossroads*. Port Moresby: Faculty of Law, UPNG.

Nuffield Council on Bioethics. 2002. *The Ethics of Patenting DNA: a Discussion Paper*. London: Nuffield Council on Bioethics.

Oakeshott, M. 1946. 'Introduction'. In T. Hobbes, [1651] *Leviathan or the Matter, Forme and Power of a Commonwealth Ecclesiastical and Civil*. Edited with an Introduction by M. Oakeshott. Oxford: Basil Blackwell.

O'Hanlon, M. 2000. 'Introduction'. In M. O'Hanlon and R. Welsch (eds.), *Hunting the Gatherers: Ethnographic Collectors, Agents and Agency in Melanesia, 1870s–1930s*. Oxford: Berghahn Books.

Ok Tedi Mining Limited 1999. 'Sustainable Development Workshop', Tabubil, 11–13 July 1999.

Ok Tedi Mining 2003. Corporate website. Available at: http://www.oktedi.com

Ollman, B. 1976. *Alienation: Marx's Conception of Man in Capitalist Society,* 2nd edn. Cambridge: Cambridge University Press.

Paine, R. 1976. 'Two Modes of Exchange and Mediation'. In B. Kapferer (ed.), *Transaction and Meaning: Directions in the Anthropology of Exchange and Symbolic Behaviour*. Philadelphia, PA: Institute for the Study of Human Issues.

Pálsson, G. n.d. 'Appropriating Family Trees: Genealogies in the Age of Genetics'. Paper presented at 'Changing Properties of Property' conference, Max Planck Institute for Social Anthropology, Halle, July 2003.

—— and K.E. Harðardóttir. 2002. 'For Whom the Cell Tolls: Debates about Biomedicine', *Current Anthropology*, 43(2): 271–301.

Parametrix, Inc. and URS Greiner Woodward Clyde. 1999. 'Draft Executive Summary: Assessment of Human Health and Ecological Risks for Proposed Mine Waste Mitigation Options at the Ok Tedi Mine, Papua New Guinea. Detailed Level Risk Assessment'. Prepared for Ok Tedi Mining, Ltd., pp. 1–15, 6 August. Available at: www.oktedi.com.

Parkin, D. 1976. 'Exchanging Words'. In B. Kapferer (ed.), *Transaction and meaning: Directions in the Anthropology of Exchange and Symbolic Behaviour*. Philadelphia, PA: Institute for the Study of Human Issues.

—— 2001. 'Escaping cultures: the paradox of creativity'. In J. Liep (ed.), *Locating cultural creativity*. London: Pluto Press.

Patel, S. 1996. 'Can the Intellectual Property Rights System Serve the Interests of Indigenous Knowledge?' In S.B. Brush and D. Stabinsky (eds.), *Valuing Local Knowledge: Indigenous Peoples and Intellectual Property Rights*. Washington DC: Island Press.

Perks, R. and G. Wetstone. 2003. *Rewriting the Rules, Year-End Report, 2002: The Bush Administration's Assault on the Environment*. Washington, DC: Natural Resources Defense Council.

Pietz, W. 1999. 'The Fetish of Civilization: Sacrificial Blood and Monetary Debt'. In P. Pels and O. Salemink (eds.). *Colonial Subjects: Essays on the Practical History of Anthropology*. Ann Arbor, MI: University of Michigan Press.

PNGLR. 1997. In the matter of an application under Section 57 of the Constitution: application by Individual and Community Rights Forum Inc (ICRAF) in re: Miriam Willingal, National Court of Justice. Papua New Guinea Law Reports, Port Moresby.

Pocock, J.G.A. 1992. 'Tangata Whenua and Enlightenment Anthropology', *New Zealand Journal of History*, 26: 28–53.

Polier, N. 1994. 'A View from the "Cyanide Room": Politics and Culture in a Mining Township in Papua New Guinea', *Identities*, 1(1): 63–84.

Posey, D. 1996. *Traditional Resource Rights: International Instruments for Protection and Compensation for Indigenous Peoples and Local Communities*. Gland, Switzerland: International Union for Conservation of Nature.

Posey, D. and G. Dutfield 1996. *Beyond Intellectual Property: Toward Traditional Resource Rights for Indigenous Peoples and Local Communities*. Ottawa: International Development Research Centre.

Pottage, A. 1998a. 'Instituting Property', *Oxford Journal of Legal Studies*, 18: 331–44.

—— 1998b. 'The Inscription of Life in Law: Genes, Patents, and Bio-Politics', *Modern Law Review*, 61: 740–65.

—— 2001. 'Persons and Things: an Ethnographic Analogy', *Economy and Society*, 30: 112–38.

Povinelli, E.A. 2001. 'Radical Worlds: the Anthropology of Incommensurability and Inconceivability', *Annual Review of Anthropology*, 30: 319–34.

—— 2002. *The Cunning of Recognition: Indigenous Alterities and the Making of Australian Multiculturalism*. Durham, NC: Duke University Press.

Powdermaker, H. 1933. *Life in Lesu: The Study of a Melanesian Society in New Ireland*. London: William and Norgate.

Puri, K. 1995. 'Cultural Ownership and Intellectual Property Rights Post-*Mabo*: Putting Ideas into Action', *Intellectual Property Journal*, 9: 293–347.

—— 1997. 'Preservation and the Conservation of Expressions of Folklore: The Experience of the Pacific Region'. UNESCO-WIPO World Forum on the Protection of Folklore Phuket, Thailand, 8–10 April, 1997.

—— 1999. 'Exploitation of Indigenous Traditional Culture'. SPC/UNESCO Symposium on the Protection of Traditional Knowledge and Expressions of Indigenous Culture in the Pacific Islands, Technical Paper No. 215. Noumea: SPC/UNESCO.

—— 2001. 'Draft Model Law for the Pacific'. Draft published as *Model Law for the Protection of Traditional Knowledge and Expressions of Culture*. In Working and Information Papers, 2nd Working group for Legal Experts on the Protection of Traditional Knowledge and Expressions of Culture, Noumea, New Caledonia, 2003.

Rabinow, P. 1996a. 'Severing the Ties: Fragmentation and Dignity in Late Modernity'. In P. Rabinow (ed.), *Essays on the Anthropology of Reason*. Princeton, NJ: University of Princeton Press.

—— 1996b. *Making PCR. A Story of Biotechnology*. Chicago, IL: University of Chicago Press.

—— 2000. 'Epochs, Presents, Events'. In M. Lock, A.Young and A. Cambrosio (eds.). *Living And Working with the New Medical Technologies: Intersections of Inquiry*. Cambridge: Cambridge University Press.

—— 2002. 'Midst Anthropology's Problems'. The 2001 David M. Schneider Distinguished Lecture. *Cultural Anthropology*, 17(2): 135–49.

Radin, M.J. 1982. 'Property and Personhood', *Stanford Law Review*, 34: 957–1015.

—— 1993. *Reinterpreting Property*. Chicago, IL: University of Chicago Press.

—— 1996. *Contested Commodities: Trade in Sex, Children, Body Parts and Other Things*. Cambridge, MA: Harvard University Press.

Raine, K. 1962. *Blake and Tradition*. Washington DC: The National Gallery of Art.

Rapp, F. 1990. 'Whitehead's Concept of Creativity and Modern Science'. In F. Rapp and R. Weihl (eds.), *Whitehead's Metaphysics of Creativity*. Albany, NY: State of New York Press.

Reed, A. 1999. 'Anticipating Individuals: Modes of Vision and Their Social Consequence in a Papua New Guinean Prison', *Journal of the Royal Anthropological Institute* (n.s.), 5: 43–56.

—— 2002. 'Smoking Kina: the Spirit of Tobacco in a Papua New Guinea Prison'. (University of Surrey, ms, written in response to 3rd PTC colloquium.)

Rifkin, J. 2001. 'Shopping for Humans', *Guardian Weekly*, 164/22.

Riles, A. 2000. *The Network Inside Out*. Ann Arbor: Michigan University Press.

—— 2004. 'Law as Object'. In D. Brenneis and S. Merry, (eds.), *Law and Empire in the Pacific: Fiji and Hawaii*. Santa Fe, NM: School of American Research Press.

Riordan, T. 1995. 'A Recent Patent on a Papua New Guinea Tribe's Cell Line Prompts Outrage and Charges of "Biopiracy"', *The New York Times*, 27 November: D2.

Robbins, J. 2001. 'Secrecy and the Sense of an Ending: Narrative, Time, and Everyday Millenarianism in Papua New Guinea and in Christian Fundamentalism', *Comparative Studies in Society and History*, 43: 525–51.

Rogers, P. 1972. *Defoe: The Critical Heritage*. London: Routledge and Kegan Paul.
Rose, C.M. 1994a. *Property and Persuasion: Essays in the History, Theory and Rhetoric of Ownership*. Boulder, CO: Westview Press.
────── 1994b. 'Possession as the Origin of Property'. In C.M. Rose, *Property and Persuasion: Essays on the History, Theory, and Rhetoric of Ownership*. Boulder, CO: Westview Press.
────── 1994c. 'Seeing Property'. In C.M. Rose, *Property and Persuasion: Essays on the History, Theory, and Rhetoric of Ownership*. Boulder, CO: Westview Press.
────── 2000. 'Expanding the Choices for the Global Commons: Comparing New-fangled Tradable Emission Allowance Schemes to Old-fashioned Common Property Regimes', *Duke Environmental Law & Policy Review*, 10: 45–72.
Rose, M. 1993. *Authors and Owners: The Invention of Copyright*. Cambridge, MA: Harvard University Press.
Rosen, L. 1997. 'The Right to be Different: Indigenous Peoples and the Quest for a Unified Theory'. *The Yale Law Journal*, 107(1): 227–59.
Ross, A. 1985. *The Life and Strange Surprizing Adventures of Robinson Crusoe*, D. Defoe, 1719. Edited with an introduction. London: Penguin.
Roulet, F. 1999. *Human Rights and Indigenous Peoples: A Handbook on the UN System*. Copenhagen: International Work Group for Indigenous Affairs.
Rousseau, J.-J. 1997 [1762]. *The Social Contract and Other Later Political Writings*. Edited and trans. V. Gourevitch. Cambridge: Cambridge University Press.
────── 1762. *Émile, ou De l'education*. Amsterdam.
Rowlands, R. 1998. 'The Power of Origins: Questions of Cultural Rights'. Inaugural lecture, University College, London.
Rumsey, A. and J. Weiner (eds.). 2001a. *Emplaced Myth: Space, Narrative, and Knowledge in Aboriginal Australia and Papua New Guinea*. Hawaii: University of Hawaii Press,
────── 2001b. *Mining and Indigenous Lifeworlds in Australia and Papua New Guinea*. Bathurst: Crawford House Publishing.
Sahlins, M. 1981. *Historical Metaphors and Mythical Realities*. Ann Arbor, MI: University of Michigan Press.
────── 1995. *How "Natives" Think: about Captain Cook, for example*. Chicago, IL: University of Chicago Press.
────── 1999. 'What is Anthropological Enlightenment? Some Lessons of the Twentieth Century', *Annual Review of Anthropology*, 28: i–xxiii.
Salisbury, R. 1976. 'Transactions or Transactors? An Economic Anthropologist's view'. In B. Kapferer (ed.), *Transaction and Meaning: Directions in the Anthropology of Exchange and Symbolic Behaviour*. Philadelphia, PA: Institute for the Study of Human Issues.
Santos, R.V. 2002 'Indigenous Peoples, Postcolonial Contexts and Genomic Research in the Late 20th Century: A View from Amazonia 1960–2000', *Critique of Anthropology*, 22(1): 81–104.
Saussure, F. 1983. *Course in General Linguistics*, trans. R. Harris, London: Duckworth.
Schieffelin, E.L. 1993. 'Performance and the Cultural Construction of Reality: A New Guinea Example'. In S. Lavie, K. Narayan and R. Rosaldo (eds.), *Creativity/Anthropology*. Ithaca, NY: Cornell University Press.
Schieffelin E.L. and R. Crittenden. 1991. *Like People You See in a Dream: First Contact in Six Papuan Societies*. Stanford, CA: Stanford University Press.
Scott, J.C. 1998. *Seeing Like a State: How Certain Schemes to Improve the Human Condition have Failed*. New Haven, CT: Yale University.

Sengi, D. 1996. 'The Challenge of the Hagahai Blood Saga'. In J. Friedlaender (ed.), 'Genes, People, and Property'. *Cultural Survival Quarterly*, 20(2): 40. Excerpted from 'Viewpoint', *Uni Tavur* (student newspaper of University of Papua New Guinea), 4 August, 1995.

Senie, H.F. 2002. *The Tilted Arc Controversy: Dangerous Precedent?* Minneapolis, MN: University of Minnesota Press.

Shapin, S. and S. Schaffer. 1985. *Leviathan and the Air Pump: Hobbes, Boyle and the Experimental Life*. Princeton, NJ: Princeton University Press.

Sherman, B. and L. Bentley. 1999. *The Making of Intellectual Property Law: the British Experience, 1760–1911*. Cambridge: Cambridge University Press.

Shiva, V. and Holla-Bhar, R. 1996. 'Piracy by Patent: The Case of the Neem Tree'. In E. Goldsmith and J. Mander (eds.), *The Case against the Global Economy and for a Turn towards Localization*. San Francisco, CA: Sierra Club.

Sillitoe, P. 1998. 'The Development of Indigenous Knowledge', *Current Anthropolog,y* 39(2): 223–52.

Simet, J. 2000. 'Copyrighting Traditional Tolai Knowledge?' In K. Whimp and M. Busse (eds.), *Protection of Intellectual, Biological and Cultural Property in Papua New Guinea*. Australian National University, Canberra: Asia Pacific Press and Port Moresby: Conservation Melanesia Inc.

―――― n.d. 'Custodians by Obligation'. Paper given to pre-PTC Conference Workshop, *Becoming Heirs: Making Inheritance Self-evident*, University of Manchester, December 2001.

Simon, B. n.d. 'Global Steps to Local Empowerment in the Next Millennium: An Assessment of UNESCO's 1989 *Recommendation on the Safeguarding of Traditional Culture and Folklore*'. Available at http://www.folklife.si.edu/unesco/simon/htm.

Simpson, T. (on behalf of the Forest Peoples Programme). 1997. *Indigenous Heritage and Self-Determination: The Cultural and Intellectual Property Rights of Indigenous Peoples*. Copenhagen: International Work Group for Indigenous Affairs.

Sismondo, S. 2004. *An Introduction to Science and Technology Studies*. Oxford: Blackwell.

Smith, C. 2001. 'Foreword'. *Creative Mapping Document 2001*. UK Government/Department of Culture, Media and Sport.

Smith, L.T. 1998. *Decolonizing Methodologies: Research and Indigenous Peoples*. New York and Dunedin: Zed Books and University of Otago Press.

Sneath, D. n.d. 'Proprietary Regimes and Sociotechnical Systems: Rights over Land in Mongolia's "Age of the Market"'. Presented at Wenner-Gren symposium on 'Changing Property Relations at the Turn of the Millenium', Ronda (Spain), 2001.

Soto, H. de 2000. *The Mystery of Capital: Why Capitalism Triumphs in the West and Fails Everywhere Else*. New York: Basic Books.

Spragens, T.A. 1973. *The Politics of Motion: The World of Thomas Hobbes*. London: Croom Helm.

Ssorin-Chaikov, N. 2000. 'Bear Skins and Macaroni: the Social Life of Things at the Margins of a Siberian State Collective'. In P. Seabright (ed.), *The Vanishing Rouble: Barter Networks and Non-Monetary Transactions in Post-Soviet Societies*. Cambridge: Cambridge University Press.

Stevenson, M. 1999. 'Carving Out a Future'. *Paradise Magazine*, 135: 25.

Strathern, M. 1985. 'John Locke's Servant and the Hausboi from Hagen: Some Thoughts on Domestic Labour', *Critical Philosophy* 2: 21–48.

—— 1988. *The Gender of the Gift: Problems with Women and Problems with Society in Melanesia*. Berkeley, CA: University of California Press.

—— 1991. 'One Man and Many Men'. In M. Godelier and M. Strathern (eds.), *Big Men and Great Men. Personifications of Power in Melanesia*. Cambridge: Cambridge University Press.

—— 1992. *Reproducing the Future*. Manchester: Manchester University Press.

—— 1996. 'Cutting the Network', *Journal of the Royal Anthropological Institute* (n.s.) 2: 517–35.

—— 1999a. *Property, Substance and Effect: Anthropological Essays on Persons and Things*. London: Athlone Press.

—— 1999b. 'What is Intellectual Property After?' In J. Law and J. Hassard (eds.), *Actor Network Theory and After*. Oxford: Blackwell Publishers/ Sociological Review Monograph.

—— 2000. 'Emergent Properties'. Robert and Maurine Rothschild Distinguished Lecture. Department of the History of Science, Harvard University [pamphlet].

—— 2001. 'Global and Local Contexts'. In L. Kalinoe and J. Leach (eds.), *Rationales of Ownership: Ethnographic Studies of Transactions and Claims to Ownership in Contemporary Papua New Guinea*. New Delhi: UBS Publishers' Distributors Ltd.

—— 2002. 'Externalities in Comparative Guise', *Economy and Society*, 31: 250–267.

—— n.d. 'Divided Origins and the Arithmetic of Ownership'. Paper delivered at the Critical Theory Institute, 'Futures of Property and Personhood', UC Irvine, April 2002.

Swanson, T.M. (ed.). 1995. *Intellectual Property Rights and Biodiversity Conservation: an Interdisciplinary Analysis of the Values of Medicinal Plants*. Cambridge: Cambridge University Press.

Sykes, K. 2001. 'Introduction: A Case Study Approach to Cultural Property in the New Guinea Islands Region'. In K. Sykes et al., *Culture and Cultural Property in the New Guinea Islands Region: Seven Case Studies*. New Dehli: UBS Publishers' Distributors Ltd.

—— with J. Simet and S. Kamene (eds.). 2001. *Culture and Cultural Property in the New Guinea Islands Region: Seven Case Studies*. New Delhi: UBS Publishers' Distributors Ltd.

Taubes, G. 1995. 'Scientists Attacked for "Patenting" Pacific Tribe', *Science*, 270(17): 1112.

Tauli-Corpuz, V. 1999. 'TRIPS and its Potential Impacts on Indigenous Peoples'. In *Indigenous Peoples and Intellectual Property Rights (IPR)*, Tebtebba Briefing Paper 5, Baguio City, Philippines: Tebtebba Foundation, Inc. Available at: http://www.tebtebba.org/about_us/publications/bp/bp.htm

Taylor, M. 2000. 'Foreword'. In M. Busse and K. Whimp (eds.), *Protection of Intellectual, Biological and Cultural Property in Papua New Guinea*. Canberra and Port Moresby: Asia Pacific Press and Conservation Melanesia Inc.

Tebtebba Briefing Paper No. 5, *Indigenous Peoples and Intellectual Property Rights (IPR)*. Baguio City, Philippines: Tebtebba Foundation, Inc., The Indigenous Peoples' International Centre for Policy Research and Education, pp. 1–5. Available at: http://www.tebtebba.org/about_us/publications/bp/bp.htm

Titmuss, R. 1997. [1970] *The Gift Relationship: From Human Blood to Social Policy*. Original edition with new chapters, eds. A. Oakley and J. Ashton. London: LSE Books.

Tobin, B. 2000. 'The Search for an Interim Solution'. In K. Whimp and M. Busse (eds.), *Protection of Intellectual, Biological and Cultural Property in Papua New Guinea*. Canberra and Port Moresby: Asia Pacific Press and Conservation Melanesia Inc.

Torremans P. and J. Holyoak. 1998. *Intellectual Property Law*. 2nd ed. London: Butterworths.

Tully, J. 1980. *A Discourse on Property: Locke and his Adversaries*. Cambridge: Cambridge University Press.

UK Government/DfES. 2002. '14–19: Extending Opportunities, Raising Standards'. Green paper.

UNESCO. 2002. *Declaration on Cultural Diversity*. Geneva: UNESCO.

―――― 2003. 'Preserving and Revitalizing our Intangible Heritage'. Available at: http://www.unesco.org/culture/heritage/intangible/html_eng/index_en.shtml

UNESCO-WIPO 1997. 'UNESCO-WIPO World Forum on the Protection of Folklore'. Geneva.

Vaidhyanathan, S. 2001. *Copyrights and Copywrongs: The Rise of Intellectual Property and How it Threatens Creativity*. New York: New York University Press.

Vail, J. 1993. 'The Impact of the Mt. Kare Goldrush on the People of the Tari District'. In T. Taufa and C. Bass (eds.), *Population, Family, Health and Development*. Port Moresby: University of Papua New Guinea.

Verdery, K. 1998. 'Property and Power in Transylvania's Decollectivization'. In C.M. Hann (ed.), *Property Relations: Renewing the Anthropological Tradition*. Cambridge: Cambridge University Press.

―――― 2003. *The Vanishing Hectare: Property and Value in Postsocialist Transylvania*. Ithaca and London: Cornell University Press.

―――― n.d. 'The Obligation of Ownership: Restoring Rights to Land in Postsocialist Eastern Europe'. Presented at Wenner-Gren symposium on 'Changing Property Relations at the Turn of the Millennium', Ronda (Spain), 2001.

Viveiros de Castro, E. 1998. 'Cosmological Deixis and Amerinidian Perspectivism', *Journal of the Royal Anthropological Institute* (n.s.), 4: 469–88

Wagner, R. 1975. *The Invention of Culture*. Englewood Cliffs, NJ: Prentice-Hall.

―――― 1986. *Symbols that Stand for Themselves*. Chicago, IL: University of Chicago Press.

Weatherall, K. 2001. 'Culture, Autonomy and Djulibinyamurr: Individual and Community in the Construction of Rights to Traditional Designs', *Modern Law Review*, 62(4): 191–214.

―――― 2001. *An Anthropology of the Subject: Holographic Worldview in New Guinea and its Meaning and Significance for the World of Anthropology*. Berkeley, CA: University of California Press.

Weber, M. 1989a [1905]. 'Protestant Asceticism and the Spirit of Capitalism'. In W.G. Runciman (ed.), *Weber: Selections in Translation*. Cambridge: Cambridge University Press.

―――― 1989b [1905]. 'The Concept of "Following a Rule"'. In W.G. Runciman (ed.), *Weber: Selections in Translation*. Cambridge: Cambridge University Press.

Weiner, J. 1999. 'Culture in a Sealed Envelope: the Concealment of Australian Aboriginal Heritage Tradition in the Hindmarsh Island Bridge Affair', *Journal of Royal Anthropological Institute* (n.s.), 5: 193–210.

―――― n.d. 'The Foi Incorporated Land Group: Law and Custom in Group Definition and Collective Action in the Kutubu Oil Project Area, PNG'. Paper given to 2nd PTC Colloquium, *Inter-Gender and Inter-Generational Transactions*, Girton College, Cambridge, June 2000.

Weiss, K.M. 1996. 'Biological Diversity is Inherent in Humanity'. In J. Friedlaender (ed.), 'Genes, People, and Property'. *Cultural Survival Quarterly*, 20(2): 26–28.

West Ningerum Pressure Association. 2000. 'Petition on the Demand of Compensation Claims'. 27 September 2000.

Whimp, K. and M. Busse (eds.). 2000. *Protection of Intellectual, Biological and Cultural Property in Papua New Guinea*. Canberra and Port Moresby: Asia Pacific Press and Conservation Melanesia Inc.

Whitehouse, H. 1996. 'Apparitions, Orations and Rings: Experience of Spirits in Dadul'. In J. Mageo and A. Howard (eds.), *Spirits in Culture, History, and Mind*. New York: Routledge.

Winthrop, R. 2002a. 'Exploring Cultural: Rights: an Introduction'. *Cultural Rights and Indigenous Identity in the Americas*, special issue, *Cultural Dynamics*, 14: 115–20.

—— 2002b. 'Defining a Right to Culture, and Some Alternatives'. *Cultural Rights and Indigenous Identity in the Americas*, special issue, *Cultural Dynamics*, 14: 161–83.

WIPO. 1997. '1967, 1982, 1984: Attempts to Provide International Protection for Folklore by Intellectual Property Rights'. UNESCO-WIPO World Forum on the Protection of Folklore, Phucket, Thailand, 8–10 April 1997. WIPO http://www.wipo.int

Wissink, D. 2000. 'The Ok Tedi Development Foundation'. Paper given to the 2000 PNG Mining & Petroleum Investment Conference, Sydney, December 2000.

Young, C. 2002. 'Business Index'. In *Ways of Working. Placing Artists in Business Contacts* (CD-ROM). London: Arts Council of England.

Young, M. 1994. 'From Riches to Rags: Dismantling Hierarchy in Kalauna', *History and Anthropology*, 7: 263–78.

Ziman, J. 2002. 'The Microeconomics of Academic Science'. In P. Mirowski and E-M. Sent (eds.), *Science Bought and Sold: Essays in the Economics of Science*. Chicago, IL: University of Chicago Press.

General Index

A
'Are'Are (Solomon Islands), 77
Aborigines (Australian), 15, 42, 56, 58n4
academy, 180, 181, 182, 188
 and intellectual property, 182
accountability, 96
Actor Network Theory, 89, 124
addition, 189
adornment, 186
agency, 152, 159, 160, 165, 178
 and creativity, 152-52, 160-61, 165, 174n20
 social, 112, 127
alienation, 67-68, 70, 77, 103n9, 107n41
Angkaiyakmin (Western Province), 114, 115
anthropology
 debates in, ix
 symmetrical, 189
appearance, 11
 public, 190n2
Arnhem Land, 58n8
art, 140, 151, 178, 181
 nexus, 178
 and paintings by Bob Kain, 113, 116
 and privatisation, 181
 public, 135, 136
 Tilted Arc (Richard Serra), 71
 of William Blake, 157-58
artist, 177
auditing, 95, 101
 political, 95-97
Australia, 10. *See also* Aborigines
Australian Museum, 44
authenticity, 71, 81n11

author, 176, 177, 178
authorisation, 45, 54
authority, 55, 75
 to reproduce, 44
authorship, 104n19, 167, 175n33, 178, 182, 191n10
 multiple origins, 178
 Rai Coast, 167-68
 scientific, 89-91
Avatip (Sepik), 48

B
Baktaman (Highlands), 112
balance metaphors, 111-12, 117, 119, 121, 123-28, 130n11
barter, 103n7
benefit, 91
benefit-sharing, 53, 92, 93
Bentham, Jeremy, 12, 123-24, 130n12
Berne Convention, 81n10
BHP Billiton, 27-31
big men, 189
 of ceremony, 188
 of science, 188
biological models, 159-60, 173n18
bioprospecting, 106n29
biotechnology, 23, 26, 31, 33
 industry, 183, 184
Blake, William, 157-58
Bogia District (Madang), 47
Bolivip (Western Province), 114
boundary, 178, 179, 181, 187
 and academy and business, 183
 of exchange, 187, 188
 and multiple origins, 183
boundary work, 177, 178, 179

and ceremony, 178
and science, 177
bridewealth, 77
Broken Hill Proprietary (BHP), 110ff
business, 151, 153, 154, 155, 171, 183
  affinal obligations and, 155, 172
  creativity and, 151–53
  ventures, 155

C
capital, 21, 27, 34
CDs, 79
church fundraising, 86
citizens, 119
  corporate, 129n1
cloning
  of genes, 184
  human, 161
cocoa fermentary, 155
cold fusion, 177
collective, 6, 11–12, 24, 32, 34, 35, 85, 93
  environmental-cum-humanitarian interests, 122
  ownership, 17n14, 32
  rights, x, 24
  work, 163
combination, 152–53, 158, 163–64, 173n9
  of elements, 153
  modelling of, 152
commemoration, 61
commerce, 158
commercialisation, 184
commodification, 9, 22, 32, 36n7, 50, 94
commodities, 32, 87, 89, 101–2, 103n9, 188
common good, 65
common law. See law
commons, the, 24, 25, 31, 32, 33, 35, 65, 66, 72, 104n22, 132, 179
  'biological', 24, 25, 35
  'cultural', 32, 33
  'global', 31
  the new, 132, 142, 147
  and property, 66, 72
  seventeenth century, 142–43
  'tragedy of', 31, 35

communal, 6, 85, 93
  enterprise, 155.
  See also rights
Community Mine Continuation Agreements (CMCAs), 29–30.
  See also Ok Tedi mine
community, 18n24, 81n7
compensation, 28–29, 31, 43, 54, 55, 67, 69, 82n16, 92, 93, 110, 111, 115, 118–19, 127
  for loss of resources, 27, 28
competition, 153, 173n13
concealment and revelation, 60–82
consultation, process of, 120, 129n2
contingency and necessity, 158, 162, 164–66, 169
Convention on Biological Diversity (CBD), vii, 4, 40, 51, 56
copying, 155, 168
Copyright and Neighbouring Rights Act 2000 (PNG), 10, 52, 53–54
copyright, 2, 3, 17n16 22, 35, 43, 45, 49, 69, 70, 72, 79, 104n19, 168, 169, 190n2, 191n6
  legislation, 10, 52, 53–54
  Universal Copyright Convention, 51
corporations, 181, 182
Council for Science and Technology, 151, 173n11
creation, 176, 177, 178, 179, 180, 181, 183
  as analytic, 7–8, 13–14
  and art, 178
  and disco, 187
  and everyday discourse, 179
  and Hagahai, 188
  and intellectual property law, 179
  and object/thing, 177
  and persuasion, 178
  and PCR, 189
  and science, 178
creativity, 6, 8, 32, 34, 151–75, 190n4
  and agency, 152–53, 160–61, 165, 174n20
  appropriative, 157, 164–65, 169–71
  and business, 151–53
  distributed, 157, 163–67, 169, 170
  and evolution, 159–60
  God and, 160–61

intellectual, 154
intellectual property and, 153, 156–57, 169–70
rhetoric surrounding, 156–57, 158, 161
reproduction and 156–57, 167. *See also* innovation; transcendence
creator, 176, 177, 179, 180, 181
and disco, 186
and Hagahai, 188
and law, 176
credibility, 177, 178, 179, 181, 186, 188, 189
credit, 86
crisis, 180
in academia, 94
in IPR, 94
cult
house, 114, 163
leader, 114
spirit, 154, 167
culture, viii, 97, 186
boundaries of Fuyuge, 186
change, 162
concept, 145
expressions of, 3, 4, 15n3, 53, 180
as a human project, 173n9
indigenous, viii, ix
and knowledge, 94
and nature, 160
as problematic, viii
and property rights, 25, 31–34, 37n14
protection of, 98
and secret or sacred material, 42, 44
cultural property, vii–viii, ix, 1, 2, 5, 15n1, 41, 71, 138, 139, 184, 187
and indigenous knowledge, 184
rights, 25, 31–34, 37n14
secret or sacred, 33
cultural rights, 2, 16n7, 95, 99
custodians, 46
customary land tenure. *See* land
customary law. *See* law
customs, 57. *See also* tradition; *kastam*; *kastom*

D

dance, 41, 185
traditional, 50

Darwin, Charles, 160
debt, 86, 89, 96, 100
Defoe, Daniel, 122, 124–25
design, 44, 46, 53
development
programs, 119
projects, 118
sustainable, 111, 118, 129n4, 129n6
digital network, 79
disco, 185
and *gab*, 185, 189
as indigenous, 186
and speed, 185, 189
discoverer, 187
discovery paradigm, 116–17
display, 137
division, 189
DNA, 23, 24, 37n10, 179, 188
and patenting, 23–25, 179. *See also* HGDP
Draft Treaty, 51. *See also* UNESCO

E

economy
economic opportunity, 49
economic rights, 47, 49
globalised, 179
education, 153
school fees, 156
embodiment, 98
emissions trading, 26
engineer/bricoleur, 158–59
environment, 26–31, 38n18
environmental concerns, 12
Environmental Defense, 38n18
environmental effects, 115
environmental impact, 9
environmental issues, 111
environmental resources, 105n23
environmental responsibility, 110–11, 115, 117, 121, 128
evolution, 160, 161, 166
and creativity, 159–60
exchange, 25, 114, 140, 145, 146, 163, 164, 166, 187
of scientific data, 89ff
of skin, 114
theory, 86
value, 103n7
exclusion, degrees of, 137

F

fetishism, 68, 74
Fiji, 37n14
flexibility, 153–54
flute, 48
Fly river, 117
folklore, 17n16, 42, 43, 53, 58n4
Fore (Eastern Highlands), 187, 188
form, 176, 177, 178, 183, 186, 189
Foucault, Michel, 123
Freud, Sigmund, 142
  and Hobbes, 142
Fuyuge (Central Province), 14, 185ff

G

gab, 185
Galileo, 125, 182
game theory, 86–89, 104n12, 104n14
gender relations, xii
gene, 12–15, 35, 36n3, 37n10, 37n13, 37n14, 38n15
  patenting, 91
General Agreement on Tariffs and Trade (GATT), 151, 172n1
generations, 13, 134ff
  cross-generational debate, 138
  difference between, x, 5
  generational relations, 129n6
genetic heritage, 105n25
genetic material, 22, 183
gifts, 87, 89, 92, 101, 103n9, 187,
  and commodities, 104n14
  Euro-American economy, 90
  exchange, 11
  gift-commodity debate, 88
global warming, 26, 27
globalisation, 22, 36, 145
Goodenough Island (Milne Bay), 75
groups, exclusivity of, 98, 107n39

H

Hagahai (Madang), 9, 14, 21–25, 36n3, 37n11, 116, 188
  and creation, 188
haus tambaran (spirit house), 48
heritage, 1, 2, 15n1, 15n3, 24, 35, 43, 50, 92, 97, 98, 105n24, 132
  common, 161
  lost, 51
  secret or sacred, 43–44, 45
  hiding, 137

Hobbes, Thomas, 112, 124–26, 128, 130n13, 140, 141–43, 146
  and Freud, 142
human genome, 23, 24, 26, 35, 36n7, 179
  and commons, 179
  Human Genome Diversity Project (HGDP), 36n7
  Human Genome Organisation, 92
  Human Genome Project, 23, 105n25
human rights. *See* rights

I

Iatmul (Sepik), 73, 141
incompleteness, 113–16
  effect of, 113–14
indigenous, 32, 78, 180
  definition of, xii
  heritage, 92
  indigeneity, 78
  knowledge, 15n3, 184, 185
  peoples, 4, 17n16, 17n19, 22–25, 30, 32, 35, 37n10, 39n24, 53, 55, 98
  rights, 4
individual, 12, 13, 23–25, 30, 32, 35, 39n24, 91
  and collective, 112
  possessive, 25, 143
  right-holder, 85
  rights, x
inertia, 95, 96, 99, 100, 101, 106n32
inflation, 95, 96, 99, 101, 106n32
  monetary, 95, 99
  of values, 94
initiation, 44, 47, 48, 73. *See also* ritual
innovation, 34, 85, 97, 102n1 132, 139, 151, 153–54, 156, 168
  and business, 153–56
  designs/songs, 167–68
  musical, 154
  Nekgini, 167–68
  religious, 154
intangible, 3, 6, 61, 64, 71, 80n1
  in persons, 98–99
  resources, 79
intellect, 161–62, 164, 166
intellectual, 10, 69
  phenomenon, 169
  rights, 6

intellectual property, 1, 41, 61, 69,
      71, 72, 78–79, 90, 156, 173n10,
      182, 188. *See also* intellectual
      property rights
   and the academy, 182
   and creativity, 153, 156–57,
      169–70
   international regimes, 152
   law, 180
   system of, 90
Intellectual Property Office (IPO), 52
intellectual property rights (IPR), xi,
      3, 8, 17n15, 49, 153, 170
   crisis in, 3
   introduction of regime, 41
   introduction of to PNG, vii–viii
   protocols, ix
   questioning of 'intellectual', 43
intellectuals, 178
interest, 12–13, 66, 132–48
   fees for, 137
   as joke, 138
   as legal concern, 143
   as motor of transformation, 144
   and passions, 142, 143
   personal, 137–38
   private, 133
   senses of, 142
international community, 16n4
internet, 191n6
intersubjectivity, 170
invention, 171, 178, 183, 184, 188
   inventiveness, 97, 140
   inventors, 176, 178

J
John Moore v. Regents of the
      University of California, 23

K
Kain, Bob, artist, 113, 116
Kaluli (Southern Highlands), 73
Kambot Storyboard, 46
Kant, Immanuel, 122–23
kastam (PNG), 34
kastom (Vanuatu), 5, 18n21
Kavieng (New Ireland), 134, 135
   airport, 136
kinship, 35, 38n22, 155
   obligation, 29
   and ownership, viii, xi
   paternal and maternal, viii
   systems of, xi
Kiunga (Western Province), 117, 118
knowledge, 4, 164, 177
   anthropology of, 141
   ethnobotanical, 105n28
   indigenous, 15n3, 184, 185
   protection of traditional, ix
   ritual, 76
   scientific, 62, 94, 187
   secret or sacred, 6, 10, 136, 186,
      189
   systems, 92
   traditional, viii, ix, 2, 4, 8, 17n16,
      41, 43, 53, 145
Kula, 140
kuru, 187–89

L
labour, 25, 31, 154, 155, 156, 163.
      See also work
land, 29, 60–61, 63, 66, 78, 80n1, 95,
      116, 120, 132, 144
   and airspace, 63
   boundaries of, 60
   claims, 35
   customary tenure of, 30, 42
   and matriliny, 66
   owners, 29, 30, 78, 124, 117, 118,
      119
   ownership, 21, 38n22, 78, 80
   tenure, 42
   as *terra nugax*, 116–17, 120, 121
   as *terra nullius*, 35, 92
law, 24, 26, 29, 30, 34, 35, 38n15,
      176ff, 181, 186
   common law, xii, 29, 52, 56, 57,
      189
   customary law, xii, 10, 30, 46, 56,
      58n8, 77, 189
   intellectual property, 180
legislation
   intellectual property rights, xn4
   patent, 10, 53
   PNG, 4
Lelet Plateau (New Ireland), 13,
      134ff
Leviathan, 124, 125, 126, 140,
      141–43
liability, 95, 96
local government, 136

Locke, John, 25, 31, 72, 143, 144, 146, 161, 171
loss, 6, 66, 67, 146, 147
　of culture, 3
　of knowledge, 3, 6
　of subsistence base, 27
'lost tribe', 24, 37n11
Lower Sepik, 46

M

Madang, 47, 48
magic, 75
　names, 164
　magicians, 170
　power, 186
　spells, 76
malanggan (funerary sculpture), 73, 133ff
　carvers, 136
　as public art, 135–36
Manam Island (Madang), 47
Manambu (Sepik), 48
Mandak (New Ireland), 139
Maori (New Zealand), 77, 106n39, 107n43, 140
market, 91, 104n20
　forces, 105 n24
Marx, Karl, 67, 68, 123–24, 154, 157, 171, 173n9, 174n23
Mataatua Declaration, 17n18
material
　secret or sacred, 46, 54
mechanized world picture, 112, 117–18, 122–23, 125–28, 130n11, 130n13, 131n15
mental/material distinction, 167–69
Melanesia, vii, ix
　specificities, 12
men's houses, 61, 62
Milpurrurru and others v. Indofurn Pty Ltd, 58n6, 58n8
mining continuation agreements. See Ok Tedi mine; Community Mining Continuation Agreements
Min, 133, 134
mines
　impact, 113, 115, 117–18, 120
　legislation, 28–29
　Ok Tedi, 110–31.
　See also Ok Tedi mine

missionaries
　Catholic, 115
　Christian, 192n14
Model Law for the Protection of Traditional Knowledge and Expressions of Culture in the Pacific Islands, 4, 6, 15n3, 16n12, 52, 56
Model Provisions for National Laws on the Protection of Expressions of Folklore Against Illicit Exploitation and Other Prejudicial Action 1982, 51, 52, 55
modernist, 186
modernity, 31, 185
　and tradition, viii
molecular biology, 183, 191n13
money, 14, 85–86, 96, 100, 111, 132, 136, 155, 156
　and monetary benefits, 92
　value, 38n18
Monte Carlo method, 184
moral rights. See rights
Morobe Province, 48
Mount Kare gold rush, 39n24
Mt. Fubilan (Western Province), 115, 116, 117, 118, 121
multiple claims, 102
museums, 1, 2, 13, 35, 132, 133, 134–48ff, 185
　enhouse, 133, 147
　local, 134–39
　and Maori meeting house, 140
music, 41, 47, 54, 79, 178
　composition of, 176
　industry, 172n1
　instruments, 185
　modern, 41
　rhythm, 185ff
　sacred flute, 47
　traditional, 41, 50
Muyuw (Milne Bay), 108n54

N

names
　magical, 164
National Council of Chiefs, Vanuatu, 53
National Cultural Commission (NCC), 41, 50, 51

National Cultural Council, Vanuatu, 53
National Cultural Property (Preservation) Act, 15n1
National Cultural Property Ordinance (1965), 15n1
National IPR Committee (NIPRC), 41, 52
nature
 and culture, 160
naven ceremony, 141
negotiation
 between domains, 183
Nekgini (Madang), 172n6
 definition of work, 166
 innovation, 167–68
 palem, 163
 patuki, 164
 speakers of, 163ff
networks, 189
New Ireland, 13, 73, 133ff
New Zealand, 77
Newton, Isaac, 126
NGOs, 4, 15, 16n4, 22, 23, 32, 35, 36n2, 130n8, 132
Notsi (New Ireland), 134
novelty
 of form, 152
 and stability, 160–62

O

objectification, 63, 67–68, 72, 81n8
obligations, 165, 166
Ok Ma dam, 117, 121
Ok Tedi mine, ix, 22, 27–31, 38n19, 38n20, 110, 115
 environmental impact, 9
 Ok Tedi Development Foundation, 118–21, 127, 129n4, 129n5, 130n9
 OK Tedi Mine Continuation Agreement (MCA), 12, 111ff, 121, 127, 129n2
 Ok Tedi Mining Limited (OTML), 110–31
 shares in, 38n19
origin, 14, 81n11, 166, 178, 187
 multiple, 183, 189
 original, 74, 179
 original work, 46

originality, 176, 178
originator, 189
ownership, 2, 3, 10, 33, 65
 collective, 17n14
 communal and collective, 97ff
 multiple, 33, 155–56
 private, 32
 rights, 7

P

Paiela (Enga Province), 73
palem (Nekgini), 163
Palestine, 95–97, 101
Panopticon, 12, 123
patent, 2, 3, 9, 14, 17n16, 21–25, 31, 34–35, 36n3, 37n12, 38n15, 39n26, 43, 53, 69, 70, 79, 170, 174n20, 184, 188, 191n11
 DNA, 179
 in Hagahi cell line, 22–25
 legislation, 10, 53, 178, 184
Patents and Industrial Designs Act 2000 (PNG), 10, 53
patuki (Nekgini), 164
paying parties, 86
performance, 74
perpetual motion, 110–31 *passim*, 125
personhood, 161
 moral, 165
 and production/reproduction of the self, 156–57, 162
 Rai Coast, 166–67
persuasion, 179, 185
poetry
 of William Blake, 157–58
policy makers
 PNG, 10
politics, 23, 30–33, 36, 37n10
pollution, 22, 26–27, 29, 31, 35, 38n23
polymerase chain reaction (PCR), 183, 184, 189
 and creation, 189
 and invention, 183, 184
 as legal entity, 184
 and speed, 184
postsocialist Europe, 95
power
 magical, 186
practice theory, 143

preservation, 41, 51, 55
prestige-reward system, 90
private, 66
　appropriations, 91
　ownership, 32
　property, 21, 31, 66, 91, 97, 147
　rights, x
privatisation, 95–97, 100
　and art, 181
　globalised, 181
prohibitions, 48
property, 7, 31, 61, 90
　as an analytic, 7–8, 9–11
　and 'the commons', 66, 72
　and communication, 62, 78, 79
　as communication technology, 62ff
　cultural, 71
　cultural and intellectual, xi, 17n19
　discussion of, 4–5
　general character of, 63
　intangible, 64, 71
　intellectual, 69, 71, 72, 78–79
　interests in the body, 24
　Marxist conception of, 67–69
　negative effects of, 96
　private, 21, 31, 66, 91, 97, 147
　regime, 21, 23–26, 31, 34–36
　and scarcity, 80
　theory, 77
　and time, 61–62, 67, 76–77
Property, Transactions, Creations (PTC), vii–x
protection, 4, 6, 10, 15n1, 15n3, 49, 54, 55, 91, 92, 147, 168, 186
　of cultural heritage, xii
　of cultural property, 1
　of culture, 98
　of traditional cultures, xi
protections, 32, 35, 132, 146
puberty, 73
public, 66, 155, 164
　domain, 32, 33, 37, 50, 90, 92, 97, 104n18
　freedoms, 91
purchase
　of rights, 48

R
RAFI (Rural Advance Foundation International), 23, 36n4, 36n5, 188

Rai Coast, 154–75 *passim*, 172n6.
　See also Reite
　authorship, 167–68
　personhood, 166–67
Re Fisherman Island Case [1979], 42
Re Petition of M.T. Somare, 57
reciprocity, 133
recognition, 174n29
regulation, ix, xi
regulatory regime, 51
Reite (Madang), 13, 154–75 *passim*
repatriation, 132
reproductive model, 163–65, 167, 168
research
　university, 91
resources, 4, 9, 26, 29, 31, 33, 35, 64, 65, 66, 170
　natural, 26–31
　perception of, 3
revelation, 11
rights, 63, 69, 89ff, 101–2
　common, 91
　communal, 18n24
　communal vs. private, x
　economic, 49
　human, xii, 16n7, 17n14, 105n25
　in song, 10
　indigenous, 4
　individual, x
　intellectual, 6
　moral, 49, 70, 72, 81n10
　multiple, 85
　purchase of, 48
　use, 29, 66
risk, 21, 26, 31, 37n10
ritual, 48, 73–79 *passim*, 82n15, 82n16, 185
　efficacy of, 76
　initiation, 73
　knowledge, 76
　naven, 141
　postpartum, 75
Robinson Crusoe, 117, 121–27, 130n10
Romania, 95, 100
Rousseau, Jean-Jacques, 122–23, 127–28, 130n10, 130n11
royalties, 54

S

sacred, 137, 139, 146
   degrees of, 138
Saussurean linguistics, 143–44
schismogenesis, 141
school fees, 156
science, 91, 115, 177–90 *passim*
   authorship, 89–91
   big men, 188
   and the Cold War, 180, 187
   creation, 178
   credentials, 187
   credibility, 177
   development of, 153
   research, 180
   rewards, 99
   studies, 14
secrecy, 75, 76, 116
   and knowledge, 10
   secretive processes, 73
   secrets, 136
self-interest, 112, 119, 122, 125, 127, 132–48 *passim*
   free of, 119
Serra, Richard, 71–72, 82n13
   Serra v. United States General Services Administration, 82n13
   Tilted Arc, 71
signified/signifier distinction, 158
skin, 186, 189
   exchange of, 114
slavery, 24
Smith, Adam, 145
social change, 143–45
social contract, 12, 112, 122–23, 126–28, 141–43
Solomon Islands, 77
song, 41, 54, 155, 187
   rights in, 10
   sacred, 163
   traditional, 181
sorcery, 76, 77, 187
speeding things up, 184–87, 191n13. *See also* world, speeded up
spells. *See* magic
spirits, 163, 166, 167, 168
   cult, 154, 167
   Nekgini, 163, 167–68
   voice, 168
Suau (Milne Bay), 60–82 *passim*
subject/object relations, 179

substantivisation
   as effect, 133, 146
   and epistemology, 147
   and ontology, 145, 147
sui generis
   intellectual property rights, 105n27
   legislation, 52
   systems, 33, 34
sustainability, 28, 31, 35, 111, 118, 120, 127–28, 129n1, 129n4, 129n6
sustainable development, 111, 118, 129n4, 129n6

T

Tabar (New Ireland), 135
tabu, 144
Tabubil (Western Province), 117
Tanga (New Ireland), 60, 61
tangata whenua (people of the land, Maori), 77
tangibles, 80n1
technology, development of, 153
terra nugax, 116–17, 120, 121
terra nullius, 35, 92
theft, 73–74, 82n16, 168
   of traditional culture, 1
Tilted Arc, 71–72. *See also* Richard Serra
tourism, 2, 3, 134, 135, 147n3
Trade-Related Aspects of Intellectual Property Rights (TRIPS), vii, xn3, 17n15, 22, 31, 40, 56, 151, 172n1, 189
trading zones, 183, 185, 187
tradition, x, xi, 2, 32, 34, 85
   and knowledge, viii
   as a modern concept, viii–ix
traditional, 185, 186
   culture, 92
   indigenous knowledge, 102n1
   knowledge, 4, 8, 17n16, 41, 43, 53, 145
traditions, 179, 192n14
transaction, 63, 73, 78, 163, 184
   as an analytic, 7–9, 11–13
transactionalism, 86–69, 112, 124
transactions, 6, 14, 61, 165
   visibility of, 94
transcendence, 160–61

transmission, 139, 140
tree, 73
Trobriand Islands, 77

U

UN Draft Declaration on the Rights of Indigenous Peoples, 16n11
UNESCO, ix, xi, 4, 15n1, 16n8, 16n12, 22, 24, 32, 35, 51, 105n24
uniqueness, 71
United Nations, 16n4
Universal Copyright Convention, 51
Universal Declaration on Cultural Diversity, 105n24
universities, 181, 182
Upper Ramu, 47
US National Institute of Neurological Disorders and Stroke, 188
use rights, 29, 66

V

value, 22, 26–28, 32–35, 34n24, 37n10, 38n18, 133, 170, 178
   financial, 137, 138
   global, 152
   preservation of, 147
   transformation of, 143–44
values, 87
   cultural, 111
   environment, 121
Vanuatu, 18n21, 37n14, 5, 53
   National Council of Chiefs, 53
   National Cultural Council, 53
   kastom, 5, 18n21
Victoria Park Racing and Recreation Grounds Co. Ltd. v. Taylor, 64, 68

visibility, 133, 165, 166, 174n29, 178, 186, 188
visual
   appraisal, 68
   manifestation, 11
   properties, 61
Visual Artists Rights Act 1990, 81n10

W

Weber, Max, 122, 124
West Ningerum Pressure Association, 115
Western Province Capacity Building Program, 121
will, 152, 162
Wopkaimin (Western Province), 113
work, 166, 174n30. *See also* labour
   collective, 163
   Nekgini definition of, 166
World Bank, 21, 28
World Intellectual Property Organisation (WIPO), xi, 4, 16n12, 17n16, 22, 32, 51, 56, 145, 172n1, 179, 189
World Trade Organisation (WTO), vii, 22, 31, 40, 98, 145, 151, 172n1, 179, 189
   trade talks, 110
world, speeded up, 153–54

Y

Yonggom (Western Province), 29–31
Yumbulul v. Aboriginal Artists Agency, 45
Yumbulul v. The Reserve Bank of Australia, 44–46, 56

INDEX OF NAMES

A
Abada, S., 52
Abramson, A., 96, 105n23
Akin, D., 103n2, 104n13
Alexander, C., 106n35
Alpers M., 25
Altman, D., 26
Anderson, W., 36n3, 187, 188, 192n15, 192, n17, 192n19
Appadurai, A., 103n8, 175n33
Araho, N., 2, 8
Arieti, S., 152, 162
Arizpe, L., xin5

B
Bainbridge, D., 107n41
Ballard, C., 27, 110
Banks, G., 27, 110
Barron, A., 33, 172n5, 176, 177, 179, 190n2
Barry, A., 153
Barth, F., 112, 124
Bateson, G., 73, 141
Battaglia, D., 69
Beck, U., 26, 31, 154
Belejack, B., 36n5
Bentham, J., 130n12
Bentley, L., 107n42, 177, 180, 190n1
Berlin, B., 36n5
Bhat, A., 22, 23, 37n1212
Biagioli, M., 90, 93, 94, 104n17, 104n19, 182, 184
Biersack, A., 62, 73, 78
Blake, C., 71
Blake, J., xin5, xiin17, 85, 93, 102n1
Blakeney, M., 4, 16n11, 16n13, 17n16, 58n6, 58n8, 106n29
BMA, 91, 105n23

Bolton, L., 5, 18n21, 18n22
Bourdieu, P., 143, 146
Boyd, D., 37n11
Brandt, F., 125
Brandt-Rauf, S., 89
Brennan, T., 18n31, 95, 106n32
Breton, S., 103n11
Brown, M., 3, 6, 16n7, 17n18, 32, 34, 35, 36n5, 71, 102n1
Browne, N., 129n3
Brush, S., xin6, 4, 16n7, 32, 92
Burton, J., 115, 116, 117
Busse, M., xiin17, 4, 18n23, 34
Byrne, J., 27

C
Callon, M., 103n7
Cambrioso, A., 185
Carrier, J., 17n17
Cetus Corporation, 191n13
Chapman, P., 28
Cheal, D., 90
Chief Ombudsman (PNG), xiin18, 41, 50, 181, 186
CIPR, 3, 17n16
Clark, J., 103n11
Clay, B., 139
Clifford, J., 133
Clinton, W., 110
Cohen, A., 103n9
Comaroff, J., 103n9
Coombe, R., xn3, 3, 15n1, 16n7, 16n9, 17n18, 51, 71, 93, 180
Cowan, J., xin5, 2, 16n7, 95
Coxon, K., 153, 162
Crittenden, R., 116
Cronon, W., 117
Cunningham, H., 23

D
Daes, E., xin5, 4, 17n19, 92
Damon, F., 108n54
de Coppet, D., 77
de Soto, H., 21
Derlon, B., 133
Dijksterhujs, E., 126
Divecha, S., 28
Dombrowski, K., 71
Dominguez, V., 32, 34
Dove, M., 33, 39n25
Drabkin, I., 125
Drahos, P., 3, 93, 104n21
Dutfield, G., xiin9, 4, 17n18, 102n1, 105n27
Dwyer, P., 104n12

E
Edgerton, D., 180
Eisenberg, R., 105n23
Ellen, R., xin6
Ellinson, D., 58n8
Eriksen, T., xin5
Ernst, T., 18n30, 78
Escobar, A., 35
Evans, G., 28

F
Fausto, C., 101
Feeny, D., 31
Filer, C., 16n8, 17n17, 18n30, 38n22, 87, 121
Fleischmann, M., 190n3
Forty, A., 133
Foster, R., 71, 105n26, 107n39
Fox, S., 157
Franklin, S., 159
Freudenthal, G., 123, 126, 131n15
Friedlaender, J., 23
Friedman, J., 174n21

G
Gadjusek, C., 36n3, 183, 184, 187, 188, 192n15
Gane, K., 25
Garrity, B., 69, 106n39, 107n43
Gell, A., 77, 140, 173n15, 178
Gieryn, T., 177
Goddard, M., 103n8, 103n9
Goldman, M., 31
Gordon, J., 27

Görlich, J., 103n7, 104n14
Graeber, D., 68, 144
Gray, K., 63, 64, 68, 107n42
Greaves, T., xin6, 16n7, 17n18, 50
Greely, H., 24, 36n7, 38n16
Gregory, C., 103n8, 107n45, 108n53, 108n55, 189
Grossman, H., 131n15
Gudeman, S., 4, 5, 66, 81n7
Gunn, M., 148n8
Guterson, H., 183

H
Hadden, R., 131n15
Hagström, W., 89, 90
Hann, C., 8, 17n17, 66
Hannerz, U., 162
Harðardóttir, K., 37n13, 191n6
Hardin, G., 31
Harris, H., xin6
Harrison, S., 5, 17n17, 17n18, 17n20, 34, 73, 82n16, 97, 106n38
Harvey, P., 133
Hastrup, K., 160
Hayden, C., 37n10, 105n28, 148n10
Heath, A., 124
Helgason, A., 18n24
Higgins, R., 28, 38n21
Hilgartner, S., 89, 91
Hill, C., 142
Hirsch, E., 18n30, 78
Hobbes, T., 146
Holding, A., 60, 61
Holla-Bhar, R., 32
Holyoak, J., 43
Hong, S., 182
Horowitz, G., 71
Hughes, T., 178
Humphrey, C., 17n17, 106n35, 108n51
Humphreys, D., 111

I
Ibeji, Y., 25
Ingold, T., 151, 152, 159, 160, 161, 166, 174n22

J
Jackson, J., 34
Jean-Klein, I., 95, 96, 106n33
Jenkins, C., 24, 36n3, 37n11, 192n20

Index of Names

Jolly, M., xiin19
Jorgensen, D., 133
Josephides, L., xiin19

K
Kalinoe, L., xn2, xiin14, xiin18, 5
Kambuou, R., 18n23
Kamene, S., xn2
Kant, I., 70, 78
Kapferer, B., 86, 88, 103n6, 112, 124
Kawowo, J., 16n10
Keating, P., 185
Keesing, R., 34
Kennedy, D., 71
Khorana, H., 191n13
Kimbrell, A., 38n15
King, S., 105n28
Knorr, C., 192n16
Kopytoff, I., 24
Kraemer, A., 133
Küchler, S., 18n21, 18n31, 73, 98, 107n41, 133
Kuper, A., xin7

L
Lambert, P., 71
Lanchester, J., 191n6
Latour, B., 124, 189
Laurie, G., 17n18
Leach, J., xn2, 57, 73
Leclerc, I., 159
Lévi-Strauss, C., 158, 159, 160
Lewis, P., 133
Libling, D., xin8, 64
Liep, J., 18n27, 18n29, 151, 152, 172n7, 173n8
Liloqula, R., 25
Lincoln, L., 133
Lock, M., 23, 36n9, 37n10
Löfgren, O., 173n14
Luhmann, N., 154

M
Macfarlane, A., 17n17
Macintrye, M., xiin19, 80n2
Macpherson, C., 25, 143
Maine, H., 65
Maino, Sir C., 57n1
Mangi, J., 37n11
Marconi, G., 182
Martin, E., 154

Matainaho, L., xiin11, 18n23
Matane, Sir P., 191n14
Maurer, B., 34, 96
Mazzoleni, R., 34
McGann, J., 158
McNeilly, R., 111
McSherry, C., 3, 91, 101, 104n20, 105n23
Merry, S., xin5, 16n4, 17n14
Merton, R., 89
Milne, T., 123
Milton, K., 31
Mimica, J., 160
Mirowski, P., 180, 181, 182, 191n7
Moore, A., 92
Morouta, Sir M., 110
Mosko, M., 5, 17n20, 104n14, 106n38
Muehlebach, A., 4, 16n10, 17n16
Mullis, K., 184, 191n13
Munn, N., 75

N
Negativland, 71
Nelson, R., 34
Nihill, M., 107n44
Niles, D., 185
Nonggorr, J., xiin17
Nuffield Council on Bioethics, 3, 104n22

O
O'Hanlon, M., 15n2
Oakeshott, M., 131n14
Ok Tedi Mining Limited, 129n1, 129n6
Ok Tedi Mining (website), 38n19, 38n20
Ollman, B., 67
Orlove, B., 4

P
Paine, R., 87, 103n10
Pálsson, G., 18n24, 37n13, 191n6, 192n16
Parametrix Inc., 28
Parkin, D., 16n5, 103n6
Patel, S., xin6
Perks, R., 38n23
Peteru, C., 16n12
Pietz, W., 21

PNGLR, xiin18, 42, 57
Pocock, J., 77, 78
Polier, N., 116
Pollock, J., 178
Pons, S., 190n3
Pope, A., 190n4
Posey, D., xin5, 4, 17n18, 52, 105n27
Pottage, A., 66, 80n6, 91, 105n23, 107n42, 185, 189
Povinelli, E., 34
Powdermaker, H., 134
Puri, K., 1, 16n12, 37n14, 42, 49, 52, 58n4

R

Rabinow, P., 23, 36n2, 183, 184, 191n13
Radin, M., 17n17, 67, 74, 88
Raine, K., 173n16
Rapp, F., 159
Reed, A., 76
Rifkin, J., 161
Riles, A., 89
Riordan, T., 23
Robbins, J., 76, 103n2, 104n13
Rogers, P., 130n10
Rose, C., 17n17, 26, 35, 60, 61, 62, 63, 65, 68, 71, 78, 81n8, 190n4
Rosen, L., 33
Ross, A., 122
Roulet, F., 16n11, 17n16
Rousseau, J-J., 130n10
Rowlands, R., xin5
Rumsey, A., 17n17, 187

S

Sahlins, M., 142, 143, 144, 145, 146
Salisbury, R., 87
Santos, R., 37n10
Saussure, F., 143, 144
Schaffer, S., 142, 182
Schieffelin, E., 73, 116
Scott, J., 31
Sengi, D., 25
Senie, H., 71
Sent, E-M., 180, 181, 182, 191n7
Shapin, S., 142, 182
Sherman, B., 107n42, 177, 180, 190n1
Shiva, V., 32
Sillitoe, P., 16n6
Simet, J., xn2, xiin14, 6, 85, 98, 108n56, 181
Simon, B., xin5

Simpson, T., xn3, xin5, xiin17, 4, 16n11, 17n14, 17n19, 102n1, 105n27
Sismondo, S., 177
Smith, C., 153
Smith, L., xiin20
Sneath, D., 106n35
Spragens, T., 125
Ssorin-Chaikov, N., 97, 103n8
Stabinsky, D., 16n7
Stevenson, M., 46
Swanson, T., 4
Sykes, K., xn2

T

Taubes, G., 23
Tauli-Corpuz, V., 32
Taussig, M., 103n8
Titmuss, R., 103n4
Tobin, B., xiin11
Torremans, P., 43
Tully, J., 143

U

UNESCO, xiin13
URS Greiner Woodward Clyde, 28

V

Vaidhyanathan, S., 71
Vail, J., 39n24
Van Gogh, V., 178
van Meijl, T., 17n17, 34, 36n1
Verdery, K., xiin19, 17n17, 80n5, 95, 96, 100, 106n31, 106n35
Viveiros de Castro, E., 101, 159
von Benda-Beckmann, F., 17n17, 34, 36n1

W

Wagner, R., 8, 140, 145, 146, 172n3
Weatherall, K., 98
Weber, M., 122
Weiner, J., 16n8, 17n17, 18n30, 18n32, 148n7, 187
Weiss, K., 23, 37n10
Wetstone, G., 38n23
Whimp, K., xiin17, 4, 18n23, 34
Whitehouse, H., 106n36
Winthrop, R., 2, 16n7, 95
Wissink, D., 120, 127, 129n5, 130n8
Young, M., 75, 76
Young, C., 151
Ziman, J., 183